# CliffsNotes®
# Spanish I
# Quick Review

### 2nd Edition
### By Jill Rodriguez and Ken Stewart

Houghton Mifflin Harcourt

Boston • New York

## About the Author

**Ken Stewart** is a National-Board-Certified Spanish teacher at Chapel Hill High School, NC, and has taught middle school through university. He was ACTFL's first National Language Teacher of the Year in 2005 and currently serves on the Curriculum Development and Assessment Committee to redesign the AP World Language courses and exams. He has published books with Wiley, Kaplan/Simon & Schuster, and Duke University Press as well as articles in *Hispania* and *The Language Educator*.

## Publisher's Acknowledgments

### Editorial

Project Editor: Kristi Hart

Acquisitions Editor: Greg Tubach

### Composition

Indexer: Potomac Indexing, LLC

Proofreader: Cara Buitron

Wiley Publishing, Inc. Composition Services

Library of Congress Control Number: 2011922781
ISBN 978-0-470-87875-0 (pbk)

Printed in the United States of America
DOC 10 9 8
4500542759

# Table of Contents

**Introduction** . . . . . . . . . . . . . . . . . . . . . . . . . . . . . . . . . . . . . . . . . . . . . .**ix**

    Why You Need This Book. . . . . . . . . . . . . . . . . . . . . . . . . . . . . . . . . . . ix

    How to Use This Book . . . . . . . . . . . . . . . . . . . . . . . . . . . . . . . . . . . . ix

    Hundreds of Practice Questions Online! . . . . . . . . . . . . . . . . . . . . . . x

**Chapter 1: Spelling and Pronunciation** . . . . . . . . . . . . . . . . . . . . . . . . . .**1**

    Consonants . . . . . . . . . . . . . . . . . . . . . . . . . . . . . . . . . . . . . . . . . . . . . . . 1

        Double consonants . . . . . . . . . . . . . . . . . . . . . . . . . . . . . . . . . . . . . .2

        Consonant sounds and spellings . . . . . . . . . . . . . . . . . . . . . . . . . . .2

        Cognates. . . . . . . . . . . . . . . . . . . . . . . . . . . . . . . . . . . . . . . . . . . . . . .2

        The letter *c* . . . . . . . . . . . . . . . . . . . . . . . . . . . . . . . . . . . . . . . . . . . .3

        The letter *g* . . . . . . . . . . . . . . . . . . . . . . . . . . . . . . . . . . . . . . . . . . . .3

        The letter *j* . . . . . . . . . . . . . . . . . . . . . . . . . . . . . . . . . . . . . . . . . . . .4

        The letter *h* . . . . . . . . . . . . . . . . . . . . . . . . . . . . . . . . . . . . . . . . . . .4

        The letter *d* . . . . . . . . . . . . . . . . . . . . . . . . . . . . . . . . . . . . . . . . . . .5

        The letter *t* . . . . . . . . . . . . . . . . . . . . . . . . . . . . . . . . . . . . . . . . . . . .5

        The letters *b* and *v*. . . . . . . . . . . . . . . . . . . . . . . . . . . . . . . . . . . . . .5

        Dictionary entries . . . . . . . . . . . . . . . . . . . . . . . . . . . . . . . . . . . . . .6

    Vowels. . . . . . . . . . . . . . . . . . . . . . . . . . . . . . . . . . . . . . . . . . . . . . . . . . .6

        Vowel sounds and spellings. . . . . . . . . . . . . . . . . . . . . . . . . . . . . . .6

        Diphthongs . . . . . . . . . . . . . . . . . . . . . . . . . . . . . . . . . . . . . . . . . . . .7

    Stress and Accentuation. . . . . . . . . . . . . . . . . . . . . . . . . . . . . . . . . . . .8

**Chapter 2: Gender: Nouns and Articles** . . . . . . . . . . . . . . . . . . . . . . . . .**10**

    Nouns. . . . . . . . . . . . . . . . . . . . . . . . . . . . . . . . . . . . . . . . . . . . . . . . . . 11

    Articles . . . . . . . . . . . . . . . . . . . . . . . . . . . . . . . . . . . . . . . . . . . . . . . . . 11

        Definite articles. . . . . . . . . . . . . . . . . . . . . . . . . . . . . . . . . . . . . . . . 11

        Indefinite articles . . . . . . . . . . . . . . . . . . . . . . . . . . . . . . . . . . . . . 12

    Gender . . . . . . . . . . . . . . . . . . . . . . . . . . . . . . . . . . . . . . . . . . . . . . . . . 12

        Basic rules. . . . . . . . . . . . . . . . . . . . . . . . . . . . . . . . . . . . . . . . . . . . 12

        Article and suffix changes . . . . . . . . . . . . . . . . . . . . . . . . . . . . . . 14

        Irregularities . . . . . . . . . . . . . . . . . . . . . . . . . . . . . . . . . . . . . . . . . 16

    Number and Plurality . . . . . . . . . . . . . . . . . . . . . . . . . . . . . . . . . . . . 19

        Plural forms of definite articles . . . . . . . . . . . . . . . . . . . . . . . . . 19

        Plural forms of indefinite articles . . . . . . . . . . . . . . . . . . . . . . . 19

        Plural forms of nouns . . . . . . . . . . . . . . . . . . . . . . . . . . . . . . . . . . 20

        Plural forms and accent marks . . . . . . . . . . . . . . . . . . . . . . . . . . 21

    Compound Nouns . . . . . . . . . . . . . . . . . . . . . . . . . . . . . . . . . . . . . . . 22

**Chapter 3: Replacing Nouns with Pronouns** . . . . . . . . . . . . . . . . . . . . .**24**

    Prounoun Use. . . . . . . . . . . . . . . . . . . . . . . . . . . . . . . . . . . . . . . . . . . .24

    Pronoun Cases. . . . . . . . . . . . . . . . . . . . . . . . . . . . . . . . . . . . . . . . . . .25

Subject Case Pronouns . . . . . . . . . . . . . . . . . . . . . . . . . . . .25
  English subject case pronouns. . . . . . . . . . . . . . . . . . . . . . . . . . .25
  Spanish subject case pronouns . . . . . . . . . . . . . . . . . . . . . . . .26
  Differences between English and Spanish subject case pronouns. . .28
  Replacing nouns with subject case pronouns. . . . . . . . . . . . . . . .29

**Chapter 4: Infinitive and Regular Verb Use . . . . . . . . . . . . . . . . . . . .31**
  Infinitives . . . . . . . . . . . . . . . . . . . . . . . . . . . . . . . . . . . . . . .31
  Verbs. . . . . . . . . . . . . . . . . . . . . . . . . . . . . . . . . . . . . . . . . . .33
  Regular Verbs in the Present Tense . . . . . . . . . . . . . . . . . . . . .34
  Choosing the Correct Verb Form . . . . . . . . . . . . . . . . . . . . . .37
  Present Progressive . . . . . . . . . . . . . . . . . . . . . . . . . . . . . . . .39

**Chapter 5: Basic Sentence Structure. . . . . . . . . . . . . . . . . . . . . . . . .42**
  Sentence Structure. . . . . . . . . . . . . . . . . . . . . . . . . . . . . . . . .42
  Conjunctions. . . . . . . . . . . . . . . . . . . . . . . . . . . . . . . . . . . . .43
  Punctuation. . . . . . . . . . . . . . . . . . . . . . . . . . . . . . . . . . . . .44
    Question marks . . . . . . . . . . . . . . . . . . . . . . . . . . . . . . . . . .44
    Exclamation points. . . . . . . . . . . . . . . . . . . . . . . . . . . . . . .45
    Punctuation and numbers. . . . . . . . . . . . . . . . . . . . . . . . . . .45

**Chapter 6: Irregular Verbs in the Present Tense . . . . . . . . . . . . . . . .46**
  Common Verbs Irregular in the Present Tense . . . . . . . . . . . . . .47
    Common irregular verbs. . . . . . . . . . . . . . . . . . . . . . . . . . . .47
    Irregular verbs in the *yo* form . . . . . . . . . . . . . . . . . . . . . . .48
  Stem-Changing Verbs in the Present Tense. . . . . . . . . . . . . . . .54
    *E* to *ie*. . . . . . . . . . . . . . . . . . . . . . . . . . . . . . . . . . . . . . .55
    *O* to *ue* . . . . . . . . . . . . . . . . . . . . . . . . . . . . . . . . . . . . . .58
    *E* to *i* . . . . . . . . . . . . . . . . . . . . . . . . . . . . . . . . . . . . . . .61
  Confusing Verbs: Determining Which Verb to Use . . . . . . . . . . .62
    *Ser* or *estar* . . . . . . . . . . . . . . . . . . . . . . . . . . . . . . . . . . .62
    *Conocer* or *saber* . . . . . . . . . . . . . . . . . . . . . . . . . . . . . . .63
    *Llevar, tomar,* and *sacar*. . . . . . . . . . . . . . . . . . . . . . . . . . .64

**Chapter 7: Asking and Answering Questions . . . . . . . . . . . . . . . . . .67**
  Yes or No Questions . . . . . . . . . . . . . . . . . . . . . . . . . . . . . . .67
  Interrogative Pronouns (Question Words) . . . . . . . . . . . . . . . . .69
  Question Words as Subjects . . . . . . . . . . . . . . . . . . . . . . . . . .72
  Using the Right Pronoun to Answer a Question . . . . . . . . . . . . .74

**Chapter 8: Adjectives . . . . . . . . . . . . . . . . . . . . . . . . . . . . . . . . . . .76**
  Adjective Use. . . . . . . . . . . . . . . . . . . . . . . . . . . . . . . . . . . .76
    Adjectives and gender. . . . . . . . . . . . . . . . . . . . . . . . . . . . .77
    Adjectives and number. . . . . . . . . . . . . . . . . . . . . . . . . . . . .81
    Adjective placement . . . . . . . . . . . . . . . . . . . . . . . . . . . . . .82
    Adjectives that change meaning . . . . . . . . . . . . . . . . . . . . . . .84

Adjective Types. . . . . . . . . . . . . . . . . . . . . . . . . . . . . . . . . . . . . . . .85
  Possessive adjectives . . . . . . . . . . . . . . . . . . . . . . . . . . . . . . . . . .85
  Demonstrative adjectives . . . . . . . . . . . . . . . . . . . . . . . . . . . . . .87
Adjectives from Verbs . . . . . . . . . . . . . . . . . . . . . . . . . . . . . . . . . . .90

**Chapter 9: Adverbs and Comparisons . . . . . . . . . . . . . . . . . . . . . . . . . .91**
Adverbs from Adjectives . . . . . . . . . . . . . . . . . . . . . . . . . . . . . . . . .91
  Irregular adverb . . . . . . . . . . . . . . . . . . . . . . . . . . . . . . . . . . . . .94
Adverb Placement in a Sentence . . . . . . . . . . . . . . . . . . . . . . . . . .95
  Adverbs of time . . . . . . . . . . . . . . . . . . . . . . . . . . . . . . . . . . . . .95
  Adverbs of manner . . . . . . . . . . . . . . . . . . . . . . . . . . . . . . . . . . .96
  Adverbs that modify adjectives or adverbs. . . . . . . . . . . . . . . .97
Shortened Adverbs . . . . . . . . . . . . . . . . . . . . . . . . . . . . . . . . . . . . .97
Comparisons. . . . . . . . . . . . . . . . . . . . . . . . . . . . . . . . . . . . . . . . . .98
  Comparisons with adjectives. . . . . . . . . . . . . . . . . . . . . . . . . . . .98
  Comparatives of equality . . . . . . . . . . . . . . . . . . . . . . . . . . . . . .99
  Superlatives. . . . . . . . . . . . . . . . . . . . . . . . . . . . . . . . . . . . . . . .100
  Comparisons with adverbs . . . . . . . . . . . . . . . . . . . . . . . . . . . .100
  Irregular comparisons . . . . . . . . . . . . . . . . . . . . . . . . . . . . . . .101

**Chapter 10: Direct and Indirect Object Pronouns . . . . . . . . . . . . . . .103**
Objective Cases. . . . . . . . . . . . . . . . . . . . . . . . . . . . . . . . . . . . . . .103
Direct Objects and Direct Object Pronouns . . . . . . . . . . . . . . . .104
  Direct object of a sentence . . . . . . . . . . . . . . . . . . . . . . . . . . . .104
  The personal *a* . . . . . . . . . . . . . . . . . . . . . . . . . . . . . . . . . . . .105
  Direct object pronouns. . . . . . . . . . . . . . . . . . . . . . . . . . . . . . .105
  Direct object pronoun placement . . . . . . . . . . . . . . . . . . . . . .106
  Common transitive verbs . . . . . . . . . . . . . . . . . . . . . . . . . . . . .108
Indirect Objects and Indirect Object Pronouns. . . . . . . . . . . . . .108
  Indirect object of a sentence . . . . . . . . . . . . . . . . . . . . . . . . . .109
  Indirect object pronouns. . . . . . . . . . . . . . . . . . . . . . . . . . . . .109
  Indirect object pronoun placement. . . . . . . . . . . . . . . . . . . . .110
  Special verbs with indirect object pronouns . . . . . . . . . . . . . .111
Double Object Sentences . . . . . . . . . . . . . . . . . . . . . . . . . . . . . . .114
  The use of *se* . . . . . . . . . . . . . . . . . . . . . . . . . . . . . . . . . . . . . .115
  Adding two object pronouns to verbs . . . . . . . . . . . . . . . . . . .116

**Chapter 11: The Preterite Tense . . . . . . . . . . . . . . . . . . . . . . . . . . . . .118**
Regular Verbs in the Preterite Tense . . . . . . . . . . . . . . . . . . . . . .118
Different *Yo* Forms in the Preterite Tense . . . . . . . . . . . . . . . . . .121
  Verbs that end in *–gar* . . . . . . . . . . . . . . . . . . . . . . . . . . . . . . .121
  Verbs that end in *–car*. . . . . . . . . . . . . . . . . . . . . . . . . . . . . . .122
  Verbs that end in *–zar* . . . . . . . . . . . . . . . . . . . . . . . . . . . . . .124
  *I* to *y*. . . . . . . . . . . . . . . . . . . . . . . . . . . . . . . . . . . . . . . . . . .125

Stem Changers in the Preterite Tense ........................126
    Stem-changing verbs ending in *–ir* ......................126
Irregulars in the Preterite Tense............................128
    *U*-stem verbs...........................................129
    *I*-stem verbs .........................................130
    *J*-stem verbs .........................................131
    Very irregular preterite verbs..........................132
Preterite Tense Situations .................................133
Preterite Tense Indicators .................................134

**Chapter 12: The Imperfect Tense** ............................**136**
Regular Verbs in the Imperfect .............................136
The Three Imperfect Irregulars .............................140
Imperfect Situations ......................................141
Imperfect Indicators ......................................142

**Chapter 13: Narrations in the Past**............................**144**
Verbs That Change Meaning in the Preterite..................145
Preterite-Imperfect Formulas...............................147
    Joining verbs with *mientras*............................148
    Joining verbs with *cuando*.............................149
Expressions of Time .......................................150

**Chapter 14: Prepositions** ...................................**153**
Simple Prepositions........................................153
    Preposition: *a*........................................154
    Preposition: *de* ......................................157
    Preposition: *en* ......................................160
    Preposition: *con* .....................................161
*Para* and *Por* ..........................................163
    Preposition: *para*.....................................163
    Preposition: *por* .....................................165
    Idiomatic expressions ..................................168
Compound Prepositions .....................................169
Preposition Use with Verbs.................................170
    Verbs with prepositions ................................170
    Verbs with prepositions in English but not Spanish .....172
    Verbs after prepositions ...............................173

**Chapter 15: More Pronouns: Reflexive, Prepositional,
and Demonstrative** ...........................................**175**
Reflexivity................................................175
    Reflexive pronouns......................................176
    Reciprocity.............................................177
    Reflexive verbs ........................................178
    Common reflexive verbs .................................179
Prepositional Pronouns.....................................180
Demonstrative Pronouns.....................................181

**Chapter 16: Commands** ...................................... 184
  *Tú* Commands ........................................ 184
    Regular affirmative *tú* commands .................... 184
    Irregular affirmative *tú* commands .................. 185
    Negative *tú* commands ............................. 186
    *Vosotros* commands ................................ 187
  *Usted* and *Ustedes* Commands ....................... 188
  Command Forms of Verbs .............................. 189
  Command Forms with Reflexive Pronouns .............. 192

**Chapter 17: Negatives** ...................................... 196
  Negative Words and Expressions ....................... 196
  Negative Sentences ................................... 198
  Negatives and Other Parts of Speech .................. 200
    Pronouns .......................................... 200
    Adjectives ......................................... 202
    Conjunctions: *sino* and *pero* ..................... 202

**Review Questions** .......................................... 204

**Resource Center** ........................................... 211
  Books ............................................... 211
  Internet ............................................. 212

**Glossary** .................................................. 213

**Appendix A: Thematic Vocabulary** ........................... 218
  Animals ............................................. 218
  Body and Health ..................................... 218
  Clothing ............................................ 220
  Days of the Week .................................... 221
  Family .............................................. 221
  Foods ............................................... 221
  Home ................................................ 222
  Months of the Year .................................. 224
  Nature .............................................. 224
  Neighborhood and Buildings .......................... 224
  School .............................................. 225
  Sports, Diversions, and Amusements .................. 227
  Travel .............................................. 228
  Weather and Seasons ................................. 228
  Work ................................................ 229

**Appendix B: Verb Charts** ................................... 231
  The Verb *Hablar* ................................... 231
  The Verb *Comer* .................................... 232
  The Verb *Escribir* ................................. 233
  The Verb *Ir* ....................................... 234

The Verb *Ser* .................................................235
The Verb *Dar* .................................................236
The Verb *Estar*................................................237
The Verb *Hacer*...............................................238
The Verb *Poner* ..............................................239
The Verb *Salir*................................................240
The Verb *Ver*..................................................241
The Verb *Saber* ..............................................242
The Verb *Caer*.................................................243
The Verb *Traer* ...............................................244
The Verb *Pensar* .............................................246
The Verb *Mentir* .............................................247
The Verb *Tener* ...............................................248
The Verb *Venir* ...............................................249
The Verb *Jugar* ...............................................250
The Verb *Dormir*.............................................251
The Verb *Pedir* ...............................................252
The Verb *Decir* ...............................................254
The Verb *Seguir*..............................................255

**Appendix C: Idiomatic Expressions** .........................**257**
Introduce a Topic .............................................257
Transitions ....................................................257
State an Opinion...............................................258
Conclusions....................................................259
Contrasts.......................................................260
Cause and Effect ..............................................260
Location .......................................................261
Time............................................................261
Manner and Adverbial Expressions ..........................263
Means of Transportation......................................265
Other Useful Expressions ....................................265

**Index** .............................................................**268**

# INTRODUCTION

The CliffsNotes *Spanish I Quick Review* book is meant to provide all of the foundations of basic Spanish pronunciation, spelling, vocabulary and sentence construction. Spanish grammar is systematically explained in its most simple way throughout this book, so there's no need for any prerequisite before beginning this "review" of the equivalent of two years of high school Spanish class.

## Why You Need This Book

Can you answer "yes" to any of these questions?

- Do you need to review the fundamentals of Spanish fast?

- Do you need a course supplement to the first or second year of Spanish class?

- Do you need a concise, comprehensive reference for basic Spanish grammar concepts?

If so, then CliffsNotes *Spanish I Quick Review* is for you!

## How to Use This Book

You can use this book in any way that fits your personal style for study and review-you decide what works best with your needs. You can either read the book from cover to cover, or just look for the information you want and put it back on the shelf for later. Here are just a few ways you can search for topics:

- Look for areas of interest in the book's Table of Contents, or use the index to find specific topics.

- Flip through the book looking for subject areas at the top of each page.

- Get a glimpse of what you'll gain from a chapter by reading through the Chapter Check-In at the beginning of each chapter.

- Use the Chapter Check-Out at the end of each chapter to gauge your grasp of the important information you need to know.

■ Test your knowledge more completely in the Review Questions, and look for additional sources of information in the Resource Center.

■ Use the Glossary to find key terms fast. This book defines new terms and concepts where they first appear in the chapter. If a word is boldfaced, you can find a more complete definition in the Glossary.

■ For helpful lists of verbs, phrases, and expressions, turn to the Appendices located at the back of the book.

■ Or flip through the book until you find what you're looking for. This book is organized to gradually build on key concepts.

# Hundreds of Practice Questions Online!

Prepare for your next Spanish I quiz or test with hundreds of additional practice questions online. The questions are organized by this book's chapter sections, so it's easy to use the book and then quiz yourself online to make sure you know the subject. Go to www.cliffsnotes.com/foreign-languages/spanish-i-quizzes to test yourself anytime and find other free homework help.

# Chapter 1
# SPELLING AND PRONUNCIATION

## Chapter Check-In

❏ Pronouncing different consonants and vowels

❏ Identifying spelling rules

❏ Stressing the correct syllable

❏ Writing accent marks when necessary

**S**ome people say, "I can't even spell in English, how can I hope to learn how to spell in Spanish?" Those who detest the lack of correlation between pronunciation and spelling in English will be thrilled to learn that Spanish is very consistent in its spelling and pronunciation rules. Since these rules are very simple and easy to learn, even a terrible speller of the English language can master the spelling of Spanish words.

This chapter provides you with the foundation to begin speaking and writing Spanish by presenting the ways to properly pronounce a word that you see written as well as to spell a word that you hear spoken. Your only difficulty may be overcoming the influence of years of speaking English. Spanish is a phonetic language, therefore spelling is quite predictable and easier than in English.

## Consonants

**Consonants** in Spanish are generally pronounced like English consonants, but a few exceptions are important. Also, there are some rules about consonants that eliminate spelling difficulties.

The letters *k* and *w* do not occur in Spanish words unless the word has been borrowed from another language like English or even Japanese. For example, *Karate* is considered a Spanish word even though it comes from Japanese.

## Double consonants

In Spanish, consonants are almost never doubled. For example, only the letter *f* is used to get the *f* sound in Spanish. Therefore, there is no difficulty in spelling *professor*. Can you remember whether it's a double *f* or *s* in English? And did you even consider that the spelling in English could have been a *ph* instead of *f* or *ff*?

However, there are four exceptions to the double-consonant rule: *ll, rr, cc,* and in rare cases, *nn*. *Ll* is an actual letter, the fourteenth letter of the Spanish alphabet since 1803. *Ll* is pronounced like the consonant *y* in Yerba. In some countries, the *ll* sounds like a combination of the sound of *sh* and the letter *j* in English. A single *l* sounds like the letter *l* you hear in English and Spanish words. *Rr* is not a letter but rather a double *r* intended to elicit the rolling sound that is difficult for many who are learning Spanish as a second language. You are supposed to roll your tongue for one *r* if it is the first letter of the word, and you should also roll your tongue whenever you see the letter *rr* within a word. This accounts for a spelling change sometimes when two words become one. For example, in the name of the island *Puerto Rico*, the *r* is rolled because it is the first letter of a word. The adjective for a native, *Puertorriqueño,* is only one word, so the *rr* is used to produce the rolling *r* and maintain the pronunciation.

The third occasion where you will see a double consonant in a Spanish word is when a double *c* is used to produce the *k* or *x* sound as in *diccionario* (dictionary).

## Consonant sounds and spellings

The pronunciation of Spanish consonants is easy to learn. There are many consonants that are pronounced exactly like their English equivalent, and these will not pose any problems for you. Only the consonants that can have more than one pronunciation or that are used in combinations to create a different sound are explained in the following sections. Any consonant that is not covered should be pronounced exactly like it is in English.

## Cognates

There are a lot of Spanish words that look similar to English words, and some are even spelled exactly the same. However these words, called **cognates,** are usually easier to spell in Spanish than they are in English once you learn the rules.

In Spanish, the letter *p* is always pronounced like the *p* in *prince,* and the Spanish never use the letter combination *ph* to produce the *f* sound. If the English word has a *ph,* the Spanish cognate will always use one *f.* For example, look at the Spanish words *teléfono* (telephone), *elefante* (elephant), and *filosofía* (philosophy). The letter *f* is the only way to produce the *f* sound in Spanish.

## The letter *c*

In Spanish, there are three ways to produce the sound of the English letter *k.* The letter *k* is used for words that are originally from other languages, and it is pronounced as it is in English. The letter *c* is pronounced like a *k* when it is followed by an *o, a,* or *u.* However, the letter *c* is pronounced like an *s* when it is followed by an *e* or *i.* The *qu* combination must be used to produce the *k* sound in front of an *e* or *i.* A word that the English borrowed from the Spanish, *mosquito,* has already prepared you to pronounce *qu* in Spanish without any *w* sound. Not like *quill,* but rather like *tequila.*

The following words have a sound like *k.* Notice the *qu = k* in front of *e* or *i,* and *c = k* in front of *o, a,* or *u.*

| | |
|---|---|
| *que* | what |
| *aquí* | here |
| *comer* | to eat |
| *culebra* | snake |
| *cantar* | to sing |

The letter *c* is pronounced like *s* when it is in front of *e* or *i,* as in the following words:

| | |
|---|---|
| *cinta* | tape |
| *cenar* | to dine |

To pronounce words with a double *c,* such as *diccionario* and *accidente,* the first *c* is hard because it's followed by a consonant, and the second *c* is soft because it's followed by an *i* or *e.*

## The letter *g*

The letter *g* in Spanish has issues very much like the letter *c:* The pronunciation of the letter *g* is influenced by the letter that follows it. Whether or not you realize it, you have been following a similar rule in English.

The reason the *g* in "goat" is pronounced differently than the *g* in "gem" is because in both Spanish and English, there is a hard *g* sound and a soft *g* sound. Generally, in English, a *g* that is followed by *e* or *i* is a soft *g*, and a *g* that is followed by *o, a,* or *u* is a hard *g*. This rule is the same in Spanish and is even more consistent.

The pronunciation of the hard *g* is the same in both languages. The *g* in *goma* (eraser), *ganar* (to win, earn), or *guante* (glove) is exactly like "good," "gallant," or "gum." Like in English, a Spanish *g* is soft if it is followed by an *e* or *i*. However, the soft *g* in Spanish sounds like the English letter *h*. The *g* in *gente* (people) or *gitana* (gypsy) sounds like the English *h* in "hat" or "heat."

To keep their language's pronunciation rules consistent, the Spanish had to face the dilemma of spelling a word with a hard *g* sound in front of an *e* or *i*. To resolve this dilemma, the letter *u* is placed between the *g* and *e* or between the *g* and *i*. Since the intent of the *u* is to produce the hard *g* sound, the *u* itself is not pronounced. This is a rare exception to the rule that all vowels are always pronounced. You may be already familiar with the words *guerrilla* and *guitarra*. These words can serve as examples to help you avoid the urge to say the *gway* or *gwee* sound when you see *g* and *u* together.

On extremely rare occasions when the *gway* or *gwee* sound *is* desired, the German symbol called an **umlaut** (¨), translated as *diéresis* or *crema* in Spanish, is used to indicate that the *u* should be pronounced like a *w* when it is in between a *g-i* or *g-e*. And, the umlaut is used only on the vowel *u*. Pronounce the word "bilingual," and then say *bilingüe* with the same *gw* sound, and you'll see how the umlaut works.

### The letter *j*
The letter *j* is always pronounced like the *h* in "hello" or "happy." When you need to spell a word with the sound of the English *h*, followed by an *e* or *i*, it is difficult to predict whether to use a *j* or *g*. For example, *jira* and *jefe* are spelled with a *j*, and *gimnasio* and *gema* are spelled with a *g*. Your awareness of this difficulty should cause you to focus on whether to use a *j* or a *g* when you first learn to spell the word. It is at least certain that words with the *h* sound in front of *o, a,* or *u* (*jo, ja,* and *ju*) are always spelled with a *j*, because a *g* would be a hard *g* if it's followed by *o, a* or *u* and wouldn't produce the *h* sound at all.

### The letter *h*
You may be wondering how to pronounce the Spanish letter *h* when you see it in a Spanish word. The answer is that you don't pronounce it at all.

The letter *h* is always silent. It exists because of the way the language has evolved, but now-a-days it is not pronounced, and it seems to confuse spelling issues. There really is no way to predict when a word will begin with a silent *h,* so be sure to focus on the spelling of words that you learn beginning with a silent *h.*

## The letter *d*

The letter *d* is a bit softer in Spanish. It basically sounds like an English *d,* but will not be stressed at the end of the word like we do in English. Say the word "made" out loud and you'll hear how the strength of the *d* at the end almost creates its own syllable. In Spanish, any *d* at the end of the word will barely be pronounced. Say *Madrid* without the *d* at the end and you'll sound like a native. Once again, the lack of double consonants makes spelling the *d* sound easy: It's always a single *d* in any Spanish word.

## The letter *t*

Another letter that is similar to English, but softer, is the *t.* It is especially soft when it is followed by an *r.* The sound of the *tr* in "triple" would be more like a *tl* sound in Spanish. Try to say *tratar* (to try, to treat) without moving your tongue away from the back of your teeth. Or if you don't mind having a slight accent, say the *t* like in English and keep it simple. When spelling, don't forget that the *t* will never be doubled in Spanish words.

## The letters *b* and *v*

The letters *b* and *v* sound the same in Spanish. The sound is a combination of *bv.* To make the sound, start out making the *b* sound, and slur into the *v* sound at the last second. When it comes to spelling words that contain a *b* or a *v,* many Spanish speakers have difficulty determining which letter to use, but since English speakers often have difficulty pronouncing the *bv* letter combination, it's easier to remember how to spell words correctly since *vivir* (to live) would be pronounced with a stronger *v* sound and *beber* (to drink) would be pronounced with a harder *b* sound. This pronunciation error is helpful with spelling, but until your *b*'s and *v*'s sound like some mixture of both sounds, you'll have an English accent. One helpful point about the similarity of *b* and *v* in Spanish is that sometimes it will be easy to recognize a word that is similar to English if you imagine the word with a *b* instead of a *v,* or vice versa. For example, the verb *gobernar* means "to govern."

## Dictionary entries

When looking up Spanish words in a Spanish dictionary, keep a few points in mind:

■ Remember that *ll* and *rr* are considered separate letters, so the Spanish side of some dictionaries will list words beginning with *ll* after the words beginning with a single *l* and words beginning with *rr* after words beginning with a single *r*.

■ The letter *ch* will be found in the *ch* section of most dictionaries at the end of the *c* section.

■ Another place where the dictionary listings may confuse you is when a word has the Spanish letter *ñ*. The little squiggle on the *n* is called a **tilde,** and it creates an entirely new letter that will follow the *n*'s in the dictionary. For example, you will find that the word *mañana* is listed after *manzana*. The *ñ* is pronounced like the *ny* combo in "canyon" or the *ni* combo in "onion."

# Vowels

Pronouncing Spanish vowels is simple. Each vowel has only one way to be pronounced, and it will be pronounced that way in every word. Unlike English, there are no silent vowels in Spanish, although some vowels will slur together to create a single sound. These vowel combinations are called diphthongs and will be explained later in this chapter.

You should be careful not to let your vowels become dipthongs when speaking Spanish. Spanish vowels are shorter, sharper, and more crisp than English vowels; therefore, Spanish vowels produce only one, constant sound. Also, the English *schwa* sound doesn't exist in Spanish although it is quite common in spoken English. For example, Spanish never has sounds like "pencil" [pɛnsəl]. The last syllable of "pencil" contains the relaxed *schwa* sound. To further illustrate this notion, the word *banana* is the same in Spanish and English. However, in English the last syllable is the *schwa* [ə] sound, and in Spanish all of the *a*'s are open vowels that are pronounced exactly the same in all three syllables.

## Vowel sounds and spellings

The few Spanish words that are common in English can serve as models for your pronunciation. Pronounce the word "taco." The letter *a* is always pronounced like it is in *taco*. If you have ever heard a person speaking with a heavy Spanish accent, you may have noticed that they usually say a word like "hat" or "can" sounding more like the English words "hot" or "con." That is because they are saying the letter *a* the only way it can be said in their language.

The letter *o* is also consistently pronounced like it is in *taco*. You may notice that the *o* is shorter in Spanish and doesn't end in a *wa* at the end.

Another word we have learned from the popularity of Mexican food is *burrito*. The Spanish vowels *u* and *i* are always pronounced like they are in the word *burrito*.

The only vowel left to master is the *e*. It is always pronounced like the *e* in *café* (even when there's no accent on the *e*). To see how well you're learning, go back and make sure you pronounce the *a* in *café* correctly. It should sound like the *a* in *taco*.

Notice that the *e* at the end of *café* is not silent as it is in the English word "cake." Remember that there are no silent vowels in Spanish (except for the *u* in *qu* and *gu* followed by *e* or *i*), so be careful of cognates that end in *e*, and remember to pronounce it at the end.

The letter *y* is a vowel only when it stands alone or when it is at the end of the word. It is pronounced like the *i* in "burrito" when it is a vowel, as in *ley*, for example. As a consonant, the Spanish *y* sounds just like "yellow" in English, as in *yo*.

The easiest vocabulary words to learn are also the trickiest to pronounce. A lot of Spanish words look similar to English words, and some are even spelled the same. But, as discussed earlier under "Cognates," these words are never pronounced exactly like their English equivalent. Also, a Spanish word that does sound like an English word will probably be spelled differently in Spanish to maintain the rules of their language. When you recognize a cognate and immediately determine its meaning, it is natural to just say the English word.

Here's one good way to eliminate the urge to simply pronounce a cognate in Spanish the same as you would in English. Practice by pronouncing all English words as if they were Spanish. At the end of the unit, this example will make more sense, but imagine when you see the English word "imagine" that you pronounce it "ee-mah-hee-nay" because that's how the letters would be pronounced in Spanish. Later, when you learn the word *imagina* you will be prepared to say "ee-mah-hee-nah" almost perfectly.

## Diphthongs

The strong vowels are *a, e,* and *o*. When two strong vowels are used together in a word, the result is two separate syllables with both vowels strongly pronounced. If one of the strong vowels is used beside a weak vowel, the resulting single syllable, called a **diphthong,** is a slur of the two vowels, with the stronger vowel the only one that is clearly heard.

The weak vowels are *i* and *u*. Remember that in the battle of the weak vowels, the last one gets stressed. The *u* creates the sound of an English *w*. When the *i* is used with a stronger vowel, the *i* sounds like the consonant *y* in both languages.

## Stress and Accentuation

The stress of a word follows two simple rules. Understanding them is imperative for pronouncing words and understanding why written accent marks are sometimes necessary:

■ If a word ends in any consonant other than *n* or *s,* the natural stress will be on the last syllable.

■ If a word ends in a vowel or the letter *n* or *s,* the natural stress is on the next-to-last syllable.

Accent marks may seem to be randomly placed in a word, but there are actually very easy rules to explain why they are used. The three basic rules to remember are:

■ There is only one kind of accent.

■ There is only one accent in any word.

■ An accent can be placed only on a vowel, never a consonant.

The main purpose of writing an accent mark is to indicate that this particular word is supposed to be stressed somewhere other than the syllable where it would be stressed naturally if it followed the rules (see "Stress and Accentuation" earlier in the chapter). This leads to some rules within the rules. For example, there are hundreds of words that are cognates of English words that end in *–tion,* like "nation," "liberation," and "condition." These words end in *–ción* in Spanish: *nación, liberación,* and *condición.* The rule states that a word that ends in an *n* has the natural stress on the next-to-last syllable, and these words are supposed to be stressed on the next-to-the-last syllable like in English. But, because they do not follow the general rule, an accent mark is written on the last vowel, the *o,* to show where the stress should be pronounced.

The previous lesson on diphthongs (see "Diphthongs" earlier in this chapter) and the strong and weak vowels becomes important when you are trying to decide whether or not a word needs a written accent mark. Remember that a diphthong is the single syllable created when one strong and one weak vowel or two weak vowels are pronounced together. That is why there is no accent on the word *iglesia*: The *i* is acting like the consonant *y*, so the diphthong *ia* creates a single syllable *ya* sound at the end of the word, and the natural stress is on the next-to-last syllable since the word ends in a vowel.

The second reason for writing an accent mark is to indicate that the weaker vowel is to be pronounced as well as the stronger vowel. This obviously creates two separate syllables, and the stress will be on the accented syllable.

Understanding these rules not only helps you know whether or not to write an accent when spelling a word that you hear, it will also help you pronounce a word that you are reading with the stress on the correct syllable. This will not only remind you to stress the word on that syllable, but will also help you remember that the word has an accent mark.

The third reason for writing an accent mark has nothing to do with pronunciation. It is used to differentiate between two words that would otherwise be spelled the same. For example, the word *si* means *if*, but the word *sí* means *yes*. Of course, when spoken, only the context of the sentence will provide a clue as to which of the two words is appropriate.

## Chapter Check-Out

### Q&A

For the following words, use the rules you have learned and underline where the stress would naturally fall.

1. *diccionario*
2. *anaranjado*
3. *devolver*
4. *dificultad*
5. *predominar*

**Answers: 1.** *diccion<u>a</u>rio* **2.** *anaranj<u>a</u>do* **3.** *devolv<u>e</u>r* **4.** *dificult<u>a</u>d* **5.** *predomin<u>a</u>r*

# Chapter 2

# GENDER: NOUNS AND ARTICLES

## Chapter Check-In

❏ Determining the gender of nouns

❏ Using articles to indicate the gender of a noun

❏ Learning to predict the gender of a word

❏ Making nouns and articles plural

❏ Watching for compound nouns

In this chapter you'll learn that all nouns in Spanish have **gender.** That means the word referring to a noun is either masculine or feminine. When possible, you will learn how to determine the gender of an unfamiliar noun, and you'll come to appreciate that learning the gender of a noun is as important as learning the word itself.

You'll learn to use **definite articles** and **indefinite articles** to represent the gender of a noun. These are the little words (such as *a* and *the*) that often come before nouns. Including a gender-specific article as you study new vocabulary words is imperative to your success in later chapters about adjectives and pronouns. The vocabulary words provided as examples throughout this chapter are the typical words learned by beginning students, and you will find it useful to learn the words and their gender as you study this chapter.

As you study the gender of the nouns presented in the following lessons, you may want to use your cultural color indoctrination to help you. For example, if you're from mainstream North American culture, you probably associate pink with feminine and blue with masculine. Write all the feminine words on pink cards and all the masculine words on blue cards, and you will unconsciously remember the color of the card as you learn each word. To quiz yourself, however, you should put the nouns all on neutral-colored flashcards. Look at the English word and try to remember the Spanish word on the other side with its article that specifies gender.

# Nouns

To understand the gender of nouns, it is first important to understand what a noun is. In elementary school, you probably learned that a noun is a person, place or thing. Technically, a **noun** is a word that represents a person, place, or thing. When a word represents a person, the gender of that noun will obviously be the gender (sex) of the person it represents.

However, in Spanish, any noun that represents any object will have gender. It is not that the object the word represents is either male or female, but rather that the word itself is either a masculine or feminine word. For example, one word for "computer," *la computadora,* is feminine, and another word for "computer" is masculine, *el ordenador.* "Television" can be represented by a feminine word, *la televisión,* or by a masculine word, *el televisor.*

# Articles

When you learn a new word that is a noun, learn the gender of the word as a part of the word by including a definite or indefinite article.

## Definite articles

In English, only one definite article is used to represent a specific, definite object. The definite article *the* can be used in front of any noun without regard to gender: *the* girl, *the* book, *the* man, *the* chair. In Spanish, the definite article reflects the gender of the word that follows. The definite article *el* (the, masculine) is used in front of a masculine noun, and the definite article *la* (the, feminine) is used in front of a feminine noun.

In the following list, you can tell which nouns are feminine words because they are preceded by the definite article *la,* and you can tell which are masculine nouns because they are preceded by the definite article *el.*

| | |
|---|---|
| *la chica* | the girl |
| *el libro* | the book |
| *el hombre* | the man |
| *la silla* | the chair |

## Indefinite articles

There is a masculine and feminine version of indefinite articles, which demonstrate the gender of the noun that they precede. While a definite article is very specific, an indefinite article refers to a less-specific object. In English the indefinite article is the word *a*. When you request "a book" you are being much less specific than when you request "the book." In Spanish, the indefinite article for a masculine noun is *un,* and the indefinite article for a feminine noun is *una.*

| | |
|---|---|
| *una chica* | a girl |
| *un libro* | a book |
| *un hombre* | a man |
| *una silla* | a chair |

It doesn't matter whether you choose to learn *el hombre* or *un hombre* as long as placing *el* or *un* in front of the noun helps you remember that the word is masculine. *La* or *una* helps you remember that the word that follows is a feminine word. Later on, you will care about whether you want to say "a man" or "the man," but for now, the articles are simply there to help you remember the gender of a noun.

# Gender

It will not always be possible to predict the gender of a noun by looking at the word. When you look up any Spanish noun in the dictionary, the first thing you'll find will be the letter *m* (for masculine) or *f* (for feminine). When you learn a new vocabulary word that is a noun, you must memorize the gender of the word as well as the actual spelling of the word. Sometimes, the spelling of the word itself may make it possible to ascertain the gender of a word just by looking at it.

## Basic rules

The first question you probably have is, "When is it possible to know the gender of a noun by looking at the word?" In some cases, you will be able to tell the gender of a word based on the ending of the word itself. The two most basic rules about gender are based on the last letter of the noun: A word that ends in *–o* is masculine, and a word that ends in *–a* is feminine. There are a few exceptions to this rule (for example, *la mano* and *el mapa*). Check out the following examples:

| *Masculine* | | *Feminine* | |
|---|---|---|---|
| *el abuelo* | the grandfather | *la abuela* | the grandmother |
| *el hermano* | the brother | *la hermana* | the sister |
| *el museo* | the museum | *la montaña* | the mountain |
| *el pueblo* | the town | *la playa* | the beach |
| *el libro* | the book | *la escuela* | the school |

## Feminine

In addition to the general rule that nouns ending in an *–a* are feminine, another feminine ending is the letter *–d*. Typically, a word that ends in *–dad, –tad, or –tud* will be feminine. Notice that most of these words have English equivalents that end in *–ty*. When you see a Spanish word that ends in *–dad, –tad,* or *–tud,* change the ending to *–ty* to recognize an obvious cognate (see Chapter 1).

| | |
|---|---|
| *la ciudad* | the city |
| *la dificultad* | the difficulty |
| *la facultad* | the faculty |
| *la juventud* | the youth |
| *la latitud* | the latitude |
| *la libertad* | the liberty (freedom) |
| *la magnitud* | the magnitude |
| *la oportunidad* | the opportunity |
| *la responsabilidad* | the responsibility |
| *la tranquilidad* | the tranquility |
| *la velocidad* | the velocity |

With reasonable confidence, you can bet that a word ending in any of the following combinations will be feminine: *–ie, –umbre, –ión.*

| | |
|---|---|
| *la costumbre* | the custom |
| *la inversión* | the investment |
| *la muchedumbre* | the crowd |
| *la serie* | the series |
| *la situación* | the situation |

English words that end in the suffix *–tion* are equivalent to the Spanish ending *–ción*. A Spanish word that ends in *–ción* will always be feminine, will always have an accent on the *ó,* and will usually have an English cognate that ends in *–tion.* For example:

| | |
|---|---|
| *la admiración* | the admiration |
| *la continuación* | the continuation |
| *la inspiración* | the inspiration |
| *la liberación* | the liberation |
| *la nación* | the nation |

## Masculine

In addition to nouns that end in *–o* being masculine, nouns that end in *–or, –és,* or *–ón* are generally going to be masculine as well. Here are a few examples:

| | |
|---|---|
| *el ordenador* | the computer |
| *el inglés* | the Englishman |
| *el cinturón* | the belt |

## Article and suffix changes

Occasionally, a noun's spelling will remain the same but the article will change to indicate whether the meaning is masculine or feminine. Also, sometimes a noun can be changed from masculine to feminine simply by changing the ending from an *–o* to an *–a.*

## Change the article

When a word that ends in *–e* is used to refer to a person, the same word is used for both genders. Only the article and adjectives (see Chapter 8) that modify the word will reflect the gender of the person that the noun represents.

| *Masculine* | | *Feminine* | |
|---|---|---|---|
| *el agente* | the male agent | *la agente* | the female agent |
| *el cantante* | the male singer | *la cantante* | the female singer |
| *el comerciante* | the businessman | *la comerciante* | the businesswoman |

| | | | |
|---|---|---|---|
| *el estudiante* | the male student | *la estudiante* | the female student |
| *el negociante* | the male merchant | *la negociante* | the female merchant |
| *el presidente* | the male president | *la presidente* | the female president |

It is common to add the suffix –*ista* to a noun to create a new noun that means "a specialist in . . ." or "a player of . . . ." For example, *el futbolista* is a player of *fútbol* (soccer), and *el pianista* is a player of the piano or a specialist in the piano. The unusual thing about words that end in –*ista* is that they will be used for both males and females. The article will indicate the gender of the person the noun represents. Notice that it will seem strange to use a word ending in –*a* to refer to a male. If you make a note of the nouns that break these general rules when you learn them, you'll avoid a lot of mistakes later.

| *Masculine* | | *Feminine* | |
|---|---|---|---|
| *el artista* | the male artist | *la artista* | the female artist |
| *el dentista* | the male dentist | *la dentista* | the female dentist |
| *el futbolista* | the male soccer player | *la futbolista* | the female soccer player |
| *el guitarrista* | the male guitar player | *la guitarrista* | the female guitar player |
| *el novelista* | the male novelist | *la novelista* | the female novelist |
| *el pianista* | the male piano player | *la pianista* | the female piano player |

There are a few occasions where the exact same word will have two very distinct meanings, one when the noun is used with a feminine article and another when the same noun is used with a masculine article. The spelling of the word does not change—only the gender determines which of the meanings is appropriate.

| *Masculine* | | *Feminine* | |
|---|---|---|---|
| *el capital* | the money | *la capital* | the city |
| *el cura* | the priest | *la cura* | the cure |
| *el guía* | the tour guide | *la guía* | the guidebook |
| *el orden* | the order (arrangement) | *la orden* | the order (command) |
| *el policía* | the policeman | *la policía* | the police force or policewoman |

### Change the suffix

When referring to people, you can change a word from masculine to feminine simply by changing a noun that ends in *–o* to *–a*.

| *Masculine* | | *Feminine* | |
|---|---|---|---|
| *el amigo* | the male friend | *la amiga* | the female friend |
| *el alumno* | the male student | *la alumna* | the female student |
| *el chico* | the boy | *la chica* | the girl |
| *el maestro* | the male teacher | *la maestra* | the female teacher |
| *el niño* | the boy child | *la niña* | the girl child |
| *el primo* | the male cousin | *la prima* | the female cousin |
| *el sobrino* | the nephew | *la sobrina* | the niece |

Nouns that end in *–or*, *–és*, or *–n* are generally going to be masculine (see "Masculine" earlier in this chapter). If you want to use one of these nouns to refer to a female, you can change it to a feminine form by adding an *–a* to the end of the word.

| *Masculine* | | *Feminine* | |
|---|---|---|---|
| *el alemán* | the German man | *la alemana* | the German woman |
| *el burlón* | the male joker | *la burlona* | the female joker |
| *el escultor* | the male sculptor | *la escultora* | the female sculptor |
| *el francés* | the French man | *la francesa* | the French woman |
| *el profesor* | the male professor | *la profesora* | the female professor |

Remember that you can only create a feminine version of a noun if the word represents a person. You cannot, for example, change *el libro* (the book) to *la libra* just because the book belongs to a girl. The word for book, *el libro,* is always masculine, no matter whose book it is.

## Irregularities

The gender rules, of course, have exceptions, but some are predictable exceptions. Even though a word that ends in *–a* is usually feminine, many words that end in *–ma* are actually masculine. Notice the irony that *–ma* words are masculine. It's even funnier to remember this rule since a word that ends in –*dad* is usually feminine.

Remember: –*ma* words are masculine and –*dad* words are feminine.

| | |
|---|---|
| *el clima* | the climate |
| *el drama* | the drama |
| *el idioma* | the language |
| *el poema* | the poem |
| *el problema* | the problem |
| *el programa* | the program |
| *el sistema* | the system |
| *el telegrama* | the telegram |

Some exceptions are:

| | |
|---|---|
| *la goma* | the eraser, rubberband |
| *la pluma* | the pen |

Some words may appear to be feminine but are actually masculine. They end in the letter –*a* but are indeed masculine. Unfortunately, there is no trick to remembering which ones they are, so you just need to memorize them.

| | |
|---|---|
| *el día* | the day |
| *la mano* | the hand |
| *el mapa* | the map |
| *el planeta* | the planet |
| *la foto* | the photo |
| *el tranvía* | the streetcar, trolley |

A noun that ends in the letter –*e* may be either masculine or feminine. If a noun ending in –*e* refers to an object, it is usually a masculine word, but not always. It is safest to memorize the gender of these words by learning them with an article.

| | |
|---|---|
| *el accidente* | the accident |
| *el aire* | the air |
| *el arte* | the art |
| *el baile* | the dance |
| *el café* | the coffee, café |
| *el cine* | the movie theater |
| *el coche* | the car |
| *el deporte* | the sport |
| *el estante* | the bookshelf |
| *el nombre* | the name |
| *el parque* | the park |
| *el pupitre* | the desk |
| *el viaje* | the trip |

There are more than a few feminine nouns that end in *–e*. Following are some of the most common and easiest to learn:

| | |
|---|---|
| *la calle* | the street |
| *la clase* | the class |
| *la leche* | the milk |
| *la llave* | the key |
| *la noche* | the night |
| *la suerte* | the luck |
| *la parte* | the part |

Some exceptions are easy to understand. For example, the words *la fotografía* and *la motocicleta* are typically cut short in Spanish to *la moto* (the motorcycle) and *la foto* (the photograph). The original, longer version for each of these words ends in *–a* and is obviously feminine. However, the gender of the word remains feminine even though the abbreviated version of the word ends in *–o*.

# Number and Plurality

It is common to hear the words gender and number used together when contemplating a noun. As discussed earlier in this chapter, the gender of the noun indicates whether the noun is masculine or feminine. The **number** of the noun indicates whether the noun is singular or plural. You will learn to identify the word *libro* as a singular, masculine noun, and how to make the plural version of this and all other nouns.

Before you learn how to make a noun plural, however, it's necessary to learn how to pluralize the definite and indefinite articles. A plural noun will have a plural version of the article in front of it. Comparatively, the definite article in English is the same regardless of whether the noun that follows is singular or plural.

## Plural forms of definite articles

The Spanish definite article (*el* and *la,* the) has a plural version of both its feminine and masculine forms. Therefore, the definite article has four forms in Spanish. The plural of *el* is *los* and the plural of *la* is *las*.

| | | | |
|---|---|---|---|
| *Singular, masculine* | | *Plural, masculine* | |
| *el* | the | *los* | the |
| *Singular, feminine* | | *Plural, feminine* | |
| *la* | the | *las* | the |

## Plural forms of indefinite articles

The indefinite articles in Spanish are *un* (a) and *una* (an). These are only used in front of a singular noun. When a plural noun requires an indefinite article in English, the word *some* is used as the plural of *a* or *an.* In Spanish, there is a feminine and masculine version of the singular indefinite article, and also a feminine and masculine version of the plural indefinite article.

| | | | |
|---|---|---|---|
| *Singular, masculine* | | *Plural, masculine* | |
| *un* | a | *unos* | some |
| *Singular, feminine* | | *Plural, feminine* | |
| *una* | an | *unas* | some |

## Plural forms of nouns

There are very simple rules to follow when creating the plural version of
a noun. If a noun ends in any vowel, simply add *–s* to create the plural
form.

| Singular | | Plural | |
|---|---|---|---|
| *el café* | the café | *los cafés* | the cafés |
| *la hermana* | the sister | *las hermanas* | the sisters |
| *el pupitre* | the desk | *los pupitres* | the desks |
| *la mesa* | the table | *las mesas* | the tables |

If a noun ends in any consonant (including *y*), add *–es* to create the plural
form.

| Singular | | Plural | |
|---|---|---|---|
| *la ciudad* | the city | *las ciudades* | the cities |
| *la ley* | the law | *las leyes* | the laws |
| *el mes* | the month | *los meses* | the months |
| *el rey* | the king | *los reyes* | the kings |

When *z* is followed by *e*, change the *z* to *c* when forming the plural. This
means that any word ending in *–z* will become *–ces* in its plural form.

| Singular | | Plural | |
|---|---|---|---|
| *el pez* | the fish | *los peces* | the fish (plural) |
| *el lápiz* | the pencil | *los lápices* | the pencils |
| *la voz* | the voice | *las voces* | the voices |

Spanish uses the plural version of the masculine noun to represent a
couple of mixed gender. For example:

| Singular | | Plural | |
|----------|----------|--------|----------|
| *el tío* | the uncle | *los tíos* | the aunt and uncle (or the uncles) |
| *el padre* | the father | *los padres* | the parents (or the fathers) |
| *el rey* | the king | *los reyes* | the king and queen (or the kings) |

## Plural forms and accent marks

In Chapter 1, you learned that a word ending in any consonant other than *n* or *s* will be stressed on the last syllable. A word that ends in a vowel, an *n,* or an *s* will be stressed on the next-to-last syllable. Because in Spanish the plural form of a word would be stressed on the same syllable as the singular form, it is sometimes necessary to add or remove an accent mark when the plural version adds an entire syllable, such as *–es.*

If you add *–es* to a word that had an accent mark on the last syllable, the accent mark is eliminated.

| Singular | | Plural | |
|----------|----------|--------|----------|
| *el autobús* | the bus | *los autobuses* | the busses |
| *el inglés* | the Englishman | *los ingleses* | the Englishmen |
| *la lección* | the lesson | *las lecciones* | the lessons |
| *el limón* | the lemon | *los limones* | the lemons |

Other words that didn't have an accent before the *–es* was added will require an accent in their plural form.

| Singular | | Plural | |
|----------|----------|--------|----------|
| *el examen* | the exam | *los exámenes* | the exams |
| *el origen* | the origin | *los orígenes* | the origins |

A noun that ends in *–s* will remain the same in its plural form (only the article will change) unless there is an accented vowel in front of the *–s*. If there is an accented vowel in front of the *–s*, you will add *–es* and drop the accent to create the plural form. This rule is important to remember with compound nouns (see later in this chapter) because they usually end in *–s* and usually have the same form for singular and plural.

| *Singular* | | *Plural* | |
|---|---|---|---|
| *el lavaplatos* | the dishwasher | *los lavaplatos* | the dishwashers |
| *el martes* | the Tuesday | *los martes* | the Tuesdays |
| *el parentesis* | the parenthesis | *los parentesis* | the parentheses |
| *la tesis* | the thesis | *las tesis* | the theses |
| *el rascacielos* | the skyscraper | *los rascacielos* | the skyscrapers |
| *el francés* | the Frenchman | *los franceses* | the Frenchmen |
| *el dios* | the god | *los dioses* | the gods |

# Compound Nouns

A **compound word** is one word created by adding two words together. In Spanish, **compound nouns** are often created by attaching the plural form of a noun to the base of a verb. These words always look plural and sometimes even look feminine, but a compound noun is always masculine and is the same in its singular and plural form.

For example:

> *abre* (opens) + *latas* (cans) = *el abrelatas* (the can opener) or *los abre-latas* (the can openers)
>
> *quita* (to take away, remove) + *manchas* (stains) = *el quitamanchas* (stain remover) or *los quitamanchas*
>
> *rasca* (scrapes) + *cielos* (skies) = *el rascacielos* (the skyscraper) or *los rascacielos* (the skyscrapers)

## Chapter Check-Out

To see if you have learned to identify the gender of nouns, write the appropriate definite article in the first blank. Then pluralize the article and the noun on the second blank.

For example: _____ *libro.* Plural: _____

**Answer:** *el* libro; *los libros.*

1. _____ *teléfono*. Plural: _____
2. _____ *pez*. Plural: _____
3. _____ *ciudad*. Plural: _____
4. _____ *silla*. Plural: _____
5. _____ *programa*. Plural: _____

**Answers: 1.** *el teléfono; los teléfonos* **2.** *el pez; los peces* **3.** *la ciudad; las ciudades* **4.** *la silla; las sillas* **5.** *el programa; los programas*

# Chapter 3

# REPLACING NOUNS WITH PRONOUNS

## Chapter Check-In

❑ Understanding what a pronoun does in a sentence

❑ Determining which pronoun to use

❑ Learning subject pronouns in English and Spanish

❑ Analyzing the differences in pronoun usage

**A** pronoun is a word that replaces a noun. Since pronouns basically do the same thing in Spanish as they do in English, it's helpful to review pronouns in English first. You'll learn the role that each noun plays in the sentence based on the pronouns that are used to replace the nouns. Then you'll learn what specific pronoun is used based on the role of the noun in the sentence. Finally, you'll learn how the cases of subject pronouns differ in the two languages and how pronouns are placed differently in sentences.

## Prounoun Use

Regardless of what type of pronoun you use, it is important to understand that a pronoun not only replaces a noun, but also all of the description words that go with the noun. To avoid the repetition of long and annoying noun clauses, a pronoun eliminates the noun and all the words that modify (describe) it. Obviously, a pronoun should not be used unless it is clear exactly what the pronoun is replacing. For example:

The *extremely beautiful mountain* was within sight. *It* was straight ahead.

In the sample sentence, the pronoun "it" replaces the noun "mountain" and also eliminates all of the modifiers that go with "mountain" because you don't say extremely beautiful "it." At first you will be replacing simple nouns with pronouns, so there won't be any complex or difficult modifiers. Just remember that when a noun has any modifiers, such as adjectives or articles, they will disappear when that noun becomes a pronoun.

## Pronoun Cases

Pronouns come in cases. A case of pronouns is a list of pronouns used to replace a noun that acts as a certain part of speech. If you want to use a pronoun to replace a noun that is the subject of a sentence, you must select the appropriate pronoun from the subject case of pronouns. A noun that is acting as the direct object of the sentence can only be replaced by one of the pronouns from the direct object case. This chapter focuses on the pronouns that are used as the subject of the sentence. The direct and indirect object cases of pronouns are explained in Chapter 10 after you have learned to identify these two parts of a sentence. Chapter 15 explains reflexive verbs and the reflexive case of pronouns as well as the case of pronouns used as the object of a preposition and the demonstrative pronouns case.

A noun can play several different roles in the sentence. It can be the subject, direct object, indirect object, object of a preposition, or something with a scary name called a predicate nominative. Which pronoun you use to replace a noun depends on what role the noun is playing in the specific sentence you are analyzing.

## Subject Case Pronouns

Since every sentence must have a subject, the first type of Spanish pronoun you learn to use is the **subject pronoun.** These little words are used to replace a noun that serves as the subject of the sentence.

### English subject case pronouns

The subject case pronouns listed in Table 3-1 are only used to replace a noun if the noun is serving as the subject of the sentence.

**Table 3-1   English Subject Case Pronouns**

| First Person Singular | First Person Plural |
|---|---|
| I | we |
| **Second Person Singular** | **Second Person Plural** |
| you | you |
| **Third Person Singular** | **Third Person Plural** |
| he, she, it | they |

Pronouns in the top row (I, we) are called first person pronouns. On the left is the singular first person, *I*, and on the right is the plural first person, *we*. If you think about it, when *I* have a group with *me*, the plural of *I* is *we*.

Pronouns in the second row down are second person pronouns (you, you). In English, the second person singular is the same as the second person plural, so the pronoun *you* is written twice. On the left, *you* refers to one person, and the *you* on the right refers to more than one person, like "you guys" or "y'all."

Pronouns in the third row are third person pronouns. The singular third person pronouns have one for each gender, *he* and *she*. For genderless objects, the pronoun *it* is used. The plural of the third person does not specify gender in English, so the generic pronoun *they* is used when talking about any group of people or things. The singular third person pronouns in English are different depending on the gender of the person being replaced (he and she). However, the plural version of these pronouns is the same regardless of gender (they, they).

Because objects do not have gender in English, the pronoun *it* is used to represent a thing or object that is the subject of the sentence. There is no Spanish equivalent to the subject pronoun *it* because all nouns are either masculine or feminine. If you want to say something like "it's important" or "it's raining" you simply use the *él* form of the verb with no pronoun. Chapter 4 discusses the different forms of verbs including the *él* form.

### Spanish subject case pronouns

The English pronouns do not exactly match up with Spanish pronouns so Table 3-2 presents the pronouns in a different way. The best way to learn these pronouns is to make flashcards with the English on one side and the Spanish on the other. Be sure to specify things like feminine and formal or informal.

**Table 3-2    Spanish Subject Case Pronouns**

| Singular Pronoun | English Equivalent | Plural Pronoun | English Equivalent |
|---|---|---|---|
| yo | I | nosotros | we |
|  |  | nosotras | we (feminine) |
| tú | you (in an informal manner) | vosotros | you (informal, plural) |
|  |  | vosotras | you (informal, plural, feminine) |
| usted | you (in a formal manner) | ustedes | you (plural) |
| Ud. (abbreviation of usted) | you (formal) | Uds. (abbreviation of ustedes) | you (plural) |
| él | he | ellos | they |
| ella | she | ellas | they (feminine) |

Subject pronouns in Spanish are usually not capitalized except when used as the first word of a sentence. Notice, however, that the abbreviated forms *Ud.* and *Uds.* are always capitalized, and the longer versions *usted* and *ustedes* are not capitalized except when serving as the first word in a sentence.

You probably don't think about the fact that the English pronoun *I* is always capitalized. The Spanish equivalent, *yo,* is not capitalized, unless it is the first word of the sentence.

Table 3-3 lists the pronouns in a specific order to help you conjugate verbs in later chapters. This organizational chart is called a conjugation chart. You should memorize the order and grouping of the pronouns listed. Notice that *nosotros/nosotras* is across from *yo; vosotros/vosotras* is across from *tú; él* is across from *ellos; ella* is across from *ellas;* and *usted* is across from *ustedes.* It is important to maintain this form when you write the pronouns in a conjugation chart. Also remember that *usted/Ud.* and *ustedes/Uds.* are second person pronouns in English but take the third person form of the verb in Spanish.

**Table 3-3    Subject Pronoun Conjugation Chart in Spanish**

| First Person Singular | First Person Plural |
|---|---|
| yo | nosotros/nosotras |
| **Second Person Singular** | **Second Person Plural** |
| tú | vosotros/vosotras |
| usted/Ud. | ustedes/Uds. |
| **Third Person Singular** | **Third Person Plural** |
| él | ellos |
| ella | ellas |

In Spanish, third person pronouns match the gender of the person they represent. The pronoun *él* means *he* and *ella* means *she*. When you pluralize the third person pronouns, *ellos* means *they* and is used to replace an all-male group or a group of mixed gender. When it is certain that *they* are all feminine, the pronoun *ellas* is used.

## Differences between English and Spanish subject case pronouns

To use pronouns correctly, it's helpful to have a basic understanding of the differences between English and Spanish subject case pronouns. Some of the pronouns are easy to translate.

The first person singular pronoun *I* in English is used exactly like the Spanish word *yo*, except that *yo* is always lowercase unless it starts a sentence. However, the corresponding first person plural pronoun *we* doesn't indicate gender in English. The Spanish first person plural pronoun *nosotros* is typically used to express *we* unless there is absolute certainty that the group of people that *we* represents is 100 percent female. *Nosotras* is the feminine version of *nosotros* and is used when *we* are all girls. It is tempting to abbreviate *nosotros* or *nosotras,* but you should not do so. The word *nos* is a very different word and will cause you much confusion later if you use it as an abbreviation.

In Spanish, if someone stands in front of a group and says, "You're invited to my party," the pronoun they use will give away whether they are speaking to one person or the entire group. Also, Spanish has a special pronoun to address someone in a formal or less formal manner.

The second person pronoun in English is *you*. This is an extremely vague pronoun because it can refer to either one person or a group, as in "you guys" or "y'all." The Spanish have a singular version of *you* and a plural version of *you*. The second person singular pronoun *usted* is formal and often abbreviated *Ud.* The second person plural version of you is *ustedes* (abbreviated as *Uds.*).

The pronoun *tú* is the informal way to say *you*. This is used when you talk to someone younger than you or someone who is a close friend or family member. It is safest to use the *usted* way of saying *you* unless you are certain that you won't be insulting someone by using the informal *tú* pronoun. The plural form of *tú* is *vosotros*, but it is rarely used outside of Spain. Most people don't bother to learn the *vosotros* pronoun because *ustedes* can be used as the plural form of *you* for any situation. Since Spanish is new to you, it's easier to use *ustedes* any time you want to address a group as "you guys" or "y'all."

## Replacing nouns with subject case pronouns

Remember that a subject pronoun is used to replace a noun that is the subject of the sentence. If the subject is a single person, use *él* or *ella* to replace the person's name, depending on the gender of the person. If the subject is more than one person, use the pronoun *ellos* unless all of the people included in the subject are female. If the subject is a thing rather than a person, the subject pronoun is often eliminated completely, or the subject pronouns *él* or *ella* are used to represent the gender of the noun being replaced.

## Chapter Check-Out

Use Table 3-3, the Spanish subject pronoun conjugation chart, to identify each of the following subjects. Here are two hints:

Hint 1: To determine if it is first, second, or third person, count from the top down.

Hint 2: To determine if it is plural or singular, look to see if it's on the right (plural) or left (singular) side of the chart.

Identify the following subject pronouns:

1. What pronoun in Spanish is first person plural?
2. What pronoun in Spanish is third person singular (masculine)?
3. What pronoun in Spanish is first person singular?
4. What pronoun in Spanish is third person plural (feminine)?

**Answers: 1.** *Nosotros* is the first person plural. It is the equivalent to "we" in English. In Spanish, there is also a feminine version, *nosotras*, which is used only when it is clear that all involved are female. **2.** *Él* is the third person singular masculine form. It is the English pronoun "he." **3.** *Yo* is the first person singular. It means "I." **4.** *Ellas* is the third person plural. In English, the word "they" is used regardless of gender, but in Spanish, *ellas* is used when they are all girls.

# Chapter 4

# INFINITIVE AND REGULAR VERB USE

## Chapter Check-In

❏ Understanding and using infinitives

❏ Creating a conjugation chart with pronouns

❏ Conjugating verbs in the present tense

❏ Using the present progressive tense

**V**erbs are the action and linking words found in all languages, but the forms that verbs take and the way they are used in sentences are different between Spanish and English. Most people learn regular verbs in present tense sentences first, but must be introduced to the verb in its infinitive form before changing the form of the verb to go with the subject. For example, the verb *to speak* is an infinitive, but in a present tense sentence, the form changes to *speaks* with certain subjects such as "He speaks English" or "She speaks French." In Spanish, the verb will also change slightly depending on what the subject of the sentence is. Using the correct form of the verb to go with the subject is called **verb conjugation.** While some of us try to avoid the good old-fashioned verb conjugation chart, most find they are able to visualize the patterns of verbs if they learn to list the forms consistently in chart form. If you've heard the word "conjugation" over and over again but are not completely certain what it means, you will appreciate this chapter because it clarifies the concept for you and then prepares you to actually create and complete conjugation charts for your own study purposes.

## Infinitives

The most basic form of a verb is called an **infinitive** in English or *infinitivo* in Spanish. While both languages have similar names for the infinitive, they do not create the infinitive form of the verb the same way. In English, the word "to" must be placed in front of a verb to create an infinitive. For example, the sentence you just read includes the infinitive "to create." In Spanish, an infinitive is only one word. *Hablar* is the Spanish equivalent to the English infinitive "to speak," *beber* is "to drink," and *escribir* is "to write." You will be able to recognize the infinitive form of verbs in Spanish because they always end in one of three ways: *–ar, –er,* or *–ir.* The above examples of infinitives include one of each type. Because *hablar* ends in *–ar,* it is called an **–ar verb**. *Beber* is an **–er verb** and *escribir* is an **–ir verb**. The type of infinitive the verb has (*–ar, –er,* or *–ir*) will determine the conjugation patterns of the verb in different tenses. You will learn what conjugation is and how to use the infinitive to determine the patterns of the verb's conjugation later in this chapter.

The main reason you need to know about infinitives is because the verbs you learn will be written in their infinitive form. It will be helpful to learn the list of simple verbs in Table 4-1 because they are used in the examples in this chapter.

**Table 4-1   Common Infinitives**

| –ar *Verbs* | –er *Verbs* | –ir *Verbs* |
| --- | --- | --- |
| *ayudar* (to help) | *aprender* (to learn) | *abrir* (to open) |
| *bailar* (to dance) | *beber* (to drink) | *decidir* (to decide) |
| *caminar* (to walk) | *comer* (to eat) | *escribir* (to write) |
| *cantar* (to sing) | *comprender* (to understand) | *recibir* (to receive) |
| *contestar* (to answer) | *correr* (to run) | *vivir* (to live) |
| *comprar* (to buy) | *leer* (to read) | |
| *estudiar* (to study) | *responder* (to answer) | |
| *ganar* (to win/to earn) | *vender* (to sell) | |
| *hablar* (to speak) | | |
| *necesitar* (to need) | | |
| *preguntar* (to ask a question) | | |
| *trabajar* (to work) | | |
| *viajar* (to travel) | | |

The specific verbs that you learn will depend on your purpose for learning Spanish. Some of the most useful verbs are included in Appendix A.

When you look for a verb in the dictionary, you will find the infinitive form listed. To avoid a rather lengthy "T" section in the English side of your dictionary, the verb is listed without the word "to" since all infinitives start with the word "to" in English. You will notice, however, that if you look for the word "write" in the Spanish side of your dictionary, you will find the infinitive *escribir*. In the Spanish side of the dictionary, the verb will always be listed as an infinitive. If you see a verb in a Spanish sentence that you want to look up, first you will have to determine the infinitive form. For example, *vive* is not in the dictionary because it is a form of the verb *vivir*. Since all verbs must end in *–ar, –er,* or *–ir,* you can usually find the correct infinitive in the dictionary without much difficulty.

## Verbs

In some aspects, Spanish uses infinitives in sentences the same way as English. Those similar usages are what you will learn in your first two years of Spanish. There are certain verbs that can be followed by an infinitive. You can create simple two-verb sentences in both languages by conjugating the first verb to go with the subject and simply placing the infinitive after the conjugated verb.

The most common verbs that can be followed by an infinitive are as follows:

| | |
|---|---|
| *desear* | to want |
| *esperar* | to hope |
| *necesitar* | to need |
| *poder* | to be able |
| *querer* | to want |

These verbs will typically be followed by a verb in its infinitive form, much like the English equivalent. To learn how to conjugate a verb, see "Regular Verbs in the Present Tense" later in this chapter.

For example:

| | |
|---|---|
| *El desea aprender.* | He wants to learn. |
| *María espera ganar.* | Maria hopes to win. |
| *Nosotros necesitamos trabajar.* | We need to work. |
| *Julio puede bailar.* | Julio is able to dance. |
| *Marco quiere comer.* | Mark wants to eat. |

Other uses of the infinitive with prepositions are addressed in Chapter 14.

# Regular Verbs in the Present Tense

Regular verbs follow predictable patterns. The pattern that a verb follows depends on the last two letters of the infinitive form of the verb. Verbs that end in *–ar* are the most common and most predictable, so they are presented first. To conjugate an *–ar* verb follow these two steps:

1. Remove the *–ar* ending from the infinitive. What is left is called the base of the verb.

2. Using the regular endings shown in Table 4-2, you would place the base of the verb in front of those endings.

**Table 4-2   Regular *–ar* Verb Endings**

| Singular Pronoun | Ending | Plural Pronoun | Ending |
|---|---|---|---|
| yo | –o | nosotros or nosotras | –amos |
| tú | –as | vosotros or vosotras | –áis |
| usted (Ud.) | –a | ustedes (Uds.) | –an |
| él | –a | ellos | –an |
| ella | –a | ellas | –an |

The verb *hablar* (to speak) is a regular *–ar* verb, so it will serve as a good illustration of creating a conjugation chart using the steps above. First, remove the *–ar* ending, and what's left is the base *habl–*. When you put the base together with ending *–o* for *yo*, for example, you have the conjugated verb form *hablo*.

Table 4-3 shows the conjugation chart for the verb *hablar* in the present tense.

**Table 4-3    Conjugation Chart for the Verb *Hablar***

| Singular Pronoun | Verb | Plural Pronoun | Verb |
| --- | --- | --- | --- |
| yo | hablo (I speak) | nosotros or nosotras | hablamos (we speak) |
| tú | hablas (you [informal] speak) | vosotros or vosotras | habláis (you [informal] speak) |
| usted (Ud.) | habla (you [formal] speak) | ustedes (Uds.) | hablan (you [formal] speak) |
| él | habla (he speaks) | ellos | hablan (they speak) |
| ella | habla (she speaks) | ellas | hablan (they speak) |

Verbs ending in *–er* are the second most common type of verb. To conjugate a regular *–er* verb, you use the same two-step process as you did with *–ar* verbs, but the endings are different for *–er* verbs. The patterns of *–er* verbs are very similar to *–ir* verbs, which will make it easy to learn their endings. So if you want to conjugate a regular *–er* verb, simply remove the *–er* ending from the infinitive and place the base of the verb in front of the endings presented in Table 4-4.

**Table 4-4    Regular *–er* Verb Endings**

| Singular Pronoun | Ending | Plural Pronoun | Ending |
| --- | --- | --- | --- |
| yo | –o | nosotros or nosotras | –emos |
| tú | –es | vosotros or vosotras | –éis |
| usted (Ud.) | –e | ustedes (Uds.) | –en |
| él | –e | ellos | –en |
| ella | –e | ellas | –en |

Now, take a look at Table 4-5 for the conjugated form of the verb *comer* (to eat).

**Table 4-5    Conjugation Chart for the Verb *Comer***

| Singular Pronoun | Verb | Plural Pronoun | Verb |
|---|---|---|---|
| yo | como (I eat) | nosotros or nosotras | comemos (we eat) |
| tú | comes (you [informal] eat) | vosotros or vosotras | coméis (you [informal] eat) |
| usted (Ud.) | come (you [formal] eat) | ustedes (Uds.) | comen (you [formal] eat) |
| él | come (he eats) | ellos | comen (they eat) |
| ella | come (she eats) | ellas | comen (they eat) |

Verbs of the third type are called *–ir* verbs. In the present tense a verb ending in *–ir* will be conjugated the same as an *–er* verb in all forms except for two. As illustrated in Table 4-6, the endings used for the *nosotros/nosotras* (the first person plural) and *vosotros/vosotras* (the second person plural) forms of the verb are different for *–ir* verbs.

**Table 4-6    Regular *–ir* Verb Endings**

| Singular Pronoun | Ending | Plural Pronoun | Ending |
|---|---|---|---|
| yo | –o | nosotros or nosotras | –imos |
| tú | –es | vosotros or vosotras | –ís |
| usted (Ud.) | –e | ustedes (Uds.) | –en |
| él | –e | ellos | –en |
| ella | –e | ellas | –en |

*Escribir* (to write) was one of the *–ir* verbs presented earlier as an infinitive. The forms of the verb *escribir* in Table 4-7 will serve as an example for any regular *–ir* verb.

**Table 4-7    Conjugation Chart for the Verb** *Escribir*

| Singular Pronoun | Verb | Plural Pronoun | Verb |
|---|---|---|---|
| *yo* | *escribo* (I write) | *nosotros* or *nosotras escribimos* (we write) | *excribimos* (we write) |
| *tú* | *escribes* (you [informal] write) | *vosotros* or *vosotras escribís* (you [informal] write) | *escribís* (you [informal] write) |
| *usted (Ud.)* | *escribe* (you [formal] write) | *ustedes (Uds.)* | *escriben* (you [formal] write) |
| *él* | *escribe* (he writes) | *ellos* | *escriben* (they write) |
| *ella* | *escribe* (she writes) | *ellas* | *escriben* (they write) |

# Choosing the Correct Verb Form

Obviously, you will not always have a pronoun as a subject. Sometimes you will use the actual noun as the subject. To determine which form of the verb to use when a noun is the subject, just consider what pronoun you would use if you were to change that noun to a pronoun in a second sentence about the subject. For example, you want to write the sentence, "John dances well." What pronoun would go in the blank if the next sentence were, "_____ does it every day." You probably responded "he" immediately. If you wanted to write this sentence in Spanish, you would ask yourself, "What is the Spanish subject pronoun that means 'he'?" Hopefully you'll remember *él* and then use the form of the verb that goes with *él*. (If you need a review of pronouns, see Chapter 3.) You do not have to write the pronoun; just use the actual noun and the form of the verb that goes with the pronoun you know would replace that noun. Here's another example:

*María canta bien.* Mary sings well.

The form *canta* is used with *ella*, the subject pronoun that would represent *María*.

When more than one name is the subject, the *ellos/ellas* form of the verb is required. For example:

*Lupe y Soledad cantan bien.* Lupe and Soledad sing well.

The form *cantan* is used with *ellas*, the subject pronoun that would replace *Lupe y Soledad*. Whenever a list of names is the subject, the *ellos/ ellas* form of the verb is used. If you think about it, the same thing happens in English. Consider the example, "Jane, Taneka, and Heather go to the store. They go shopping every day." Notice that the verb form "go" is used for both sentences because the subjects are the same even if one is stated in pronoun form.

When a sentence starts with any name(s) and the pronoun *I*, the subject of the sentence is basically *we*. In Spanish, the *nosostros/nosotras* form of the verb will be used any time the subject is one or more names + *yo*.

For example:

> *Juanita, Julia, y yo cantamos.* Juanita, Julia, and I sing.
>
> *Julia y yo cantamos bien.* Julia and I sing well.

Take note that a verb with an *–s* on the end of it in the English sentence does not necessarily have an *–s* on the end in the Spanish translation. It is a common mistake to want to write "she sings" with *cantas*. Since she is the pronoun *ella*, you must use the form of the verb that goes with *ella*: *canta*. Just remember that the form of the verb that ends in *–s* in Spanish goes with the pronoun *tú*.

> *Él canta.* He sings.
>
> *Tú cantas.* You sing.

The secret to using the correct verb form is to refuse to think in English. Here are some tips to keep in mind when conjugating a verb with a noun:

- Determine the subject of the sentence and what pronoun would replace it.

- Determine which ending of the verb goes with that pronoun, and add it to the base of the verb you want to use in the sentence.

- Don't even think about what the English verb form would be.

When the subject of a sentence is *it*, the Spanish will simply use the *él/ella* form of the verb and write absolutely no pronoun. The subject is understood because of the form of the verb. This will happen with sentences about weather and seasons: It is cloudy *(está nublado)*. It is summer *(es verano)*. Any time you're writing a sentence that starts with "it," just use the *él/ella* form of the verb and forget about using any pronoun.

Any time the subject can be easily ascertained, the pronoun is eliminated. Because three pronouns: *él, ella,* and *usted* all share the same form of the verb, it is important to use the subject or subject pronoun any time the identity of the subject is difficult to determine. You can't just write *canta* unless it's really obvious who's singing from some prior sentence. The same is true for *ellos, ellas,* and *ustedes.* The verb form *cantan* is shared by all three, so it's important to use these pronouns for clarity. However, you'll often see sentences that begin without any subject when a previous sentence has made the subject obvious. For example:

> *Trini escribe muy bien. Esribe novelas y dramas.*
> Trini writes very well. She writes novels and plays.

In the second sentence, it is assumed that the subject is the most recently named noun. It is the responsibility of the speaker to write at least a pronoun for the second sentence if the subject is not the last possible subject mentioned in the first sentence.

# Present Progressive

In English the **present progressive** is often used to indicate an action in progress or ongoing. If the present tense is used to state "I bathe," it has a slightly different meaning than if the present progressive tense is used: "I am bathing." The understood meaning of the present progressive is that the action of the verb is happening at that point in time. There are other cases in English sentences where the present progressive indicates that the action of the verb is not necessarily occurring at that exact moment of time, but rather is an ongoing process that is much like the simple present indicative tense. For example, "He is studying French" has the same basic meaning as "He studies French." But if one asks what he is doing right now, it would also be appropriate to use the present progressive to answer: "He is studying French."

The Spanish use the present progressive similarly. The present progressive construction is created the same way in Spanish as it is in English. This makes the present progressive very easy to learn and understand.

To use a verb in the present progressive, you must first conjugate the verb *estar* to go with the subject. Then you use the present participle form of the main verb. The **present participle** in Spanish ends in *–ando* (for *–ar* verbs) or *–iendo* (for both *–er* and *–ir* verbs) and is the equivalent of an English verb ending in *–ing*. For example: *Juan estudia* (John studies) is the present tense. *Juan está estudiando* (John is studying) is the present progressive construction. You must have both parts in this contruction, or else it will not make sense.

An *–ir* verb that stem changes in the present tense will have an *e>i* or *o>u* stem in the present participle form. Here are some examples of *–ir* verbs:

| *Infinitive* | *Present Participle* |
|---|---|
| *morir* (to die) | *muriendo* (dying) |
| *dormir* (to sleep) | *durmiendo* (sleeping) |
| *decir* (to say, to tell) | *diciendo* (saying, telling) |
| *sentir* (to feel, to regret) | *sintiendo* (feeling, regretting) |
| *mentir* (to tell a lie) | *mintiendo* (telling a lie) |
| *pedir* (to request) | *pidiendo* (requesting) |

All other verbs that stem change in the present tense will not have any stem change in the present participle form.

| *Infinitive* | *Present Participle* |
|---|---|
| *cerrar* (to close) | *cerrando* (closing) |
| *pensar* (to think) | *pensando* (thinking) |
| *jugar* (to play) | *jugando* (playing) |
| *perder* (to lose) | *perdiendo* (losing) |

If you want to use a verb in the present progressive, you are really only conjugating the verb *estar,* and adding the exact same present participle form to each of the different forms of *estar.* For example, Table 4-8 shows how the verb *trabajar* (to work) is used in the present progressive.

**Table 4-8   Present Progressive of the Verb *Trabajar***

| | | |
|---|---|---|
| *yo estoy trabajando* (I am working) | *nosotros/nosotras* | *estamos trabajando* (we are working) |
| *tú estás trabajando* (you are working) | *vosotros/vosotras* | *estáis trabajando* (you are working) |
| *usted está trabajando* (you are working) | *ustedes* | *están trabajando* (you are working) |
| *él está trabajando* (he is working) | *ellos* | *están trabajando* (they are working) |
| *ella está trabajando* (she is working) | *ellas* | *están trabajando* (they are working) |

If you read or hear a Spanish sentence in the present progressive and it doesn't sound right, it may be that English would have used the present tense. So, if you try thinking of the present tense form of the verb that's in its present participle form, the sentence may be easier for you to understand.

## Chapter Check-Out

### Fill in the blank

Use your knowledge of the conjugation charts to fill in the blanks with the correct form of the verb in parenthesis.

1. *Yo* _____ *español. (hablar)*
2. *Tú* _____ *libros. (vender)*
3. *Cecilia* _____ *en Puerto Rico. (vivir)*
4. *Miguel y yo* _____ *muchos tacos. (comer)*
5. *Sarita, Violeta, y Andrés* _____ *mucho. (estudiar)*

For numbers 6–10, go back to numbers 1–5 and use the present progressive.

**Answers: 1.** *hablo* **2.** *vendes* **3.** *vive* **4.** *comemos* **5.** *estudian* **6.** *estoy hablando* **7.** *estás vendiendo* **8.** *está viviendo* **9.** *estamos comiendo* **10.** *están estudiando*

# Chapter 5

# BASIC SENTENCE STRUCTURE

## Chapter Check-In

- ❑ Understanding sentence structure
- ❑ Using subjects and verbs
- ❑ Joining thoughts with conjunctions
- ❑ Adding punctuation

**C**reating a correct sentence is not always as simple as translating the words of an English sentence and writing them in the same order in Spanish. Fortunately, the basic sentence structure is generally the same, but there are some basic concepts you must understand in order to avoid making common mistakes when writing or speaking in complete sentences. This chapter covers simple, affirmative sentences. Negative sentences and questions pose more difficulties for English speakers and will be covered in later chapters.

## Sentence Structure

The only requirements for a complete sentence are a subject and a verb. Just like in an English sentence, in Spanish the subject (when stated) comes (usually) before the verb. There are many other parts of speech that can make a sentence more complex, but those are discussed in later chapters. For now, simply think of a sentence as:

<u>Subject</u> + **verb** + rest of sentence

In the following sample sentences, the subject is <u>underlined</u> and the verb is in bold type.

<u>Julieta</u> **bebe** una coca cola.
<u>Julieta</u> **drinks** a Coke.

<u>Tú</u> **compras** un televisor.
<u>You</u> **buy** a TV.

<u>Berto y Gonzalo</u> **viajan** a Lima.
<u>Berto and Gonzalo</u> **travel** to Lima.

<u>Diego</u> **trabaja** en un hospital.
<u>Diego</u> **works** in a hospital.

Remember that the **subject** is the person or thing that is responsible for the action of the verb. The **verb** is usually an action word and will be conjugated in the correct form to go with the subject (see Chapter 4 for rules on conjugation; see Chapter 6 for rules on the most common linking verbs: *ser* and *estar*).

## Conjunctions

The easiest way to make a sentence more complex is by using conjunctions to join two words or even two phrases. A conjunction links nouns, clauses, and phrases using "and," "but," and "or." These three English conjunctions are used to join parts of a sentence or even two sentences.

For example:

- Jill **and** Brad are my neighbors.
- Brad **or** Jill mows the lawn once a week.
- Brad mows in the morning, **but** Jill prefers the evening.

The most basic Spanish conjunctions are:

| | |
|---|---|
| *y* | and |
| *pero* | but |
| *o* | or |

These three conjunctions are used in the same way as English conjunctions. Remember that if the conjunction *y* (and) is used to create a compound subject, the verb will be in a plural form. However, if the conjunction *o* (or) is used, the subject is considered singular, and the verb will be in a singular form.

*Estela y Coleta bailan tango.*

Estela and Coleta dance the tango. (Notice that *bailan* is an *ellos* form of the verb.)

*Miguelita o Marisol baila el flamenco hoy.*

Miguelita or Marisol dances the flamenco today. (Notice that *baila* is the *ella* form of the verb.)

While *y* and *o* can be used to join nouns or sentences together, *pero* can only be used to join sentences together.

*Juan baila pero Marco canta.*

Juan dances but Marco sings.

There are two irregularities with conjunctions. The conjunction *o* changes to *u* in front of words beginning with *ho–*, or *o–*. And, the conjunction *y* changes to *e* in front of any word beginning with *hi–* or *i–*.

For example:

| | |
|---|---|
| *Lola e Inéz* | Lola and Inez |
| *Madre e hija* | Mother and daughter |
| *Miami u Orlando* | Miami or Orlando |
| *Adiós u hola* | Goodbye or hello |

## Punctuation

You can't have a complete sentence without punctuation, and, luckily, punctuation rules are very similar in both Spanish and English. On the basic level, a period is used at the end of a sentence, and a comma is used for the same reasons you would use a comma in English. However, there are some differences between Spanish and English.

### Question marks

One unusual punctuation mark is the upside-down question mark (¿) that precedes a Spanish question. The question is followed by the same question mark (?) used in English. Because Spanish questions often look exactly like sentences, the upside-down question mark is necessary to identify that what follows is a question.

## Exclamation points

The upside-down exclamation point (¡) is another unusual punctuation mark. It precedes a Spanish exclamatory sentence and is followed by the same exclamation point (!) used in English. The emphasis indicated by an exclamation point at the end of the sentence is reinforced by an upside-down exclamation point at the beginning so that the reader knows to say the sentence with emotion before the sentence is over.

## Punctuation and numbers

There is a rather confusing aspect of punctuation that occurs only with numbers. The Spanish use a comma to indicate a decimal point and a period where we use a comma in numbers. For example:

| English Number | Spanish Number |
|---|---|
| 1,000 | 1.000 |
| 2.43 | 2,43 |
| 2,345,678 | 2.345.678 |
| $6,455.00 | $6.455,00 |

## Chapter Check-Out

Translate the following sentences into Spanish. Be sure to use the correct conjunction and to consider whether to conjugate the verb to go with a singular or plural subject.

1. John and Mary cook.
2. Gomez and Hidalgo teach the class.
3. Charlotte or Orlando wins the game.
4. He plays the guitar but she plays the piano.
5. The boy and the girl study.

**Answers: 1.** *Juan y María cocinan.* **2.** *Gómez e Hidalgo enseñan la clase* **3.** *Charlotte u Orlando gana el partido.* **4.** *Él toca la guitarra pero ella toca el piano.* **5.** *El chico (niño) y la niña estudian* (or *Los niños estudian*).

# Chapter 6

# IRREGULAR VERBS IN THE PRESENT TENSE

## Chapter Check-In

❑ Conjugating irregular verbs

❑ Learning the patterns of *yo* irregulars

❑ Conjugating stem-changing verbs

❑ Differentiating between two verbs with one English translation

This chapter prepares you to deal with some of the irregularities of verbs in the present tense. You will learn that certain irregular verbs follow no pattern. Unfortunately, when you learn one of these verbs, you will have to learn each specific form of the verb without being able to predict the endings.

There are other verbs that are technically "irregular," but they have such predictable irregularities that once you learn the patterns these verbs will be as easy to conjugate as regular verbs.

Another issue that arises with verbs is based on the meaning of the verb rather than the conjugation. It is common for English to have one verb with several different meanings. Some Spanish verbs prove to be challenging because there are two completely different Spanish verbs—each with a specific meaning—that are translated with the exact same word in English. This chapter prepares you to differentiate the meanings of those two verbs and determine which one is appropriate in a specific situation.

# Common Verbs Irregular in the Present Tense

There is an exception to every rule, except the rule that states there's an exception to every rule. You can go crazy contemplating this paradox, but, as you study language, you become convinced that the statement is true. The good news about Spanish is that many of the exceptions to the rules are predictable. The most commonly used irregular verbs and the most important patterns to irregular verbs follow.

## Common irregular verbs

Some verbs are so irregular that you will not be able to recognize when a conjugated form goes with the infinitive of the verb. The most irregular verbs in Spanish are also the most common, so you see the conjugated forms of these verbs often. Eventually, you will come to know the conjugated forms of these verbs so well that it may be difficult to remember the infinitive form. The verb *ir* means "to go." Notice that the entire verb looks like the *–ir* infinitive ending, but it is conjugated nothing at all like a normal *–ir* verb. Also, notice that the conjugated forms of the verb *ir* in Table 6-1 look more like they come from some *–ar* verb with a *v* in it.

**Table 6-1    Conjugation Chart for the Verb *Ir***

| | |
|---|---|
| *yo voy* (I go) | *nosotros/nosotras vamos* (we go) |
| *tú vas* (you [informal] go) | *vosotros/vosotras vais* (you [informal, plural] go) |
| *usted (Ud.) va* (you [formal] go) | *ustedes (Uds.) van* (you [formal, plural] go) |
| *él va* (he goes) | *ellos van* (they go) |
| *ella va* (she goes) | *ellas van* (they [feminine] go) |

Once you get used to thinking that *voy, vas, va, vamos, vais,* and *van* all mean *go* or *goes,* it's hard to remember that the infinitive that means "to go" is the verb *ir.*

Another really irregular verb is *ser,* which means "to be." Be aware that each word that follows a pronoun in Table 6-2 is the entire form of the verb.

**Table 6-2    Conjugation Chart for the Verb *Ser***

| | |
|---|---|
| *yo soy* (I am) | *nosotros/nosotras somos* (we are) |
| *tú eres* (you [informal] are) | *vosotros/vosotras sois* (you [informal, plural] are) |
| *usted (Ud.) es* (you [formal] are) | *ustedes (Uds.) son* (you [formal, plural] are) |
| *él es* (he is) | *ellos son* (they are) |
| *ella es* (she is) | *ellas son* (they [feminine] are) |

As luck would have it, the most common form, *es,* sounds a lot like its English equivalent "is."

Not only is *ser* irregular in its conjugated forms, it also has to compete with the verb *estar,* which also means "to be." An explanation of when to use *ser* and when to use *estar* is later in the chapter.

### Irregular verbs in the *yo* form

Several common verbs in Spanish are completely regular verbs except for the *yo* form. These are usually called *yo* irregulars. To help you remember the irregular *yo* form as you work through this section, verbs with the same irregular *yo* form are grouped together. For a reminder on the regular endings of verbs, see Chapter 4.

#### *–oy* verbs

There are two extremely important verbs that are irregular only because the *yo* form of the verb ends in *–oy*: *dar* (to give) and *estar* (to be). As you can see in Tables 6-3 and 6-4, the rest of the forms of the verbs have regular endings.

**Table 6-3    Conjugation Chart for the Verb *Dar***

| | |
|---|---|
| *yo doy* (I give) | *nosotros/nosotras damos* (we give) |
| *tú das* (you [informal] give) | *vosotros/vosotras dais* (you [informal, plural] give) |
| *usted (Ud.) da* (you [formal] give) | *ustedes (Uds.) dan* (you [formal, plural] give) |
| *él da* (he gives) | *ellos dan* (they give) |
| *ella da* (she gives) | *ellas dan* (they [feminine] give) |

**Table 6-4    Conjugation Chart for the Verb *Estar***

| | |
|---|---|
| *yo estoy* (I am) | *nosotros/nosotras estamos* (we are) |
| *tú estás* (you [informal] are) | *vosotros/vosotras estáis* (you [informal, plural] are) |
| *usted (Ud.) está* (you [formal] are) | *ustedes (Uds.) están* (you [formal, plural] are) |
| *él está* (he is) | *ellos están* (they are) |
| *ella está* (she is) | *ellas están* (they [feminine] are) |

Notice that the verb *estar* has accent marks on all forms except the first person *yo* and the first person plural *nosotros/nosotras*.

### *–go* verbs

There are many verbs with a *yo* form that ends in *–go* even though there is not a single letter *g* in the infinitive. Most of these verbs are regular in all of the rest of their forms.

The four simplest and most common *–go* verbs are:

| | |
|---|---|
| *hacer* | to make, to do |
| *poner* | to put |
| *valer* | to be worth |
| *salir* | to leave |

The verbs *hacer, poner,* and *valer* are all regular *–er* verbs with an irregular *yo* form that ends in *–go*. Tables 6-5, 6-6, and 6-7 show how to conjugate each verb.

**Table 6-5    Conjugation Chart for the Verb *Hacer***

| | |
|---|---|
| *yo hago* (I make/do) | *nosotros/nosotras hacemos* (we make/do) |
| *tú haces* (you [informal] make/do) | *vosotros/vosotras hacéis* (you [informal, plural] make/do) |
| *usted (Ud.) hace* (you [formal] make/do) | *ustedes (Uds.) hacen* (you [formal, plural] make/do) |
| *él hace* (he makes/does) | *ellos hacen* (they make/do) |
| *ella hace* (she makes/does) | *ellas hacen* (they [feminine] make/do) |

### Table 6-6　Conjugation Chart for the Verb *Poner*

| | |
|---|---|
| *yo pongo* (I put) | *nosotros/nosotras ponemos* (we put) |
| *tú pones* (you [informal] put) | *vosotros/vosotras ponéis* (you [informal, plural] put) |
| *usted (Ud.) pone* (you [formal] put) | *ustedes (Uds.) ponen* (you [formal, plural] put) |
| *él pone* (he puts) | *ellos ponen* (they put) |
| *ella pone* (she puts) | *ellas ponen* (they [feminine] put) |

### Table 6-7　Conjugation Chart for the Verb *Valer*

| | |
|---|---|
| *yo valgo* (I am worth) | *nosotros/nosotras valemos* (we are worth) |
| *tú vales* (you [informal] are worth) | *vosotros/vosotras valéis* (you [informal, plural] are worth) |
| *usted (Ud.) vale* (you [formal] are worth) | *ustedes (Uds.) valen* (you [formal, plural] are worth) |
| *él vale* (he is worth) | *ellos valen* (they are worth) |
| *ella vale* (she [it] is worth) | *ellas valen* (they [feminine] are worth) |

*Salir* is a *–go* verb like *poner, hacer,* and *valer.* However, because it is an *–ir* verb, it will have the regular endings for an *–ir* verb, which differ slightly from *–er* verbs in the *nosotros/nosotras* and *vosotros/vosotras* forms, as shown in Table 6-8.

### Table 6-8　Conjugation Chart for the Verb *Salir*

| | |
|---|---|
| *yo salgo* (I leave) | *nosotros/nosotras salimos* (we leave) |
| *tú sales* (you [informal] leave) | *vosotros/vosotras salís* (you [informal, plural] leave) |
| *usted (Ud.) sale* (you [formal] leave) | *ustedes (Uds.) salen* (you [formal, plural] leave) |
| *él sale* (he leaves) | *ellos salen* (they leave) |
| *ella sale* (she leaves) | *ellas salen* (they [feminine] leave) |

The next two verbs, *caer* (to fall) and *traer* (to bring), follow the regular –*er* verb patterns of a –*go* verb, except for the irregular *yo* form, which adds an *i* to the conjugated form, as shown in Tables 6-9 and 6-10.

**Table 6-9   Conjugation Chart for the Verb *Caer***

| | |
|---|---|
| *yo caigo* (I fall) | *nosotros or nosotras caemos* (we fall) |
| *tú caes* (you [informal] fall) | *vosotros or vosotras caéis* (you [informal, plural] fall) |
| *usted (Ud.) cae* (you [formal] fall) | *ustedes (Uds.) caen* (you [formal, plural] fall) |
| *él cae* (he falls) | *ellos caen* (they fall) |
| *ella cae* (she falls) | *ellas caen* (they [feminine] fall) |

**Table 6-10   Conjugation Chart for the Verb *Traer***

| | |
|---|---|
| *yo traigo* (I bring) | *nosotros/nosotras traemos* (we bring) |
| *tú traes* (you [informal] bring) | *vosotros/vosotras traéis* (you [informal, plural] bring) |
| *usted (Ud.) trae* (you [formal] bring) | *ustedes (Uds.) traen* (you [formal, plural] bring) |
| *él trae* (he brings) | *ellos traen* (they bring) |
| *ella trae* (she brings) | *ellas traen* (they [feminine] bring) |

Three common –*go* verbs also fall under another irregular category called **stem-changing verbs.** The conjugation patterns of stem-changing verbs is explained later in this chapter, but the irregular –*go* ending of the *yo* form follows to keep the list of -*go* verbs together.

| | |
|---|---|
| *tener* (to have [possession]) | *yo* form: *tengo* |
| *venir* (to come) | *yo* form: *vengo* |
| *decir* (to say, to tell) | *yo* form: *digo* |

### –zco verbs

Normally you can't predict that a verb will be irregular in its *yo* form unless you already know the verb. There is one rule that is consistent, however. If the infinitive of the verb ends in a vowel followed by *–cer* or *–cir*, the *yo* form of the verb ends in *–zco*. Here are the infinitive forms of some of the most common *–zco* verbs:

| | |
|---|---|
| *agradecer* | to thank |
| *aparecer* | to appear |
| *conocer* | to know, to be aquainted with (a person or place) |
| *desaparecer* | to disappear |
| *desconocer* | to be ignorant of |
| *establecer* | to establish |
| *merecer* | to deserve |
| *obedecer* | to obey |
| *ofrecer* | to offer |
| *permanecer* | to remain |
| *pertenecer* | to belong |

These verbs are all conjugated exactly like *conocer*, which is the example used in Table 6-11. Use this table as model when you need to conjugate the other *–zco* verbs.

### Table 6-11    Conjugation Chart for the Verb *Conocer*

| | |
|---|---|
| *yo conozco* (I know) | *nosotros/nosotras conocemos* (we know) |
| *tú conoces* (you [informal] know) | *vosotros/vosotras conocéis* (you [informal, plural] know) |
| *usted (Ud.) conoce* (you [formal] know) | *ustedes (Uds.) conocen* (you [formal, plural] know) |
| *él conoce* (he knows) | *ellos conocen* (they know) |
| *ella conoce* (she knows) | *ellas conocen* (they [feminine] know) |

There are many verbs that end in *–ducir*. Because they all have the same ending, a vowel followed by *–cir*, they are conjugated the same way. All their forms are regular except the *yo* form, which ends in *–zco*.

Four common *–ducir* verbs are presented in the following list. The verb *producir* is conjugated in Table 6-12. Use that table as a model to conjugate the other three, as well as any other *–ducir* verb.

| | |
|---|---|
| *conducir* | to drive |
| *introducir* | to insert |
| *producir* | to produce |
| *traducir* | to translate |

**Table 6-12  Conjugation Chart for the Verb *Producir***

| | |
|---|---|
| *yo produzco* (I produce) | *nosotros/nosotras producimos* (we produce) |
| *tú produces* (you [informal] produce) | *vosotros/vosotras producís* (you [informal, plural] produce) |
| *usted (Ud.) produce* (you [formal] produce) | *ustedes (Uds.) producen* (you [formal, plural] produce) |
| *él produce* (he produces) | *ellos producen* (they produce) |
| *ella produce* (she produces) | *ellas producen* (they [feminine] produce) |

### *ver* and *saber*

Two other verbs have unique *yo* forms. Both *ver* (to see) and *saber* (to know [a fact]) are regular *–er* verbs in all forms except the *yo* form, but their *yo* forms are completely different, as shown in Tables 6-13 and 6-14.

**Table 6-13  Conjugation Chart for the Verb *Ver***

| | |
|---|---|
| *yo veo* (I see) | *nosotros/nosotras vemos* (we see) |
| *tú ves* (you [informal] see) | *vosotros/vosotras veis* (you [informal, plural] see) |
| *usted (Ud.) ve* (you [formal] see) | *ustedes (Uds.) ven* (you [formal, plural] see) |
| *él ve* (he sees) | *ellos ven* (they see) |
| *ella ve* (she sees) | *ellas ven* (they [feminine] see) |

**Table 6-14    Conjugation Chart for the Verb *Saber***

| | |
|---|---|
| *yo sé* (I know) | *nosotros/nosotras sabemos* (we know) |
| *tú sabes* (you [informal] know) | *vosotros or vosotras sabéis* (you [informal, plural] know) |
| *usted (Ud.) sabe* (you [formal] know) | *ustedes (Uds.) saben* (you [formal, plural] know) |
| *él sabe* (he knows) | *ellos saben* (they know) |
| *ella sabe* (she knows) | *ellas saben* (they [feminine] know) |

# Stem-Changing Verbs in the Present Tense

To this point, the irregular verbs presented in this chapter have the irregularity in the endings of the conjugated verb form. However, there is a different kind of predictable verb conjugation where the stem of the verb changes. These verbs have all the regular endings (even the *yo* form!) but have a change occur in the stem of the verb in certain forms. The **stem** of the verb is what remains when you remove the *–ar, -er,* or *–ir* ending from the infinitive form of the verb.

Because it is the stem of the verb that changes, these verbs are called **stem-changing verbs** or **stem-changers.** It is impossible to identify that a verb is a stem-changer simply by looking at the infinitive unless you have previously learned this particular verb and remember that it is a stem-changer.

Stem-changing verbs could be *–ar, –er,* or *–ir* verbs. You can, at least, count on the stressed syllable in the stem being the one that changes. Stem-changing verbs are so common that most dictionaries give the stem change up front in the entry, even before the verb's translation.

The hardest part about stem-changers is that you have to memorize the verbs that have stem changes. Once you memorize the type of stem change a verb has, the actual patterns of the stem-changing verbs are quite simple, and all the endings are regular, so conjugating these verbs is easy.

There are basically three ways that the stem of a verb can change in the present tense. The verbs covered in this section are grouped according to the type of stem change they have. While you learn the meanings of the verbs, learn what kind of stem change it has as well.

## *E* to *ie*

The most common stem change is *e* to *ie* (represented by *e>ie*). That means the stressed letter *e* in the stem of the verb will change to *ie* in certain conjugated forms of the verb. These stem-changing verbs are listed with the stem change in parentheses after the infinitive. You should remember the verbs with the *e>ie* as a part of the infinitive so that you'll be able to conjugate them correctly. If a verb has two *e*'s in the stem, it is always the second *e* that stem changes. In the tables in this section, the *e* that changes to *ie* is underlined.

The patterns for stem-changing verbs are very consistent. All forms of the verb will stem change except for *nosotros/nosotras* and *vosotros/vosotras*. The best way to see the patterns is to consider a few examples.

The verb *pensar* (to think) is typical of an *–ar* verb with an *e>ie* stem change. Where the stem change occurs, the *ie* is underlined in Table 6-15. Notice that *pensamos* and *pensáis* do not have a stem change.

**Table 6-15  Conjugation Chart for the Verb *Pensar***

| | |
|---|---|
| *yo pienso* (I think) | *Nosotros/nosotras pensamos* (we think) |
| *tú piensas* (you [informal] think) | *vosotros/vosotras pensáis* (you [informal, plural] think) |
| *usted (Ud.) piensa* (you [formal] think) | *ustedes (Uds.) piensan* (you [formal, plural] think) |
| *él piensa* (he thinks) | *ellos piensan* (they think) |
| *ella piensa* (she thinks) | *ellas piensan* (they [feminine] think) |

The following list contains commonly used *–ar* verbs that stem change *e>ie* exactly like pensar:

| | |
|---|---|
| *cerrar* | to close |
| *comenzar* | to begin (interchangeable with *empezar*) |
| *confesar* | to confess |
| *despertar* | to wake up |
| *empezar* | to begin (interchangeable with *comenzar*) |
| *gobernar* | to govern |
| *negar* | to deny |
| *recomendar* | to recommend |

The verb *perder* (to lose) is a typical *–er* verb with an *e>ie* stem change. The forms of this verb are presented in Table 6-16, which serves as an model for the list of common *–er* verbs that follow the table.

**Table 6-16  Conjugation Chart for the Verb *Perder***

| | |
|---|---|
| *yo pierdo* (I lose) | *nosotros/nosotras perdemos* (we lose) |
| *tú pierdes* (you [informal] lose) | *vosotros/vosotras perdéis* (you [informal, plural] lose) |
| *usted (Ud.) pierde* (you [formal] lose) | *ustedes (Uds.) pierden* (you [formal, plural] lose) |
| *él pierde* (he loses) | *ellos pierden* (they lose) |
| *ella pierde* (she loses) | *ellas pierden* (they [feminine] lose) |

The following list presents common *-er* verbs that stem change *e>ie*:

| | |
|---|---|
| *ascender* | to ascend (to go up) |
| *descender* | to descend (to go down) |
| *defender* | to defend |
| *encender* | to light, to turn on |
| *entender* | to understand |
| *querer* | to want, to love |

Notice in this list that the *–er* ending is not part of the stem, so *perder* and *querer* have only one *e* in the stem. When verbs like *defender* and *entender* have two *e*'s in the stem, the second one will stem change. See Table 6-17 for an example.

**Table 6-17  Conjugation Chart for the Verb *Defender***

| | |
|---|---|
| *yo defiendo* (I defend) | *nosotros/nosotras defendemos* (we defend) |
| *tú defiendes* (you [informal] defend) | *vosotros/vosotras defendéis* (you [informal, plural] defend) |
| *usted (Ud.) defiende* (you [formal] defend) | *ustedes (Uds.) defienden* (you [formal, plural] defend) |
| *él defiende* (he defends) | *ellos defienden* (they defend) |
| *ella defiende* (she defends) | *ellas defienden* (they [feminine] defend) |

The –*ir* verbs that stem change *e>ie* all follow the same patterns as the verb *mentir* (to lie [to tell an untruth]). See Table 6-18 for the forms of the verb.

**Table 6-18   Conjugation Chart for the Verb *Mentir***

| | |
|---|---|
| *yo miento* (I lie) | *nosotros/nosotras mentimos* (we lie) |
| *tú mientes* (you [informal] lie) | *vosotros/vosotras mentís* (you [informal, plural] lie) |
| *usted (Ud.) miente* (you [formal] lie) | *ustedes (Uds.) mienten* (you [formal, plural] lie) |
| *él miente* (he lies) | *ellos mienten* (they lie) |
| *ella miente* (she lies) | *ellas mienten* (they [feminine] lie) |

The following are some of the most common –*ir* verbs that have an *e>ie* stem change:

| | |
|---|---|
| *preferir* | to prefer |
| *sentir* | to feel, to regret |
| *sugerir* | to suggest |

Notice that the verb *preferir* has two *e*'s in the stem. Just as with –*er* verbs, whenever there are two *e*'s in the stem of an –*ir* verb, it is the second one that stem changes. See Table 6-19 for the forms of the verb.

**Table 6-19   Conjugation Chart for the Verb *Preferir***

| | |
|---|---|
| *yo prefiero* (I prefer) | *nosotros/nosotras preferimos* (we prefer) |
| *tú prefieres* (you [informal] prefer) | *vosotros/vosotras preferís* (you [informal, plural] prefer) |
| *usted (Ud.) prefiere* (you [formal] prefer) | *ustedes (Uds.) prefieren* (you [formal, plural] prefer) |
| *él prefiere* (he prefers) | *ellos prefieren* (they prefer) |
| *ella prefiere* (she prefers) | *ellas prefieren* (they [feminine] prefer) |

*Tener* (to have) and *venir* (to come) are *e>ie* stem changers but also have an irregular *yo* form. You encountered these two verbs with the –*go* verbs earlier in this chapter in "Irregular verbs in the *yo* form." That is because the *yo* form of each of these verbs ends in –*go*, even though the rest of the forms follow the *e>ie* stem-changing patterns. These verbs are very common, so be sure to learn the conjugation charts in Tables 6-20 and 6-21.

**Table 6-20   Conjugation Chart for the Verb *Tener***

| | |
|---|---|
| yo tengo (I have) | nosotros/nosotras tenemos (we have) |
| tú ti*e*nes (you [informal] have) | vosotros/vosotras tenéis (you [informal, plural] have) |
| usted (Ud.) ti*e*ne (you [formal] have) | ustedes (Uds.) ti*e*nen (you [formal, plural] have) |
| él ti*e*ne (he has) | ellos ti*e*nen (they have) |
| ella ti*e*ne (she has) | ellas ti*e*nen (they [feminine] have) |

**Table 6-21   Conjugation Chart for the Verb *Venir***

| | |
|---|---|
| yo vengo (I come) | nosotros/nosotras venimos (we come) |
| tú vi*e*nes (you [informal] come) | vosotros/vosotras venís (you [informal, plural] come) |
| usted (Ud.) vi*e*ne (you [formal] come) | ustedes (Uds.) vi*e*nen (you [formal, plural] come) |
| él vi*e*ne (he comes) | ellos vi*e*nen (they come) |
| ella vi*e*ne (she comes) | ellas vi*e*nen (they [feminine] come) |

Notice how similar the forms are for both *tener* and *venir*. The only differences are in the *nosotros/nosotras* and *vosotros/vosotras* endings because *venir* is an *–ir* verb and *tener* is an *–er* verb.

### *O* to *ue*

The second most common type of stem change is *o* to *ue* (*o>ue*). Here are some common *–ar* verbs that stem change *o>ue*:

| | |
|---|---|
| *acordarse* | to remember |
| *acostarse* | to go to bed, to lie down |
| *almorzar* | to eat lunch |
| *contar* | to count, to tell a story |

| | |
|---|---|
| *costar* | to cost |
| *demostrar* | to show (interchangeable with *mostrar*) |
| *encontrar* | to find |
| *jugar* | to play (a sport or game) |
| *mostrar* | to show (interchangeable with *demostrar*) |
| *probar* | to prove, to test, to try, to try out |
| *recordar* | to remember, to recall, to remind |
| *volar* | to fly |

Common –*er* verbs that stem change *o>ue* are:

| | |
|---|---|
| *devolver* | to return an object, to give something back |
| *envolver* | to wrap up |
| *mover* | to move |
| *poder* | to be able |
| *resolver* | to resolve |
| *soler* | to be accustomed to, to tend to |
| *volver* | to return |

Table 6-22 shows the conjugation forms for the verb *poder* (to be able). Those verb forms can be followed for the other common –*er* verbs as well.

**Table 6-22    Conjugation Chart for the Verb *Poder***

| | |
|---|---|
| *yo puedo* (I can) | *nosotros/nosotras* podemos (we can) |
| *tú puedes* (you can [informal]) | *vosotros/vosotras podéis* (you [informal, plural] can) |
| *usted (Ud.) puede* (you [formal] can) | *ustedes (Uds.) pueden* (you [formal, plural] can) |
| *él puede* (he can) | *ellos pueden* (they can) |
| *ella puede* (she can) | *ellas pueden* (they [feminine] can) |

Common *-ir* verbs that stem change *o>ue* are:

*dormir*      to sleep

*morir*       to die

Table 6-23 shows the conjugation forms for the verb *promover* (to move). Those verb forms can be followed for the other common *-er* verbs as well.

**Table 6-23   Conjugation Chart for the Verb *Promover***

| | |
|---|---|
| *yo prom<u>ue</u>vo* (I promote) | *nosotros/nosotras promovemos* (we promote) |
| *tú prom<u>ue</u>ves* (you [informal] promote) | *vosotros/vosotras promovéis* (you [informal, plural] promote) |
| *usted (Ud.) prom<u>ue</u>ve* (you [formal] promote) | *ustedes (Uds.) prom<u>ue</u>ven* (you [formal, plural] promote) |
| *él prom<u>ue</u>ve* (he promotes) | *ellos prom<u>ue</u>ven* (they promote) |
| *ella prom<u>ue</u>ve* (she promotes) | *ellas prom<u>ue</u>ven* (they [feminine] promote) |

The verb *jugar* is usually listed with the *o>ue* stem-changing verbs because it follows the same pattern. However, as you can see, there is no *o* to change to *ue* in the verb *jugar*. It is the only *u>ue* stem changer in the language. *Jugar* means "to play a sport," so of course it's a popular word in both Spanish- and English-speaking cultures. Table 6-24 shows the unusual verb forms of *jugar*.

**Table 6-24   Conjugation Chart for the Verb *Jugar***

| | |
|---|---|
| *yo j<u>ue</u>go* (I play) | *nosotros/nosotras jugamos* (we play) |
| *tú j<u>ue</u>gas* (you [informal] play) | *vosotros/vosotras jugáis* (you [informal, plural] play) |
| *usted (Ud.) j<u>ue</u>ga* (you [formal] play) | *ustedes (Uds.) j<u>ue</u>gan* (you [formal, plural] play) |
| *él j<u>ue</u>ga* (he plays) | *ellos j<u>ue</u>gan* (they play) |
| *ella j<u>ue</u>ga* (she plays) | *ellas j<u>ue</u>gan* (they [feminine] play) |

## *E* to *i*

Contemplate this rule: All *e>i* stem changing verbs are *–ir* verbs, but not all *–ir* verbs are *e>i* stem changers. Consider the list of *e>ie* stem changers earlier in this chapter, some of them are *–ir* verbs.

This means that when you learn an *–ir* verb that stem changes, you must remember whether it stem changes *e>ie* or *e>i*. Fortunately, the list of *e>i* stem-changing verbs is short, and only *–ir* verbs can stem change *e>i*.

Common *e>i* stem changing verbs are:

| | |
|---|---|
| *despedirse de* | to say goodbye |
| *impedir* | to impede, to prevent |
| *medir* | to measure |
| *reír* | to laugh |
| *repetir* | to repeat |
| *seguir* | to follow, to continue |
| *servir* | to serve |
| *sonreír* | to smile |
| *vestir* | to dress |

Table 6-25 shows the forms of the verb *servir* (to serve). Use this table as a model for all *–ir* verbs that are *e>i* stem changers.

**Table 6-25    Conjugation Chart of the Verb *Servir***

| | |
|---|---|
| *yo sirvo* (I serve) | *nosotros/nosotras servimos* (we serve) |
| *tú sirves* (you [informal] serve) | *vosotros/vosotras servís* (you [informal, plural] serve) |
| *usted (Ud.) sirve* (you [formal] serve) | *ustedes (Uds.) sirven* (you [formal, plural] serve) |
| *él sirve* (he serves) | *ellos sirven* (they serve) |
| *ella sirve* (she serves) | *ellas sirven* (they [feminine] serve) |

# Confusing Verbs: Determining Which Verb to Use

When you learn Spanish, there are a few instances where two specific verbs are translated to the same English verb and are not interchangeable. It is important to learn the situations where each verb is appropriate because, in some cases, the meaning of the sentence is altered if you use the wrong verb.

## *Ser* or *estar*

Both of the verbs *ser* and *estar* mean "to be," but each indicates a specific type of "being." *Ser* is used to describe more permanent states of being, and *estar* is generally used for more temporary states; but there are some exceptions.

Learning all the rules can be difficult, especially when there are many different sets to learn, but acronyms can make it easier. An **acronym** is a pronounceable word formed by the first letters of a set of specific phrases or series of words used to help you remember the details of the information.

In Table 6-26, the first letters of each reason spell out the acronym "C-NOTE" to help you remember the reasons for using the verb *ser*. Table 6-2 showed how to conjugate the verb *ser* in the present tense. Consider the examples in Table 6-26, and look for the form of *ser* in each sentence to see how it is used.

**Table 6-26   Reasons for Using *Ser* (C-NOTE)**

| Reason | Sample Sentence |
| --- | --- |
| **C**haracteristics | *Ellos <u>son</u> altos y delgados.* (They are tall and thin.) |
| **N**ationality/origin | *Lolita <u>es</u> Colombiana.* (Lolita is Colombian.) |
| **O**ccupation | *Su padre <u>es</u> abogado.* (His father is a lawyer.) |
| **T**ime | *<u>Son</u> las cinco y media. Es la una y cuarto.* (It's five thirty. It's a quarter after one.) |
| **E**vent location | *La fiesta <u>es</u> en mi casa.* (The party is at my house.) |

Think of the *E* as representing *Event location* because this is an exception to the rule that *estar* is used for locations.

Generally the verb *estar* indicates a temporary state of being, but when you see the specific reasons for using *estar*, you will notice that the location of a building or geographical feature is indicated with *estar*, and this is not exactly temporary. Table 6-4 presented all the conjugated forms of *estar*. Consider the examples in Table 6-27 to see how the verb is used in sentences.

**Table 6-27    Reasons for Using *Estar* (TLF)**

| Reason | Sample Sentence |
|---|---|
| **T**emporary conditions | *La comida está caliente.* (The meal is hot.) |
| **L**ocation (except for events) | *El parque está aquí.* (The park is here.) |
| **F**eelings/emotions/health | *Durante un examen, yo estoy nerviosa.* (During a test, I am nervous.) |

## *Conocer or saber*

*Conocer* and *saber* are two verbs that can be translated to the English verb "to know." *Conocer* is the verb to use when you could just as correctly say "to be acquainted with." It is most often used with people, but can also refer to familiarity with a place. Use the verb *conocer* any time you want to say that you know a person or that you know your way around a place. Whenever *conocer* is followed by a person or a word that refers to a person, the verb will be followed by the preposition *a*.

> *Yo conozco a Manuel.*
> I know (am acquainted with) Manuel.

> *Conoces bien la ciudad de Guatemala.*
> You are well acquainted with Guatemala City.

*Saber* is used to indicate knowledge of a fact or knowledge of how to do something. It is often followed by an infinitive. When used with an infinitive, it should be thought of as "to know how" because the word "how" is not used in these situations in Spanish. When *saber* is used in the preterite tense (see Chapter 11), it means "found out" because it refers to the first moment something was known.

> *Sabes construir una casa muy bien.*
> You know how to build a house very well.

> *Yo sé la dirección.*
> I know the address.

> *No vamos a la piscina porque no sabemos nadar.*
> We don't go to the pool because we don't know how to swim.

### Llevar, tomar, and sacar

*Llevar, tomar,* and *sacar* all can be translated as "to take," but each verb has a specific purpose, and you must know when each one is appropriate.

Spanish differentiates verbs according to what is being taken. *Llevar* means to transport something or someone from one place to another. It is not used to refer to taking a means of transportation, but rather the action of taking a person or an object to a different location. If a person is being taken somewhere, *llevar* is followed by the preposition *a*.

> *Marla lleva a su sobrina a la playa.*
> Marla takes her niece to the beach.

> *Juan y Andrés llevan los refrescos a la fiesta.*
> John and Andrew take the drinks to the party.

> *Llevas a un amigo a la fiesta.*
> You are taking a friend to the party.

*Tomar* is used when taking a means of transportation or when taking something by mouth, such as medicine or a bite of food or a drink.

*El nunca toma un taxi.*
He never takes a taxi.

*Es importante tomar vitaminas.*
It's important to take vitamins.

*Toman muchas bebidas frías durante el verano*
They take "in" many cold drinks during the summer.

*Sacar* is most often translated as "to take out," so you would use it to say things like "take out the garbage" or "take out your homework." Remember that there is no need to use the preposition "out" after *sacar*, even though in most cases where this verb is used in English it is followed by "out." *Sacar* is also used when taking a photograph, even though the English expression does not include the preposition "out."

*Yo saco muchas fotos durante mis vacaciones.*
I take many photographs during my vacations.

*Ustedes necesitan sacar la tarea.*
You all need to take out the homework.

*Los niños sacan la basura el viernes.*
The children take out the garbage on Friday.

The English verb "to take" is often followed by a preposition that completely changes the overall meaning. The same expressions in Spanish usually do not require a preposition, but rather a completely different verb. A good way to test the quality of your Spanish/English dictionary is to look up the verb "to take" on the English side and see if the entry specifies the different Spanish verbs that mean: to take on, to take over, to take off, to take up, etc.

## Chapter Check-Out

For sentences 1–3, conjugate the verb in parentheses in the present tense. Be sure to consider what the subject of the sentence is so that you use the correct form of the verb to go with the subject. For sentences 4–6, determine which verb is appropriate and conjugate it to go with the subject.

1. *Laura _____ bailar con su novio. (querer)*
2. *Yo _____ la música a la fiesta latina. (traer)*
3. *Nosotros _____ a la fiesta. (ir)*
4. *Yo _____ a muchas personas aquí. (conocer or saber)*
5. *Mi madre _____maestra. (ser or estar)*
6. *Silvia y Sergio _____muchas fotos durante la vacacion. (sacar, tomar or llevar)*

**Answers:** 1. *quiere* 2. *traigo* 3. *vamos* 4. *conozco* 5. *es* 6. *sacan*

# Chapter 7

# ASKING AND ANSWERING QUESTIONS

## Chapter Check-In

❏ Learning to write yes or no questions

❏ Using question words

❏ Answering questions with the right pronoun

There are several types of questions one can form depending on the type of information being requested. If a simple yes or no is all that is necessary to answer a question, it is aptly called a "yes or no question." When more information is required, a specific question word is necessary to elicit the desired response. This chapter prepares you to write yes or no questions and presents the vocabulary necessary to create more in-depth questions using question words. It is extremely important to remember that questions cannot be created in Spanish by simply translating an English question word-for-word.

## Yes or No Questions

The simplest questions to create are *yes* or *no* questions. They are actually much simpler in Spanish than they are in English. Consider the sentence, "Johnny speaks Italian." How would you make an English yes or no question out of it? You put the word "does" in front and change the form of the verb *speak*.

> **Does** <u>Johnny</u> **speak** Italian?

Of course, you already know how to make a sentence into a question in English, but it's helpful to realize that part of what you do to make a question is switch the subject with a part of the verb.

Most people struggle when they try to write a yes or no question in Spanish, because they stumble over the first word of the question in English: Yes or no questions usually start with either do or does. This word does not translate in a Spanish question because there is no need for a helping verb to create a question. The Spanish language creates questions by simply switching the subject and verb. As soon as you see a question starting with do or does in English, you will need to apply a simple three-step process to create the Spanish equivalent.

1. Remove the "do" or "does" from the English question.
2. Translate the remaining sentence into Spanish, carefully conjugating the verb to match the subject.
3. Switch the subject with the verb, and add the question marks.

Now, use that three-step process to change an English question into a Spanish question. Here's the English example:

**Do** I **study** a lot?

Here's how the process is broken down step by step:

1. Remove the "do" or "does" from the English question.
I **study** a lot.

2. Translate the remaining sentence into Spanish, carefully conjugating the verb to match the subject.
Yo **estudio** mucho.

3. Switch the subject with the verb, and add the question marks.
¿**Estudio** yo mucho?

Here's another example:

**Does** she **need** a friend?

And, here is the step-by-step translation:

1. Remove the "do" or "does" from the English question.
She **needs** a friend.

2. Translate the remaining sentence into Spanish, carefully conjugating the verb to match the subject.
Ella **necesita** una amiga.

**3.** Switch the subject with the verb, and add the question marks.

¿**Necesita** <u>ella</u> una amiga?

In a Spanish question, the verb is placed in front of the subject. You may have heard new learners of English mistakenly create questions like, "Speak you Spanish?" because they are incorrectly applying the rules of their language to English. When you get used to creating questions in Spanish, you will learn to appreciate their simplicity.

# Interrogative Pronouns (Question Words)

**Interrogative pronouns** simply mean question words. Whether or not you realize it, a question word is actually a pronoun because it is used in place of the noun that would be the answer to the question.

Following is a complete list of question words. Notice that they all have accent marks.

| | |
|---|---|
| ¿quién? | (singular, to ask about one person) who? |
| ¿quiénes? | who? plural (used when you assume the answer is more than one person) |
| ¿qué? | what? |
| ¿cuál? | which?, what? |
| ¿cuáles? | which ones?, what? (in front of a plural noun) |
| ¿cómo? | how? |
| ¿dónde? | where? |
| ¿cuándo? | when? |
| ¿cuánto? | how much? (used in front of a singular, masculine noun) |
| ¿cuánta? | how much? (used in front of a singular, feminine noun) |
| ¿cuántos? | how many? (used in front of a plural, masculine noun) |
| ¿cuántas? | how many? (used in front of a plural, feminine noun) |
| ¿por qué? | why? (because of what?) |
| ¿para qué? | why? what for? (for what purpose?) |

Most of the question words have exact equivalents in Spanish and English. But there are a few issues you must understand in order to use the correct question word in context. There are three Spanish interrogative pronouns that can be translated to the English word *what: qué, cuál,* and *cómo.* Unfortunately, they are not just interchangeable, but there are some simple rules to govern their usage.

■  *What* **rule 1:** Always use *qué* to mean *what* directly in front of any noun.

> *¿Qué libro lee usted?*
> What book do you read?

> *¿Qué comida comen ellos?*
> What food do they eat?

■  *What* **rule 2:** *Qué* is used in front of any form of the verb *ser* when asking for a definition or an explanation. That is, when you're really asking "What does it mean?" or "What is it?"

■  *What* **rule 3:** *Cuál* is used in front of any form of the verb *ser* (see Chapter 6) when you're asking for a choice or specific answer. For example, consider the difference between the following two answers to a question about your address. The sample questions that generate them use the *es* form, which means *is,* of the verb *ser.*

**A:** My address is the house number, the street name, city, state, and zip code where I live.

**B:** My address is 555 Kingston Lane, Carrollton, Ohio 44615.

Answer A is obviously the response to a question asking for a definition or explanation of the word "address." This is the type of answer elicited from the following question:

> *¿Qué es dirección?*
> What is "your address?" (give me an explanation or definition of address)

Answer B is clearly the type of response to the question, "What is your address?" Any question asking for a specific response, as in the following example, requires the question word "*cuál.*"

> *¿Cuál es tu dirección?*
> What is your address? (give me a specific place)

■ *What* **rule 4:** *Cómo* is often used as a response when someone fails to hear a comment and would like it repeated. In English when someone says something you don't hear, you say, "What?" If this happens in Spanish, the one word response, "*¿Cómo?*" is appropriate. That does not, however, mean that *cómo* can be used to mean "What?" in any other situation.

The importance of knowing how to ask a question is obvious, but a large number of people tend to mix up the question words or simply can't remember them. Try to use *mnemonic* (memory) tricks to help you remember the question words. The following examples are silly, and therein lies their beauty. Although they won't elicit the exact question word, they will certainly jar your memory. You should try to think of your own mnemonic devices for the rest of the question words.

> **How** did he get into a **coma**?
> *Cómo* = how

> **Who** dates **Barbie**? Ken!
> *Quién* = who

> **What** do they sell at **K**-mart?
> *Qué* = what

> **When** can I buy a **condo**?
> *Cuándo* = when

Most questions that have a question word are created exactly like a yes or no question with the question word in front. Take the question "Does he speak Italian?" *¿Habla él italiano?* There are several question words that could be placed in front of the question to elicit more information than a yes or no answer. The following examples show how different question words can elicit different answers:

> *¿Cómo está tu familia?*
> How is your family?

> *¿Dónde habla él italiano?*
> Where does he speak Italian?

*¿Cuándo habla él italiano?*
When does he speak Italian?

*¿Por qué habla él italiano?*
Why does he speak Italian?

All of the sample questions can be created simply by switching the subject and the verb to create a yes or no question and then placing the specific question word in front.

## Question Words as Subjects

There are other question words that are used a little differently. They actually serve as the subject of the question. Here is a list of the question words that can be used as subjects:

| | |
|---|---|
| *quién* | who (singular) |
| *quiénes* | who (plural) |
| *cuánto* | how much (singular) |
| *cuánta* | how much (singular) |
| *cuántos* | how many (plural) |
| *cuántas* | how many (plural) |
| *cuál* | which (singular) |
| *cuáles* | which ones (plural) |

The question "Who speaks Italian?" uses the pronoun *who* as a subject. Just like in English, the Spanish question *¿Quién habla español?* uses the pronoun *quién* as the subject.

These questions are created exactly the same in Spanish and English. However, since there are both a singular and plural version of *who* in Spanish, there is one thing you don't think about in English that you'll have to think about in Spanish. You know that you're supposed to conjugate the verb "to go" with the subject (see Chapter 4). When the subject is a question word, the verb is conjugated in either the *él/ella* or *ellos/ellas* form based on whether the question word is singular or plural.

The singular version of "who," *quién* is meant to represent one person, so use the *él/ella* form of the verb you would use if one person were the subject of the sentence. The plural version of "who," *quiénes,* is meant to represent several people, so you would use the *ellos/ellas* form of the verb with it. When the question words *quién* and *quiénes* are used without prepositions, they always will be the subject of the sentence (for more information on prepositions, see Chapter 14). Here are examples of *quién* and *quiénes* as subjects of a sentence:

> *¿Quiénes aprenden español?*
>
> Who learns Spanish? (assuming that more that one person is learning Spanish)

> *¿Quién baila con María?*
>
> Who dances with María? (assuming that only one person is dancing with María)

Notice that when the question word serves as the subject, there is no need to switch the subject and verb.

A few other question words can act as the subject of the sentence too, such as *cuánto* and *cuánta.* Be careful to consider the gender and number of the noun that *cuánto* represents. For example, if you already established you were talking about rain *(la lluvia),* you could say:

> *¿Cuánta cae cada verano? (cuánta* is the subject, *cae* is the verb)
>
> How much falls each summer? *(how much* is the subject, *falls* is the verb)

The question word *cuánta* can be used in another type of question. This is simply a yes or no question with the question word placed in front. For example:

> Does Marta eat meat? *(Marta* is the subject, *eat* is the verb)
>
> *¿Come carne Marta? (Marta* is the subject, *come* is the verb)

You can also put the question word "how much" in front of this yes or no question:

> How much does Marta eat?
>
> *¿Cuánto come Marta?*

In the example above, you could also say "How much meat does Marta eat?"

> *¿Cuánta (carne) come Marta?*

Here *¿cuánta?* is used to refer to *la carne,* not that fact that Marta is female.

The question words *cuál* and *cuáles* are also used to ask questions.

> What's today's date?
> *¿Cuál es la fecha de hoy?*

> Which songs (which ones) do you prefer?
> *¿Cuáles canciones prefieres?*

## Using the Right Pronoun to Answer a Question

When you have to answer a question, you must first carefully listen to or look at the subject used in the question to determine the correct subject to use in your response. You could either memorize Table 7-1 to determine how to answer a question, or just think about it in English because it is exactly the same. However, it is always better to understand than to memorize. Once you understand Table 7-1, you can refer to it while you're still learning, but you'll quickly find you no longer need it.

**Table 7-1    Determining the Subject for the Response to a Question**

| If the subject of the question is . . . | Answer with . . . |
| --- | --- |
| *tú* or *usted* | *yo* |
| *ustedes* | *nosotros/nosotras* |
| any name(s) *y tú* | *nosotros/nosotras* or name(s) *y yo* |
| any name(s) *y usted* | *nosotros/nosotras* or name(s) *y yo* |
| *yo* | *tú* or *usted* |
| *nosotros/nosotras* | *ustedes* |
| any name(s) *y yo* | *ustedes,* or name(s) *y usted* |

For example:

> *¿Hablas tú español?*          *Sí, yo hablo español.*
> Do you speak Spanish?          Yes, I speak Spanish.

| | |
|---|---|
| *¿Hablan ustedes español?* | *Sí, hablamos español.* |
| Do you guys speak Spanish? | Yes, we speak Spanish. |
| | |
| *¿Hablan Marco y tú español?* | *Sí, hablamos español.* or *Sí, Marco y yo hablamos español.* |
| Do you and Marco speak Spanish? | Yes, we speak Spanish. or Yes, Marco and I speak Spanish. |

Since there are some options, you'll have to decide the specific pronoun depending on the context of the question.

When a question is asked about someone else, either their name or the third person pronoun is used. To answer these questions, you don't have to change the subject or the verb form. Simply answer yes or no, and put the subject back in front of the verb to make it back into a sentence. If there is a question word, add in the requested information.

| | |
|---|---|
| *¿Baila ella?* | *Sí, ella baila.* |
| Does she dance? | Yes, she dances. |
| | |
| *¿Trabaja María?* | *Sí, María trabaja.* |
| Does María work? | Yes, María works. |
| | |
| *¿Cuándo trabaja María?* | *María trabaja mañana.* |
| When does María work? | Maria works tomorrow. |

## Chapter Check-Out

Write the following questions in Spanish.

1. Do you study?
2. When does Daniel work?
3. Do Martin and I dance?
4. Do Ana and Jaime swim?
5. Why does she win?

**Answers: 1.** *¿Estudias (tú)? ¿Estudias?* or *¿Estudia (usted)?* **2.** *¿Cuándo trabaja Daniel?* **3.** *¿Bailamos Martín y yo?* **4.** *¿Nadan Ana y Jaime?* **5.** *¿Por qué gana ella?*

# Chapter 8
# ADJECTIVES

## Chapter Check-In

❑ Creating the correct form of an adjective to match the noun it modifies

❑ Placing adjectives correctly in a sentence

❑ Understanding demonstrative and possessive adjectives

❑ Creating an adjective from a verb

To describe something in any language, you need to learn how to use adjectives. This chapter presents the most commonly used Spanish adjectives and explains how to create the appropriate form of an adjective to match the gender and number of the noun it describes. A Spanish adjective often follows the noun it modifies (describes), so this will be an adjustment to English speakers. However, there are some circumstances in Spanish sentences when the adjective must be placed before the noun. A few easy-to-learn rules concerning the placement of adjectives are included in this chapter to help you avoid scrambling your Spanish sentences.

## Adjective Use

An **adjective** is a word that modifies (describes) a noun. There are different types of adjectives that indicate possession, demonstrate distance, and make comparisons. A Spanish adjective will change its ending to match the gender and number of the noun it describes. When you look up an adjective in the dictionary, it is always listed in its singular masculine form. It is up to you to know the rules to change an adjective to its feminine and/or plural form. If you want to use an adjective correctly in a complete sentence, you must consider the gender of the noun you want it to describe. Then you must choose the correct form of the adjective and place it either in front of or behind that noun based on the rules explained in this chapter.

## Adjectives and gender

It's important to know that adjectives in dictionaries and vocabulary lists are always presented in their singular masculine form. In this form, most adjectives end in –o, but a few end in –e or a consonant. This section provides some extremely common adjectives you need to learn in order to understand the examples used throughout this chapter. The examples in each list utilize vocabulary from Chapter 2. Remember that the article in front of the noun will indicate the gender of the noun and the adjectives that follow the noun will match that gender.

Some useful adjectives that end in –o are:

| | |
|---|---|
| *alto* | tall |
| *amarillo* | yellow |
| *anaranjado* | orange |
| *barato* | cheap |
| *blanco* | white |
| *bonito* | pretty |
| *caro* | expensive |
| *cómico* | funny |
| *cómodo* | comfortable |
| *corto* | short (in length) |
| *delgado* | thin |
| *delicioso* | delicious |
| *divertido* | amusing |
| *duro* | hard |
| *extranjero* | foreign |
| *feo* | ugly |
| *generoso* | generous |
| *gordo* | fat |
| *guapo* | attractive (handsome) |
| *hermoso* | beautiful |
| *largo* | long |

| | |
|---|---|
| *limpio* | clean |
| *loco* | crazy |
| *negro* | black |
| *pardo* | brown |
| *rico* | rich |
| *rojo* | red |
| *sucio* | dirty |

If an adjective ends in *–o* in its singular masculine form, the final *–o* will change to *–a* when the adjective is used to describe a feminine noun. As it will be explained later in this chapter, if the noun is plural, the adjective must also be plural, in which case the adjective will end in *–os* or *–as*. The following examples use some of the nouns whose gender is described in Chapter 2. The definite article is included here to remind you of the gender of the noun so you can review the gender rules as you read these examples. To use an adjective correctly, you have to know the gender of the noun it modifies.

| | |
|---|---|
| *el chico guapo* | the attractive boy |
| *la chica guapa* | the attractive girl |
| *el coche blanco* | the white car |
| *la montaña blanca* | the white mountain |
| *el libro divertido* | the amusing book |
| *la situación divertida* | the amusing situation |

Some commonly used adjectives that end in *–e* are:

| | |
|---|---|
| *agradable* | pleasant |
| *alegre* | happy |
| *elegante* | elegant |
| *enorme* | enormous |
| *excelente* | excellent |
| *fuerte* | strong |
| *importante* | important |

| | |
|---|---|
| *impresionante* | impressive |
| *independiente* | independent |
| *inteligente* | intelligent |
| *interesante* | interesting |
| *pobre* | poor |
| *responsable* | responsible |
| *simple* | simple |
| *triste* | sad |
| *verde* | green |

Adjectives that end in *–e* do not change endings for feminine nouns. In their singular forms they are used exactly the same to modify both masculine and feminine nouns. Consider the following examples:

| | |
|---|---|
| *el abuelo inteligente* | the intelligent grandfather |
| *la abuela inteligente* | the intelligent grandmother |
| *el parque enorme* | the enormous park |
| *la ciudad enorme* | the enormous city |
| *el pueblo interesante* | the interesting town |
| *la muchedumbre interesante* | the interesting crowd |

A few adjectives end in consonants. For example:

| | |
|---|---|
| *azul* | blue |
| *difícil* | difficult |
| *fácil* | easy |
| *gris* | gray |
| *feliz* | happy |
| *popular* | popular |

Adjectives that end in a consonant usually will not change endings to indicate gender except for those indicating nationality.

| | |
|---|---|
| *el hermano popular* | the popular brother |
| *la hermana popular* | the popular sister |
| *el problema difícil* | the difficult problem |
| *la situación difícil* | the difficult situation |
| *el mapa azul* | the blue map |
| *el boligrafo azul* | the blue pen |

The adjectives of nationality that end in a consonant are special and will often change depending on the gender of the person to whom they refer. Unlike other adjectives ending in a consonant, you actually add the letter –*a* after the consonant at the end of an adjective of nationality to use it with a feminine noun. It is also possible that other descriptive adjectives ending in a consonant will also change in the feminine form.

| | |
|---|---|
| *el señor español* | the Spanish gentleman |
| *la señora española* | the Spanish lady |
| *un chico juguetón* | a playful guy |
| *una chica juguetona* | a playful girl |

In the following examples, note that adding a syllable to the end of a word usually changes where the stress of the word will fall. If an adjective of nationality has an accent mark on the last syllable, it will disappear when you add –*a* to the end. This occurs quite often with adjectives of nationality.

| | |
|---|---|
| *el negociante inglés* | the English businessman |
| *la actriz inglesa* | the English actress |
| *el cine japonés* | the Japanese cinema |
| *la ciudad japonesa* | the Japanese city |
| *el libro francés* | the French book |
| *la novela francesa* | the French novel |

Some adjectives that indicate nationality end in –*o* and are used like any other adjectives. Simply change the –*o* ending to –*a* if the adjective is describing a feminine noun. Notice in all the following examples that Spanish does not require the capitalization of adjectives of nationality, but English does.

| | |
|---|---|
| *el hombre colombiano* | the Colombian man |
| *la mujer colombiana* | the Colombian woman |
| *el muchacho mexicano* | the Mexican boy |
| *la muchacha mexicana* | the Mexican girl |

Adjectives of nationality that end in –*e* are also like other adjectives. The same form is used for both genders.

| | |
|---|---|
| *el padre nicaragüense* | the Nicaraguan father |
| *la madre nicaragüense* | the Nicaraguan mother |
| *el amigo canadiense* | the Canadian friend (male) |
| *la amiga canadiense* | the Canadian friend (female) |

## Adjectives and number

You may have noticed that all of the examples so far have been singular nouns. Once you understand the rules for creating the different gender forms of adjectives, you are ready to tackle plurals. An adjective will become plural if the noun it modifies is plural. To see how to pluralize a noun, turn to Chapter 2. In English, when a noun becomes plural, the definite article and adjectives do not change. "The red pen" becomes "The red pens." Only the noun "pens" is pluralized.

In the Spanish equivalent, when the noun "pens" becomes plural, so do the article "the" and the adjective "red." The definite article *el* becomes *los* and *la* becomes *las* when the noun is plural, and the adjective that follows the noun will be in its plural form also.

| | |
|---|---|
| *Las camisas rojas* | the red shirts |

The plural forms of adjectives are created the same way as the plural forms of nouns. If an adjective ends in any vowel, add –*s* to make it plural.

| | |
|---|---|
| *los muchachos mexicanos* | the Mexican boys |
| *las muchachas mexicanas* | the Mexican girls |
| *los coches blancos* | the white cars |
| *las montañas blancas* | the white mountains |

If an adjective ends in any consonant, add *–es* to make it plural.

| | |
|---|---|
| *los problemas difíciles* | the difficult problems |
| *las situaciones difíciles* | the difficult situations |
| *los hermanos populares* | the popular brothers |
| *las hermanas populares* | the popular sisters |

When you create the plural form of an adjective that ends in *–z*, don't forget the rule that "*z* changes to *c* when followed by *e.*"

| | |
|---|---|
| *la solución eficaz* | the effective solution |
| *las soluciones eficaces* | the effective solutions |
| *el hombre sagaz* | the wise man |
| *los hombres sagaces* | the wise men |

## Adjective placement

Generally, an adjective of quality (which includes most adjectives) is placed after the noun it modifies in a Spanish sentence, as shown in the examples in the preceding section. However, there are a few simple rules to learn about the types of adjectives that must be placed in front of a noun.

Adjectives of quantity are placed in front of the noun they quantify. This includes all numbers and any adjectives that indicate amount. The following are some common adjectives of quantity:

| | |
|---|---|
| *mucho, mucha* | much, a lot |
| *muchos, muchas* | many, a lot |
| *poco, poca* | little, few |
| *bastante* | enough (does not change forms) |
| *suficiente* | enough (does not change forms) |
| *alguno, alguna, algunos, algunas* | some |
| *varios, varias* | several |

The word "apocope" means "cut short." Some adjectives are called **apocopated** because their endings are cut short in specific circumstances.

The apocopated adjectives listed below are usually placed in front of a noun, and, if that noun is singular and masculine, only then should you drop the final *–o* of the adjective.

| | |
|---|---|
| **bueno** | good |
| *la buena chica* | the good girl |
| *el buen chico* | the good boy |
| **malo** | bad |
| *la mala situación* | the bad situation |
| *el mal problema* | the bad problem (remember that *problema* is masculine) |
| **primero** | first |
| *la primera hija* | the first daughter |
| *el primer hijo* | the first son |
| **tercero** | third |
| *la tercera clase* | the third class |
| *el tercer ejemplo* | the third example |
| **uno** | one |
| *una pluma* | one pen (a pen) |
| *un libro* | one book (a book) |
| **alguno** | some |
| *alguna libertad* | some freedom |
| *algún dinero* | some money (notice that the shortened form has an accent mark because of the pronunciation rules) |
| **ninguno** | none, not any, no (to negate a noun) |
| *ninguna cámara* | no camera |
| *ningún tiempo* | no time |

While those adjectives drop the *–o* only in front of a singular masculine noun, there is one adjective that is cut short in front of any singular noun.

The adjective *grande* (great, large) can be used both in front of a noun or after it. It's unique because *grande* becomes *gran* when placed before any singular noun, regardless of gender. The full form of *grande* is used when placed after the noun. The meaning of the adjective may change to "large" according to the context. You will learn other adjectives that change meaning based on where they're placed later in this chapter.

| | |
|---|---|
| *el gran héroe* | the great hero |
| *la gran oportunidad* | the great opportunity |
| *el gran canal* | the large canal |
| *el piano grande* | the large piano |
| *la ciudad grande* | the large city |

In these sentences, the adjective is not shortened even if the noun is singular and masculine because the adjective is not in front of the noun.

| | |
|---|---|
| *Juana es la tercera.* | Juana is third. |
| *Julio es el primero.* | Julio is first. |
| *Marco es malo.* | Mark is bad. |
| *Alicia es buena.* | Alicia is good. |

One other circumstance that affects the placement of an adjective is when it is modified by an adverb. When an adverb such as *bien, más,* or *muy* precedes an adjective, both words will usually follow the noun. (You'll learn more about adverbs in Chapter 9.)

| | |
|---|---|
| *el chico más guapo* | the most handsome boy |
| *la chica muy bonita* | the very pretty girl |

## Adjectives that change meaning

If you place the adjective incorrectly in a sentence, most of the time you will not alter the meaning of the sentence. You may sound a little silly to a native speaker, but you will still express what you mean to say. However, a few adjectives change meaning depending on where they're placed in the sentence. Imagine telling your teacher that she's large when you meant to say she's great—just because you put the adjective in the wrong place! Here is the complete list so you won't make mistakes like this in your own conversations.

| | |
|---|---|
| *el antiguo maestro* | the former teacher |
| *el abuelo antiguo* | the old-fashioned grandfather |
| *el pobre hombre* | the poor man (unfortunate) |
| *el hombre pobre* | the poor man (impoverished) |
| *el gran salón* | the great ballroom |
| *el salon grande* | the large ballroom |
| *diferentes libros* | various books |
| *libros diferentes* | different books |
| *el nuevo coche* | the new car (new to you) |
| *el coche nuevo* | the brand new car |

## Adjective Types

There are two more types of adjectives that are placed in front of the noun. Possessives and demonstratives are very specific types of adjectives that are extremely useful. It is imperative to learn how to use possessive adjectives and demonstrative adjectives to even approach mastery in the language. Luckily, they are very easy to learn.

### Possessive adjectives

**Possessive adjectives** indicate the owner of the noun they modify. They are usually placed in front of the noun and must match the gender and number of the noun they describe, not the gender and number of the owner of the noun. Table 8-1 provides a complete list.

**Table 8-1   Possessive Adjectives in Front of a Noun**

| | |
|---|---|
| *mi, mis* (my) | *nuestro, nuestra, nuestros, nuestras* (our) |
| *tu, tus* (your) | *vuestro, vuestra, vuestros, vuestras* (your) |
| *su, sus* (your) | *su, sus* (your) |
| *su, sus* (his) | *su, sus* (their) |
| *su, sus* (her) | *su, sus* (their) |

The order of the adjectives is the same as the order of the pronouns refer-ring to the owner. If the person who owns it is *yo*, the possessive adjective is *mi* or *mis*. If the owner is *tú*, the possessive adjective is *tu* or *tus*. If the owner is *él, ella*, or *usted*, the possessive adjective is *su* or *sus*. Just remem-ber that the number of the adjective matches the number of the noun being owned, not the owner. Once you decide to use the adjective *su*, you only make it plural if it is in front of a plural noun. It doesn't matter how many people own the noun. If *they* own a book, "their book" is written *su libro*. If *he* owns many books, "his books" is written *sus libros*.

It's also tricky because the possessive adjective *su* is used to mean his, her, their, and your. Remember that *él, ella* and *usted* share the same conju-gated form of the verb, and they also share the same possessive adjective. If you (*usted*) own a book "your book" is written *su libro*. If you (*tú*) own a book, "your book" is written *tu libro*.

Notice that the subject pronoun *tú* has an accent and means "you." The possessive adjective *tu* has no accent and means "your." Since *nuestro* and *vuestro* end in *–o*, they will change to match both the number and gender of the noun they modify. That is why there are four forms of these adjectives.

A different form of possessive adjective is used when it follows the noun. This most commonly occurs with a linking verb such as *ser* or *estar*, but it also can happen when the noun is preceded by an article. Notice in Table 8-2 that all possessive adjectives have four forms. Be careful to use the form of possession to match the gender and number of the noun it follows.

**Table 8-2    Long-form Possessive Adjectives after a Noun**

| | |
|---|---|
| *mío, mía, míos, mías* (my, mine) | *nuestro, nuestra, nuestros, nuestras* (our, ours) |
| *tuyo, tuya, tuyos, tuyas* (your, yours) | *vuestro, vuestra, vuestros, vuestras* (your, yours) |
| *suyo, suya, suyos, suyas* (your, yours) | *suyo, suya, suyos, suyas* (your, yours) |
| *suyo, suya, suyos, suyas* (his) | *suyo, suya, suyos, suyas* (their, theirs) |
| *suyo, suya, suyos, suyas* (her, hers) | *suyo, suya, suyos, suyas* (their, theirs) |

Notice in the following examples that the long form of the possessive adjective is used in conjunction with an article.

| | |
|---|---|
| *mi libro = el libro mío* | my book |
| *tu pluma = la pluma tuya* | your pen (informal you) |
| *nuestro amigo = el amigo nuestro* | our friend |
| *vuestra hermana = la hermana vuestra* | you all's sister |
| *su madre = la madre suya* | his, her, their or your (formal) mother |

As mentioned earlier, a common usage of this version of possessive adjective is after a form of the linking verbs *ser* or *estar*. Notice that the English possessive is different when it follows a form of "to be" (*is* or *are*). For example, "my book" becomes "the book is mine." In Spanish, the possessive adjectives from Table 8-2 are placed after the noun whether there's a linking verb or not.

| | |
|---|---|
| *el libro mío* | my book |
| *El libro es mío.* | The book is mine. |
| *las fotografías bonitas tuyas* | your pretty pictures |
| *Las fotografías bonitas son tuyas.* | The pretty pictures are yours. |
| *la casa nuestra* | our house |
| *La casa es nuestra.* | The house is ours. |
| *las niñas suyas* | his girls, her girls, their girls, your (formal) girls |
| *Las niñas son suyas.* | The girls are his, the girls are hers, the girls are theirs, the girls are yours. |

## Demonstrative adjectives

A **demonstrative adjective** is a word that demonstrates the proximity or distance of the noun it modifies. *This* (singular) and *these* (plural) are used to indicate that the noun being modified is *here*. To indicate something is farther away—*there*—the demonstrative adjectives are *that* (singular) and *those* (plural).

In Spanish, you will need to indicate the gender as well as the number of the noun being modified by a demonstrative adjective. The word for *this* has a masculine and feminine form (*este* and *esta*), and the word for *these* has a masculine and feminine form (*estos* and *estas*).

The words for *that* (*ese, esa*) and *those* (*esos, esas*) also indicate gender and number, and are actually just like the "closer" words except that they're missing the letter *t*. Remember the rule with a rhyme: "*this* and *these* both have *t*'s, but *that* and *those* don't."

Demonstrative adjectives are placed before the noun. Here are some examples:

| | |
|---|---|
| *Este libro es interesante.* | This book is interesting. |
| *Esta silla es anaranjada.* | This chair is orange. |
| *Estos estudiantes son inteligentes.* | These students are intelligent. |
| *Estas peliculas son aburridas.* | These movies are boring. |
| *Ese mapa es viejo.* | That map is old. |
| *Esa niña es adorable.* | That little girl is adorable. |
| *Esos restaurantes son caros.* | Those restaurants are expensive. |
| *Esas playas son bonitas.* | Those beaches are pretty. |

In Spanish there are actually three distances: here, there, and far away. If you want to indicate that a noun is "way over there," you use the singular demonstrative adjective *aquel/aquella,* or the plural *aquellos/aquellas.* There is no English equivalent to these words, so it's best to translate them as "that _____ way over there" or "those _____s way over there." The following sentences exemplify this concept. Notice that sometimes it sounds better to say "far away" instead of "way over there."

| | |
|---|---|
| *Aquel chico es guapo.* | That boy (way over there) is attractive. |
| *Aquella nación es rica.* | That nation (far away) is wealthy. |
| *Aquellos libros son viejos.* | Those books (way over there) are old. |
| *Aquellas montañas son blancas.* | Those mountains (way over there) are white. |

Table 8-3 shows which demonstrative adjective should be used with each of the three distances, which are all adverbs.

## Table 8-3    Distances and Demonstrative Adjectives

| Distance | Demonstrative Adjective |
|---|---|
| *aquí* = here<br>Indicates that the object is close to the speaker. | Use: *este, esta, estos,* or *estas* |
| *allí* = there<br>Indicates that the object is close to the person being addressed or that it is relatively far from both, the speaker and the person addressed. | Use: *ese, esa, esos,* or *esas* |
| *Allá/allí* = way over there (far away)<br>Indicates that the object is far from both the speaker and the person being addressed.<br><br>Sometimes *Allá/allí* are used to mean the same distance, according to different dialects. | Use: *aquel, aquella, aquellos,* or *aquellas* |

These adverbs are a good clue as to which demonstrative adjective is appropriate for the sentence because they usually appear together, as in these examples:

| | |
|---|---|
| *este libro aquí* | this book here |
| *ese libro ahí* | that book over there |
| *aquellos libros allí* | those books over yonder |

Table 8-4 organizes all the demonstrative adjectives by gender and number. The singular feminine forms and both plural forms of all the demonstrative adjectives consistently have "normal" endings (*–a, –os, –as*). It is the singular masculine forms that are a bit strange: *este, ese, aquel.* Learning these forms is important because in Chapter 15 you will learn about demonstrative pronouns, and they have a form that looks like what you would expect for the singular masculine form of these adjectives.

## Table 8-4    Demonstrative Adjectives

| Singular | Masculine | Feminine | Plural | Masculine | Feminine |
|---|---|---|---|---|---|
| this | *este* | *esta* | these | *estos* | *estas* |
| that | *ese* | *esa* | those | *esos* | *esas* |
| that (way over there) | *aquel* | *aquella* | those (way over there) | *aquellos* | *aquellas* |

# Adjectives from Verbs

The **past participle** is a form of the verb that usually ends in *–ado* or *–ido*. To form a past participle of an *–ar* verb, remove the *–ar* and add *–ado, –ada, –ados, –adas.* To create the past participle form of an *–er* or *–ir* verb, remove the infinitive ending and add *–ido, –ida, –idos, –idas.* Note that these adjectives have four forms and often correspond to the *–ed* ending of English adjectives.

The past participle of most verbs can function as an adjective. Once you have formed the past participle version of the verb, you have the singular, masculine form of the adjective, which ends in *–o.* Remember to change the ending to *–a* for feminine nouns and add *–s* for plural nouns.

| | | |
|---|---|---|
| *parar* = to stop | *el coche parado* | the stopped car |
| *organizar* = to organize | *la oficina organizada* | the organized office |
| *perder* = to lose | *las llaves perdidas* | the lost keys |
| *vestir* = to dress | *los chicos bien vestidos* | the well-dressed boys |

## Chapter Check-Out

For sentences 1–3, write the correct form of the adjective in parentheses. The adjective will always be provided in its singular, masculine form, and you may or may not have to change it to match the gender of the word it modifies.

1. *Esa mujer es _____. (español)*
2. *Hablamos italiano en _____ familia. (nuestro)*
3. *_____ chicas viven aquí. (este)*

For numbers 4–6, translate the sentence to Spanish. Be careful to put the adjective in the appropriate place in addition to using the correct form of the adjective to match the noun it modifies.

4. Those girls have many handsome boyfriends.
5. My intelligent brother has many books.
6. Those buildings (far away) are tall.

**Answers: 1.** *española* **2.** *nuestra* **3.** *estas* **4.** *Esas chicas tienen muchos novios guapos.* **5.** *Mi hermano inteligente tiene muchos libros.* **6.** *Aquellos edificios son altos.*

# Chapter 9
# ADVERBS AND COMPARISONS

## Chapter Check-In

❑ Creating adverbs from adjectives

❑ Using adverbs in a sentence

❑ Making comparisons using adverbs and adjectives

**A**dverbs are words that modify verbs. They can also be used to modify another adverb or an adjective, and can be created from adjectives. This chapter presents common adverbs and shows how some adverbs are formed from adjectives. Both adjectives and adverbs can be used to create comparisons. This chapter prepares you to write comparisons of nouns by using adjectives and to compare actions by using adverbs.

## Adverbs from Adjectives

In the sentence "He is quick," the adjective "quick" describes the pronoun "he." If the sentence changes to describe something he does, such as "he works quickly," the adverb "quickly" is used because it modifies the verb "works." In English, many adverbs are created by adding the suffix "–ly" to an adjective. Many adverbs in Spanish are created by adding the suffix *–mente* to the end of an adjective. When you see a Spanish word that ends in *–mente,* try picturing "–ly" on the end of the word and you may recognize a simple cognate that looks very similar to its English equivalent.

In both languages, there are some adverbs that are simple, independent words, but many adverbs are based on an adjective. To create this type of adverb in Spanish, you must use the feminine form of the adjective, if it exists. For example, the word *finalmente,* does not have a feminine form. Chapter 8 discusses how to create the feminine form of adjectives, and the basic rules are included with the examples in this section.

Add –*mente* to the end of the singular, feminine form (whenever possible) of an adjective, and you have an adverb. Adverbs do not vary in form even though you must use the feminine form of the adjective to create the adverb. Table 9-1 uses several examples to demonstrate how to create an adverb from an adjective that ends in –*o*.

**Table 9-1   Forming Adverbs from Regular Adjectives Ending in –*o***

| Eng. Adjective = Span. Adjective. | Feminine form | Span. Adverb = Eng. Adverb |
|---|---|---|
| necessary = *necesario* | *necesaria* | *necesariamente* = necesarily |
| lazy = *perezoso* | *perezosa* | *perezosamente* = lazily |
| quick = *rápido* | *rápida* | *rápidamente* = quickly |
| sincere = *sincero* | *sincera* | *sinceramente* = sincerely |

An adjective that ends in an –*e* is the same in its feminine form, so you just need to add –*mente* to make it into an adverb, as shown in Table 9-2.

**Table 9-2   Forming Adverbs from Adjectives Ending in –*e***

| Eng. Adjective = Span. Adjective | Span. Adverb = English Adverb |
|---|---|
| happy = *alegre* | *alegremente* = happily |
| brillant = *brilliante* | *brillantemente* = brillantly |
| diligent = *diligente* | *diligentemente* = diligently |
| sweet = *dulce* | *dulcemente* = sweetly |
| strong = *fuerte* | *fuertemente* = strongly |
| poor = *pobre* | *pobremente* = poorly |
| sad = *triste* | *tristemente* = sadly |

An adjective that ends in a consonant normally does not add an –*a* to the end to make it feminine (unless it is an adjective of nationality). Therefore, as you can see in Table 9-3, you just add –*mente* to an adjective that ends in a consonant to make the adverb form.

**Table 9-3    Forming Adverbs from Adjectives Ending in a Consonant**

| Eng. Adjective = Span. Adjective | Span. Adverb = English Adverb |
|---|---|
| courteous = *cortés* | *cortésmente* = courteously |
| weak = *débil* | *débilmente* = weakly |
| easy = *fácil* | *fácilmente* = easily |
| happy = *feliz* | *felizmente* = happily |

Notice in the following examples that an adverb created from an adjective that has a written accent mark will retain the same written accent.

| | |
|---|---|
| *Paco es débil.* | Paco is weak. |
| *Paco canta débilmente.* | Paco sings weakly. |
| *David es rápido.* | David is quick. |
| *David corre rápidamente.* | David runs quickly. |

A few specific adverbs have no suffix and are identical to the adjective. The following words can be used as adjectives or adverbs. When used as adverbs, they look like a singular masculine form of the adjective, but since they actually modify a verb, they do not have gender and will not change endings.

| | |
|---|---|
| *mucho* | much (a lot) |
| *poco (un poco)* | little (a little) |
| *demasiado* | too much |
| *tanto* | so much |
| *más* | more |
| *menos* | less |

Table 9-4 shows those words in action as an adverb and as an adjective.

**Table 9-4    Words that Serve as Adverbs and Adjectives**

| Adverb | Adjective |
|---|---|
| Alicia gana mucho. | Alicia juega muchos partidos. |
| Alicia wins a lot. | Alicia plays many games. |
| El álgebra es un poco difícil. | Julio come poca carne. |
| Algebra is a little difficult. | Julio eats little meat. |
| Leemos demasiado. | Tenemos demasiados libros. |
| We read too much. | We have too many books. |
| Ella habla tanto. | Ella ve tantas películas. |
| She talks so much. | She watches so many movies. |
| Juana trabaja más que yo. | Ella está más bien feliz. |
| Juana works more than I do. | She's rather happy. |
| La plata cuesta menos que el oro. | José está menos enfermo hoy que ayer. |
| Silver costs less than gold. | José is less ill today than yesterday. |

## Irregular adverb

There is one irregular adverb that is troublesome in both languages. The adverb form of "good" is "well," which is irregular in English. Not only is the adverb "well" formed irregularly, but the adjective form "good" is often used incorrectly to modify verbs. To describe a noun or a pronoun, you must use the adjective "good." To describe a verb, you must use the adverb "well."

For example, "The book is good" uses the adjective "good" to modify the noun "book." In "The author writes well," the adverb "well" modifies the verb "writes." It is common to hear the incorrect sentence, "he writes good." The same problem occurs in Spanish. The word *bueno* is the equivalent to the English adjective "good," and the adverb form of *bueno* is irregular, also. The adverb *bien* is the equivalent to the English adverb "well."

A similar phenomenon occurs with the adjective *malo* (bad) and the adverb *mal* (badly). It is somewhat easier to remember that *malo* is the adjective form because it ends in –*o,* so you would have to determine the gender of the noun it modifies in order to use the right form of the adjective. If you can't find a noun and realize that *malo* modifies a verb, you must use the adverb *mal* instead.

In the following examples, notice that *mejor* (better) and *peor* (worse) are extremely unusual. The same word can be used as an adjective or adverb, but it does not change endings when used as an adverb.

| Adverb | Adjective |
|---|---|
| *Jaime y Carmen bailan mejor que sus vecinos.* | *Jaime y Carmen son mejores bailarines que sus vecinos.* |
| Jaime and Carmen dance better than their neighbors. | Jaime and Carmen are better dancers than their neighbors. |
| *Susana y Consuela cocinan peor que su madre.* | *Las comidas son peores que las que preparó mi madre.* |
| Susana and Consuela cook worse than their mother. | The meals are worse than the ones my mom prepared. |

# Adverb Placement in a Sentence

The basic rule pertaining to the placement of adverbs in a sentence is to place adverbs after verbs but in front of adjectives or other adverbs, but variations are possible. The adverb is placed immediately after the verb when the verb has an object, as in the first example, or the adverb has a short form, as in the second.

> *El examen es horriblemente difícil.*
> The exam is horribly difficult.

> *Mis abuelos hablan bien el castellano.*
> My grandparents speak Castillian well.

## Adverbs of time

Since the main job of adverbs is to modify verbs, adverbs may include words that indicate the time in which the action of the verb is done. The following list includes some of the adverbs that are not based on adjectives. Add these to your list of important vocabulary words.

| | |
|---|---|
| *ahora* | now |
| *anoche* | last night |
| *antes* | before |
| *aún* | even, yet |

| | |
|---|---|
| *ayer* | yesterday |
| *entonces* | then |
| *luego* | then, later |
| *mañana* | tomorrow |
| *nunca* | never |
| *pronto* | soon |
| *siempre* | always |
| *tarde* | late |
| *temprano* | early |
| *todavía* | still, yet |

While other types of adverbs are generally placed after the verb, the placement of adverbs of time is generally pretty flexible. They can either precede or follow the verb of the sentence without changing the meaning.

| | |
|---|---|
| *Él todavía habla.* | He still speaks. |
| *Él habla todavía.* | He speaks still. |
| *Siempre corremos en el parque.* | We always run in the park. |
| *Corremos siempre en el parque.* | We always run in the park. |

## Adverbs of manner

Adverbs of manner tell how something is done. Many of the adverbs created from adjectives are adverbs that indicate the manner in which a verb is done. When an adverb is modifying a verb, it will immediately follow the verb it modifies unless there is a direct object after the verb. If there happens to be a direct object after the verb, the adverb will follow the direct object.

| | |
|---|---|
| *Ramón come rápidamente.* | Ramón eats quickly. |
| *Adela canta tristemente.* | Adela sings sadly. |
| *Nyscelle baila felizmente.* | Nyscelle dances happily. |
| *Gonzalo habla español perfectamente.* | Gonzalo speaks Spanish perfectly. |

## Adverbs that modify adjectives or adverbs

When an adverb is used to modify an adjective or another adverb, it will be placed in front of the adjective or adverb it modifies. Many of these adverbs act as **intensifiers.** For example, the adverb "very" can intensify the adjective "intelligent;" it also can modify the adverb "intelligently" as in, "He speaks very intelligently." The same is true in Spanish.

| | |
|---|---|
| *Él es muy inteligente.* | He is very intelligent. |
| *Él habla muy inteligentemente.* | He speaks very intelligently. |

The following are some common adverbs that can be used to intensify (modify) an adjective or an adverb.

| | |
|---|---|
| *completamente* | completely |
| *extremadamente* | extremely |
| *muy* | very |
| *sumamente* | extremely |
| *totalmente* | totally |

## Shortened Adverbs

Adding *–mente* to the feminine form of an adjective creates a pretty long word. This creates a rather cumbersome sentence when several adverbs ending in *–mente* are used in the same sentence, so the Spanish language has a rule to shorten adverbs when more than one is used. When two or more adverbs end in *–mente,* the suffix *–mente* is used only with the last adverb, all preceding adverbs lose the *–mente* and keep the singular feminine form of the adjective.

| | |
|---|---|
| *Marco trabaja rápida y diligentemente.* | Marco works quickly and diligently. |
| *Laura juega al fútbol inteligente y fuertemente.* | Laura plays soccer intelligently and powerfully. |
| *El policía obra justa y lealmente.* | The policeman serves justly and loyally. |
| *Los padres ayudan generosa y responsablemente.* | The parents help generously and responsibly. |

# Comparisons

A comparison can be created using adjectives or adverbs. The basic construction of comparison sentences is the same for both.

## Comparisons with adjectives

The sentence structure for a superiority comparison using an adjective looks like this:

> **Subject + linking verb + *más* + adjective + *que* + noun (or pronoun)**
>
> *Marla es más interesante que Rosa.*
>
> Marla is more interesting than Rosa.

The expression "more interesting" sounds idiomatically correct because interesting is a long adjective. Be aware that in English a shorter adjective will be written with a suffix *–er* to indicate comparisons. It sounds better to say "taller" than "more tall" because "tall" is such a short adjective. In Spanish, it doesn't matter how long or short the adjective is, the expression "more . . ." is always used, except in the few instances when a comparative word is more appropriate, such as *mejor* (better) or *peor* (worse), for example.

> *Victoria es más alta que Samuel.*
>
> Victoria is taller (more tall) than Samuel.

> *Victoria es más inteligente que Sara.*
>
> Victoria is more intelligent than Sara.

The sentence structure of an inferiority comparison using an adjective looks like this:

> **Subject + linking verb + *menos* + adjective + *que* + noun (or pronoun)**
>
> *Martín es menos guapo que Gonzalo.*
>
> Martín is less attractive than Gonzalo.

> *Martina es menos loca que Diego.*
>
> Martina is less crazy than Diego.

In the preceding examples, notice that when the two people or things being compared are of different genders, the adjective must match the gender of the subject of the sentence.

## Comparatives of equality

A comparative of equality means that the people or things being compared have equal characteristics or possessions. To express a comparison of equality, you will use an adjective with the expression "*tan . . . como*" even though in English you use the same word twice: "as . . . as" to create equivalent expressions, as shown here:

> **Subject + linking verb + *tan* + adjective + *como* + noun (or pronoun)**
>
> *Susana es tan popular como su hermano.*
>
> Susana is as popular as her brother.

In the followinig examples, the adjective matches the subject of the sentence.

> *Gabriela es tan loca como su padre.*
>
> Gabriela is as crazy as her father.

> *Ramón es tan rico como ella.*
>
> Ramón is as rich as she (is).

When a comparison of nouns indicates equivalence, the same formula is used, except that *tan* becomes the adjective *tanto (–a, –os, –as)* and must match the gender and number of the noun that follows it.

> **Subject + linking verb + *tanto* + noun + *como* + noun (or pronoun)**
>
> *Mateo tiene tantos televisores como Marisol.*
>
> Matt has as many televisions as Marisol.

> *El maestro tiene tanta paciencia como un santo.*
>
> The teacher has as much patience as a saint.

## Superlatives

A **superlative** is the maximum level of the adjective. In English, a superlative is created with a definite article in front of an adjective, and the suffix *–est* is attached to the end of it. The *tallest,* the *prettiest,* or the *smartest* can be qualified by a prepositional phrase "in the class" or "at the party." This is done in Spanish with a formula very similar to comparisons, except the definite article *(el, los, la, las)* precedes the *más* or *menos,* and *de* or *en* are used instead of *que.* Superlatives only work with adjectives, not adverbs. The formula for creating a superlative expression is as follows:

**Subject + linking verb + definite article + *más* +adjective + *de* + rest of sentence.**

*Eva es la más alta de la escuela.*

Eva is the tallest in the school.

*Ignacio y Mateo son los más guapos de todos.*

Ignacio and Matt are the most handsome of all.

In English a negative superlative is always created by using the term "the least." In Spanish the same formula as previously shown is used with *menos* before the adjective. The formula for creating a negative superlative expression is as follows:

**Subject + linking verb + definite article + *menos* +adjective + *de* + rest of sentence.**

*Pepe es el menos alto de la escuela.*

Pepe is the least tall in the school.

## Comparisons with adverbs

Remember, adverbs use the feminine form of the adjective whenever possible *(perezosamente).* When there is no feminine form, the adjective just takes on the suffix *–mente.* Look at the examples following each formula to see how to create comparisons between adverbs.

■ Subject + verb +*más* + adverb + *que* + noun (or pronoun)

*Beti estudia más diligentemente que Carmen.*

Beti studies more diligently than Carmen.

*Lolita trabaja más perezosamente que Berto.*

Lolita works more lazily than Berto.

■ Subject + verb + *menos* + adverb + *que* + noun (or pronoun)

*Lola se viste menos elegantemente que Daniela.*
Lola dresses less elegantly than Daniela.

*Mercedes escribe menos cuidadosamente que su hermano.*
Mercedes writes less carefully than her brother.

When the comparison (more than, less than) results in a number following the *más que* or *menos que*, then *que* changes to *de* unless the sentence is negative, as shown in these examples:

*Tengo más <u>de</u> veinte dólares.*
I have more than twenty dollars.

*Cuesta menos <u>de</u> veinte dólares.*
It costs less than twenty dollars.

*No tengo más <u>que</u> diez dólares.*
I don't have more than ten dollars. (I have only ten dollars.)

## Irregular comparisons

In both languages, there are some comparison words that are formulated irregularly. A good example is the adjective *good*. If it followed normal rules, you would say "gooder," and little kids do this before they learn it's irregular. The adjectives in the following list have irregular comparatives. Instead of saying *más bueno,* you say *mejor.* Insead of *menos bueno,* you say *peor.*

| | |
|---|---|
| good = *bueno* | better = *mejor* |
| bad = *malo* | worse = *peor* |
| big = *grande* | older = *mayor* (when referring to age) |
| little = *pequeño* | younger = *menor* (when referring to age) |
| old = *viejo* | older = *mayor* |
| young = *joven* | younger = *menor* |

Notice that *mayor* is used when bigger really means older. If you are actually talking about size, use *más grande* (more big). The same is true with the word *little*. In English *little* can be used to refer to age, as in "my little sister." The adjective *menor* indicates less age, but to indicate less size, use *menos grande* (less big) or *más pequeño* (more small). Here are some examples:

> *Mi casa es más grande que tu casa.*
> My house is bigger than your house.

> *Yo soy mayor que mi hermano.*
> I am bigger (older) than my brother.

> *Tu casa es más pequeña que mi casa.*
> Your house is smaller than my house.

> *Tu hermana es menor que mi hermana.*
> Your sister is younger than my sister.

## Chapter Check-Out

Create the adverb form of the following adjectives:

**1.** *inteligente*

**2.** *bueno*

**3.** *feliz*

**4.** *malo*

Translate the following sentences to Spanish:

**5.** Marta is the tallest of the class.

**6.** Miguel is taller than his brother.

**7.** Felipe has more than thirty dollars.

**8.** Sarita speaks slowly.

**9.** Janina is as intelligent as the teacher.

**Answers: 1.** *inteligentemente* **2.** *bien (buenamente)* **3.** *felizmente* **4.** *mal (malamente)* **5.** *Marta es la más alta de la clase.* **6.** *Miguel es más alto que su hermano.* **7.** *Felipe tiene más de treinta dólares.* **8.** *Sarita habla lentamente.* **9.** *Janina es tan inteligente como la maestra.*

# Chapter 10

# DIRECT AND INDIRECT OBJECT PRONOUNS

## Chapter Check-In

❑ Identifying the direct and/or indirect object of a sentence

❑ Replacing direct and indirect objects with the appropriate pronouns

❑ Placing object pronouns correctly in a sentence

❑ Using double object pronouns in a sentence

**C**hapter 3 discusses how to replace the subject of a sentence with a pronoun. This chapter details how to use pronouns to replace nouns that serve as objects–either direct or indirect. You will learn how to identify the parts of a sentence and to replace a noun with the appropriate pronoun if the noun is the direct object or indirect object.

## Objective Cases

In English there is a case of pronouns called the **objective case.** Those are the pronouns to use when the noun you want to replace is either the direct object, indirect object, or object of a preposition. Table 10-1 lists those pronouns in the same order as the subject pronouns were listed in Chapter 3.

**Table 10-1    English Object Pronouns**

| Person | Singular | Plural |
|---|---|---|
| First person | me | us |
| Second person | you | you |
| Third person (masculine) | him | them |
| Third person (feminine) | her | them |
| Third person (no gender) | it | them |

Spanish also has three distinct cases of object pronouns: direct object, indirect object, and object of the preposition (object of the preposition pronouns are discussed in Chapter 15, which comes after a discussion on prepositions in Chapter 14).

# Direct Objects and Direct Object Pronouns

As you learned in Chapter 3, to determine which pronoun to use to replace a noun, you must determine what role the noun is playing in the sentence. When you want to use a pronoun to replace a noun that is the direct object of the sentence, however, you must first be able to identify that the noun is the direct object of the sentence. The **direct object** is the person(s) or things(s) that receive the action of the verb. Not every sentence has an explicitly stated direct object. If there is an answer to the question "Who or what is being verbed?" that is the direct object of the sentence.

### Direct object of a sentence

If there is a direct object in a sentence, there is a very simple way to systematically identify it along with the subject and verb. It's the following three-step process (the order is important!):

1. **To identify the verb of the sentence, ask yourself what action is taking place.** That action word is the verb of your sentence.

2. **Ask yourself who or what is responsible for the action.** The noun that answers that question is the subject of your sentence.

3. **Ask yourself who or what is being "verb-ed."** The answer to that question is the direct object of the sentence. If you can't identify a direct object, don't worry. Not every sentence has one.

This system is much easier to understand with an example or two. Remember that every sentence must have a subject and a verb, but not every sentence will have a direct object. The three-step analysis follows.

*Yolanda vende libros.* (Yolanda sells books.)

1.  **What is the action of the sentence?** *Vende* (sells). *Vende* is the verb of the sentence.

2.  **Who or what does the action?** *Yolanda. Yolanda* is the subject of the sentence.

3.  **Who or what is being sold?** *Libros* (books). *Libros* is the direct object of the sentence.

## The personal *a*

Whenever the direct object of a sentence is a person or any word referring to a person, the preposition *a* is placed in front of the direct object. This is called the **personal *a*** and will disappear when the direct object is turned into a pronoun. Notice in the following examples that the personal *a* has no translation in the English sentences.

| | |
|---|---|
| *Marta invita <u>a Laura</u>.* | Marta invites <u>Laura</u>. |
| *El padre mira <u>a los niños</u>.* | The father sees <u>the children</u>. |
| *El maestro llama <u>a los estudiantes</u>.* | The teacher calls <u>the students</u>. |
| *Mis amigos y yo ayudamos <u>a los pobres</u>.* | My friends and I help <u>the poor</u>. |

## Direct object pronouns

Once you have determined that the noun you want to replace with a pronoun is serving as the direct object of the sentence, you can select the appropriate pronoun from the direct object case of Spanish pronouns. Table 10-2 lists the Spanish direct object pronouns. To determine which pronoun is appropriate, consider what pronoun you would have used if you were using a subject pronoun, and then select the direct object pronoun from the same "spot" in the table.

**Table 10-2    Spanish Direct Object Pronouns**

| Person | Singular | Plural |
|---|---|---|
| First person (masculine and feminine) | *me* (me) | *nos* (us) |
| Second person (masculine and feminine) | *te* (you) | *os* (you) |
| Third person (masculine) | *lo* (him) | *los* (them) |
| Third person (feminine) | *la* (her) | *las* (them) |

The English equivalent to this chart is Table 10-1. There is no need for a neutral pronoun, like the English word "it," because all nouns have gender in Spanish. *Lo* means "him," but when used to replace masculine nouns that are objects, *lo* is translated as the English word "it." The direct object pronoun *la* means "her," and also means "it" when replacing a feminine noun that is an object. Just remember that *lo, la, los,* and *las* refer to both people and things.

*Lo* and *la* are also the direct object pronouns for *usted*. So you must consider the gender of the "you" that you are replacing with a pronoun. *Los* and *las* are the direct object pronouns for *ustedes,* too, and will reflect the gender of the group of people that "you (plural)" refers to.

It is especially confusing when the direct object pronouns *la, los,* and *las* look exactly like the definite article *la, los,* and *las*. Just remember when one of these words isn't followed by a noun, it is probably replacing one rather than serving as an article.

### Direct object pronoun placement

In English, a direct object always follows the verb. It does not matter whether the object has been turned into a pronoun or not. In Spanish, a direct object follows a conjugated form of a verb unless you turn it into a pronoun. When you change a direct object to a pronoun, the direct object pronoun must be moved in front of the conjugated form of the verb. If the sentence is negative, the *no* or other negative word will precede the direct object pronoun. Watch what happens in the following pairs of examples. The direct object is underlined in each sentence, but in the second sentence it has been changed to a direct object pronoun and moved to directly in front of the verb.

| | |
|---|---|
| *El señor García enseña la lección.* | Mr. Garcia teaches the lesson. |
| *El señor García la enseña.* | Mr. Garcia teaches it. |
| *Mateo invita a Gabriela.* | Mateo invites Gabriela. |
| *Mateo la invita.* | Mateo invites her. |
| *Maya escribe un libro.* | Maya writes a book. |
| *Maya lo escribe.* | Maya writes it. |
| *Anita mira a Martín.* | Anita sees Martín. |
| *Anita lo mira.* | Anita sees him. |
| *Vicente no trae las bebidas a la fiesta.* | Vicente doesn't bring the beverages to the party. |
| *Vicente no las trae a la fiesta.* | Vicente doesn't bring them to the party. |
| *El jefe no invita a las mujeres.* | The boss doesn't invite the women. |
| *El jefe no las invita.* | The boss doesn't invite them. |
| *Benjamín tiene los regalos.* | Benjamin has the gifts. |
| *Benjamín los tiene.* | Benjamin has them. |
| *Octavio lleva a los músicos.* | Octavio takes the musicians. |
| *Octavio los lleva.* | Octavio takes them. |

When there are two verbs in the sentence, the first one is conjugated and the second one is used in its infinitive form. In such sentences, the object pronouns can be placed in front of the conjugated verb or can be attached to the end of the infinitive.

| | |
|---|---|
| *Daniel la quiere llamar.* | Daniel wants to call her. |
| *Daniel quiere llamarla.* | Daniel wants to call her. |

You learned in Chapter 4 how to create the present progressive tense. When a sentence is in the present progressive tense, there will be a conjugated form of *estar* and the present participle form of the verb. Object pronouns may be placed in front of the conjugated form of *estar* or attached to the end of the verb in the present participle form (ending in *–iendo* or *–ando*). This will change the natural stress, so you must add an accent mark to the vowel preceding *–ndo* when you attach one or two object pronouns. Of course, you can always choose to place the object pronouns in front of the conjugated form of *estar* and avoid using a written accent mark. Both ways of expressing the progressive are accept-able in Spanish; it does not change the meaning.

| | |
|---|---|
| *Juan la está llamando.* | Juan is calling her. |
| *Juan está llamándola.* | Juan is calling her. |

### Common transitive verbs

There are specific verbs that require a direct object. These verbs, called **transitive verbs,** sound incomplete if you try to use them without a direct object. If you say "he brings," it is technically a sentence but sounds incomplete because the transitive verb "brings" requires a direct object. You can't help but think, "he brings what?" Here are transitive verbs that are commonly used when practicing using direct objects:

| | |
|---|---|
| *comprar* | to buy |
| *dar* | to give |
| *escribir* | to write |
| *invitar* | to invite |
| *llamar* | to call |
| *llevar* | to carry (away), to take (away), to wear |
| *mirar* | to watch, look, to look at |
| *querer (e>ie)* | to want, to love |
| *traer* | to bring |

# Indirect Objects and Indirect Object Pronouns

An **indirect object** is a word or phrase that informs to whom or for whom something is being done. It can be a person, an animal, or a thing. Not every sentence has a direct object pronoun, but there's a good chance that if a sentence does have a direct object, it will also have an indirect object. The general rule is that a sentence cannot have an indirect object unless it has a direct object; however, exceptions do exist and are dis-cussed later in the chapter.

## Indirect object of a sentence

To find the indirect object of a sentence, you must first find the direct object. Using the three-step process discussed earlier to locate the direct object, a fourth step is added to identify the indirect object:

1. **To identify the verb of the sentence, ask yourself what action is taking place.** That action word is the verb of your sentence.

2. **Ask yourself who or what is responsible for the action.** The noun that answers that question is the subject of your sentence.

3. **Ask yourself "who or what is being verb-ed?"** The answer to that question is the direct object of the sentence. You may not have a direct object, but if there is a direct object, there's a chance that there may also be an indirect object.

4. **To identify the indirect object of the sentence, ask yourself to whom or for whom is the direct object "verb-ed"?**

Remember that every sentence must have a subject and a verb, but not every sentence will have a direct object and/or indirect object. It is, however, safe to say that (except in special cases) there will not be an indirect object unless there is a direct object. Here's an example of the four-step process:

*Julio le da a María lecciones.* (Julio gives María lessons.)

1. **What is the action of the sentence?** *Da* (gives). *Da* is the verb of the sentence.

2. **Who or what does the action?** *Julio.* *Julio* is the subject of the sentence.

3. **Who or what is being given?** *Lecciónes* (lessons). *Lecciónes* is the direct object of the sentence.

4. **To or for whom or what are the lessons given?** *A María.* *María* is the indirect object of the sentence.

## Indirect object pronouns

Indirect object pronouns are somewhat different from direct object pronouns because indirect object pronouns are used even when the actual indirect object is stated. Table 10-3 lists the indirect object pronouns.

**Table 10-3    Spanish Indirect Object Pronouns**

| Person | Singular | Plural |
|---|---|---|
| First person (masculine and feminine) | *me* (me) | *nos* (us) |
| Second person (masculine and feminine) | *te* (you) | *os* (you) |
| Third person (masculine and feminine) | *le* (him, her) | *les* (them) |

As discussed earlier, English pronouns are the same for both indirect and direct objects. You can see that most of the Spanish indirect object pronouns look exactly like direct object pronouns except for the third person singular and plural. There is no differentiation between the masculine indirect object pronoun to *him* and the feminine to *her*. The pronouns *le/les* are used as the indirect object pronoun for both genders.

Because the pronoun *le* has several meanings, a clarification should be placed either at the beginning of the sentence or after the verb to indicate the gender or even the specific person. To create a clarification, the preposition *a* is followed by a subject pronoun. *A él, a ella,* or *a usted* can be used to clarify the pronoun *le,* or any noun can be used after the preposition *a* to specify exactly who the indirect object is.

The pronoun *les* has the same problem, so if it's necessary to clarify the gender of "them" or to specify "you guys," use the same method of clarification by adding *a* in front of the subject pronoun, as in *a ellos, a ellas,* or *a ustedes.*

### Indirect object pronoun placement

In the following sample sentences, the actual indirect object and the indirect object pronoun are both in bold print because they both refer to the same thing. But unlike with direct objects, you do not have to eliminate the indirect object to require a pronoun. You must use an indirect object pronoun any time there is an indirect object, but you may choose to use only the indirect object pronoun if the actual indirect object is clear. The indirect object pronoun is placed before the conjugated verb or attached to an infinitive like a direct object. The clarification is provided in Spanish by using the preposition *a + noun* or *personal subject pronoun.*

| | |
|---|---|
| *Juan le da un diamante a su novia.* | Juan gives a diamond to his girlfriend. |
| *Juan **le** da **a ella** un diamante.* | Juan gives **her** a diamond. (***A ella*** is used to clarify that ***le*** refers to **her**) |

| | |
|---|---|
| *Juan **le** da un diamante.* | Juan gives **her** a diamond. (It must have been already established that *le* refers to **her**.) |
| *Amanda **le** trae la comida (**a su abuelo**).* | Amanda brings **her grandfather** the meal. |
| *Amanda **le** trae la comida **a él**.* | Amanda brings **him** the meal. (*A él* clarifies that *le* refers to **him**.) |
| *Amanda **le** trae la comida.* | Amanda brings **him** the meal. (Used only when no clarification is necessary.) |
| *Ricardo **les** enseña la lección **a los estudiantes**.* | Ricardo teaches **the students** the lesson. |
| *Ricardo **les** enseña la lección.* | Ricardo teaches **them** the lesson. |
| *Yo siempre **les** digo la verdad **a mis hermanas**.* | I always tell **my sisters** the truth. |
| *Yo siempre **les** digo la verdad **a ellas**.* | I always tell **them (feminine)** the truth. (Used to specify that **them** refers to all girls.) |
| *Yo siempre **les** digo la verdad.* | I always tell **them** the truth. (The gender of **them** doesn't matter.) |
| *Roberto compra un coche para **ustedes**.* | Robert buys a car for **you guys**. |
| *Roberto **les** compra un coche.* | Robert buys **you guys** a car. (Used if it's already established that *les* is referring to *ustedes*.) |

Notice in these examples that you can use either the indirect object pronoun without the actual indirect object stated or the indirect object pronoun along with the actual indirect object. Note: In Spanish, you cannot say *Doy el dinero a ella*. You must use the indirect object pronoun: *Le doy el dinero (a ella)*.

## Special verbs with indirect object pronouns

There are a few special verbs that work in conjunction with an indirect object pronoun to create an idiomatic expression that is quite common in Spanish as well as its English equivalent. See if you know the meanings of the following sentences.

*Me gusta la pizza.*
*Te gustan los libros.*
*Nos gusta la música.*
*Le gusta bailar.*

You probably translate the first sentence as "I like pizza," and you are correct. "I like" is the idiomatic expression used in English to express *"me gusta,"* but in reality the verb *gustar* means to please, and the Spanish expression states "Pizza pleases me." Notice that *yo* is never used with a *gustar*-type verb. It's easier to use the verb *gustar* correctly if you understand that it doesn't exactly mean "like" even though you translate it that way. When you learn the patterns of sentences with the verb *gustar,* you will also be able to use the verbs in Table 10-4, because they are all used in sentences exactly like *gustar*.

These sentences are tricky, because the English version uses a subject pronoun and the Spanish version uses an indirect object pronoun. Try reading the Spanish sentence backward and it will be more like the English version.

| | |
|---|---|
| *Me gusta la pizza.* | Pizza pleases me. = I like pizza. |
| *Te gustan los libros.* | The books please you. = You like books. |
| *Nos gusta la música.* | The music pleases us. = We like the music. |
| *Le gusta bailar.* | Dancing pleases him. = He likes to dance. |

Because the pronoun *le* is so vague, a clarification can be placed either at the beginning of the sentence or after *gustar* to indicate the gender or even the specific person who is pleased. To create a clarification, use the preposition *a* followed by a subject pronoun. *A él, a ella,* or *a usted* can be used to clarify the pronoun *le*.

| | |
|---|---|
| *A ella le gusta la pizza.* | Pizza pleases her. = She likes pizza. |
| *A él le gusta comer.* | Eating pleases him. = He likes to eat. |
| *A usted le gusta el restaurante.* | The restaurant pleases you (formal). = You (formal) like the restaurant. |

The pronoun *les* has the same problem, so if it is necessary to clarify the gender of "them" or to specify "you guys," use the same method of clarification by adding *a ellos, a ellas,* or *a ustedes.*

| | |
|---|---|
| *A ellas les gusta correr.* | Running pleases them (feminine). = They (feminine) like to run. |
| *A ustedes les gusta mirar la tele.* | Watching TV pleases you guys. = You guys like to watch TV. |
| *A ellos les gusta el partido.* | The game pleases them. = They (masculine) like the game. |

The indirect object precedes the verb *gustar* to indicate who is pleased. But what makes these sentences stray from the Spanish norm, is that the subject of the sentence—the thing that is doing the pleasing—follows the verb. The verb is still conjugated to go with the subject, but the subject is after the verb. Usually either the *él* or *ellos* form of *gustar (gusta)* is used. *Gustan* is used when followed by a plural subject, and *gusta* is used when followed by a singular subject or an infinitive. The indirect object that precedes *gusta* or *gustan* does not affect which form of *gustar* you use. Look carefully at the following examples, and notice that *gustar* is conjugated to go with the subject that follows. If there is a clarification of the indirect object after *gustar*, ignore it. The subject follows and determines which form of *gustar* to use.

| | |
|---|---|
| *Le gustan a él las guitarras.* | The guitars please him. = He likes the guitars. |
| *Les gusta el piano.* | The piano pleases them. = They like the piano. |
| *A ellos les gusta tocar.* | Playing pleases them. = They like to play. |
| *Me gustan los músicos.* | Musicians please me. = I like the musicians. |

When *gusta* is followed by a verb in its infinitive form, the verb is actually acting like a singular noun and is called a **gerund.** In English, a verb that is acting like a noun will have the *–ing* ending, but in Spanish the infinitive is always used in those cases.

Soccer is fun. Playing is fun.

Both *soccer* and *playing* are singular nouns, as are *fútbol* and *jugar* in this translation:

El *fútbol* es divertido. *Jugar* es divertido.

So when an infinitive is used as the subject after *gustar*, the *él* form *gusta* is appropriate, as in these examples:

| | |
|---|---|
| *Nos gusta el fútbol.* | Soccer pleases us. = We like soccer. |
| *Nos gusta jugar.* | Playing pleases us. = We like to play. |

There are several common verbs in Spanish that are used exactly like *gustar*, as shown in Table 10-4. It's important to learn these verbs and the examples that follow in order to use them correctly.

**Table 10-4  Special Verbs with Indirect Object Pronouns**

| Verb | Example |
|---|---|
| *agradar* (to please) | *Me agrada caminar con mis perros.* |
| | It pleases me to walk my dogs. |
| *bastar* (to suffice, to be enough) | *Le basta tener una casa y comida.* |
| | It's enough for him to have a house and food. |
| *doler* (to pain) | *Me duele la cabeza.* |
| | My head pains me. [I have a headache.] |
| *faltar* (to be lacking, to be missing) | *Les faltan los papeles.* |
| | They are lacking the papers. |
| *parecer* (to seem [look like]) | *Te parecen niños.* |
| | They look like children to you. |
| *placer* (to please) | *Nos placen los viajes largos.* |
| | Long voyages please us. |
| *quedar* (to remain) | *Le queda a usted un minuto.* |
| | There is one minute remaining for you. |
| *sobrar* (to be left over, to be an excess) | *Nos sobran muchas hamburguesas.* |
| | Many hamburgers are left over [on us]. |
| *tocar* (to be someone's turn) | *Le toca a Adela.* |
| | It's Adela's turn. |

# Double Object Sentences

Direct object pronouns and indirect object pronouns are placed in front of the verb. Since it is common to have both an indirect and direct object pronoun in a sentence, they will both be directly in front of the verb. In such sentences, the indirect object pronoun always precedes the direct object pronoun.

When there are direct and indirect object pronouns in the same sentence, follow the formula: the I.O.P. (Indirect Object Pronoun) then the D.O.P. (Direct Object Pronoun.  Both precede the conjugated verb.

Subject + **I.O.P** + <u>D.O.P</u> + verb + rest of sentence.

In the following examples, the first sentence establishes what the actual direct object of the sentence is, and the second sentence uses a direct object pronoun to replace it. The indirect object is in bold and the direct object is underlined to help you visualize what noun changes into what pronoun and where they are placed in the sentence. Notice that once you change the direct object to a pronoun, you must remove the direct object pronoun based on the formula above. These techniques will help you understand object pronouns.

| | |
|---|---|
| *Mi padre **me** compra <u>un coche nuevo</u>.* | My dad buys **me** <u>a new car</u>. |
| Mi padre **me** <u>lo</u> compra. | My dad buys <u>it</u> for **me**. |
| *Tu madre **te** cuenta <u>muchos cuentos</u>.* | Your mom tells **you** <u>many stories</u>. |
| *Tu madre **te** <u>los</u> cuenta.* | Your mom tells <u>them</u> to you. |
| *Nuestro jefe **nos** ofrece <u>una vacación</u>.* | Our boss offers **us** <u>a vacation</u>. |
| *Nuestro jefe **nos** <u>la</u> ofrece.* | Our boss offers <u>it</u> **to us**. |

## The use of *se*

When two object pronouns beginning with the letter *l (le, les, la, lo, las, los)* are used together, the first pronoun, which is always the I.O.P., changes to *se*. The following examples tackle this situation. The indirect object is in bold and the direct object is underlined to help you visualize what noun changes into what pronoun and where they are placed in the sentence.

| | |
|---|---|
| *Sergio **le** compra a **su madre** <u>unas flores</u>.* | Sergio buys **his mom** some <u>flowers</u>. |
| *Sergio **se** <u>las</u> compra.* | Sergio buys <u>them</u> **for her**. |
| *Gabriel **les** da algunos <u>besos</u> **a sus padres**.* | Gabriel gives **his parents** <u>some kisses</u>. |
| *Gabriel **se** <u>los</u> da **a sus padres**.* | Gabriel gives <u>them</u> to **his parents**. |
| *Lorenzo **le** enseña <u>el concepto difícil</u> a **su amigo**.* | Lorenzo teaches **his friend** <u>the difficult concept</u>. |
| *Lorenzo **se** <u>lo</u> enseña.* | Lorenzo teaches <u>it</u> **to him**. |
| *Ana **les** trae <u>la comida</u> **a sus abuelos**.* | Ana brings **her grandparents** <u>the meal</u>. |
| *Ana **se** <u>la</u> trae.* | Ana brings <u>it</u> **to them**. |

Here's another way to think of it: *le* and *les* change to *se* when placed before *lo, la, los,* or *las.*

### Adding two object pronouns to verbs

Earlier in this chapter, you learned that object pronouns can be attached either to the end of a present participle form of the verb or to the end of an infinitive form of the verb, as well as placed in front of a conjugated form of the verb (see "Direct object pronoun placement" earlier in this chapter). If you are using two object pronouns, they will be together wherever you choose to place them.

Adding two pronouns to the end of an infinitive messes up the natural stress and requires you to add an accent mark to the vowel before the final –*r* of the infinitive. You can add one pronoun to an infinitive without adding an accent, but you must add a written accent if you attach two object pronouns to the end of an infinitive. For example:

| | |
|---|---|
| *Enrique va a comprar**le** <u>unas flores</u> **a su novia.*** | Enrique is going to buy his girlfriend some flowers. |
| *Enrique va a comprár**selas**.* | Enrique is going to buy them for her. |

You learned earlier that you must add an accent mark to a present participle if even one pronoun is added. Since a present participle ends in a vowel, even one pronoun added to the end will mess up the natural stress. So you must add an accent to the vowel before the –*ndo* of the gerund if you add either one or two pronouns.

| | |
|---|---|
| *Melaní está ayudándome.* | Melanie is helping me. |
| *Mis padres están comprándomelo.* | My parents are buying it for me. |

There is always a conjugated verb in every sentence, so you can always put both object pronouns in front of the conjugated form of the verb. Do not, however, place one pronoun in front of the conjugated form of the verb and attach the other object pronoun to the end of an infinitive or present participle.

| | |
|---|---|
| *Enrique **le** va a comprar <u>unas flores</u> a su novia.* | Enrique is going to buy his girlfriend some flowers. |
| *Enrique **se** <u>las</u> va a comprar.* | Enrique is going to buy them for her. |

## Chapter Check-Out

For each pair of sentences, analyze the first sentence to determine the part of speech of each noun. Then write the pronoun that would go in the blank in the second sentence. If you have trouble, underline the direct object in both sentences (like the examples in the explanations throughout this chapter). The indirect objects were in bold in the examples, but you'll have to circle the indirect object in the following sentences.

1. *Mis padres me compran un coche nuevo.*

   *Mis padres me _____ compran.*

2. *Los jóvenes les escriben muchas cartas a las mujeres.*

   *Los jóvenes ___ las escriben.*

3. *A ellos les gustan los animales.*

   *A ella ____ gustan los animales.*

4. *Marianela le envía una tarjeta a su hermano.*

   *Marianela se _____ envía.*

5. *Jerónimo les pide mucho dinero.*

   *Jerónimo ___ lo pide.*

**Answers: 1.** *lo* **2.** *se* **3.** *le* **4.** *la* **5.** *se*

# Chapter 11

# THE PRETERITE TENSE

## Chapter Check-In

☐ Conjugating regular verbs in the preterite tense

☐ Predicting spelling changes in the *yo* form

☐ Understanding stem changing verbs in the preterite

☐ Learning the patterns of irregular preterite verbs

☐ Using the preterite tense in appropriate situations

There are two past tense aspects and forms in Spanish: the preterite and the imperfect. This chapter provides a clear explanation of the preterite tense. In addition to the regular patterns of verb forms in the preterite, there are many irregular preterite forms and some spelling changes to learn. To differentiate between the two Spanish past tense aspects, you learn the situations where the preterite tense is appropriate. You will also learn a list of special vocabulary words called indicators that help you know when to use the preterite tense.

## Regular Verbs in the Preterite Tense

To conjugate a regular verb in the preterite tense, remove the infinitive ending and add the appropriate endings. For an *–ar* verb that is regular in the preterite, use the endings from Table 11-1. (Not all verbs that were regular in the present tense are regular in the preterite. Preterite irregulars are presented later in this chapter.)

**Table 11-1    Preterite Endings for Regular –ar Verbs**

| Singular Pronoun | Ending | Plural Pronoun | Ending |
|---|---|---|---|
| yo | -é | nosotros/nosotras | -amos |
| tú | -aste | vosotros/vosotras | -asteis |
| usted | -ó | ustedes | -aron |
| él | -ó | ellos | -aron |
| ella | -ó | ellas | -aron |

The endings are a little confusing because the *él, ella,* and *usted* forms end in *–ó* in the preterite tense, but the *yo* form ends in *–o* (no accent) in the present tense. Take note of the accent mark on the preterite forms because that is the only difference. The *yo* form of all regular preterite verbs always has an accent mark as well. Remember to pronounce these words with the stress on the last syllable. The *tú* form is also different in the preterite tense: it never ends in *–s* like it does in the present tense.

Regular *–ar* verbs have the same *nosotros* form in the preterite as they do in the present tense. The only way you will know whether an *–ar* verb in the *nosotros* form is in the preterite or present tense is the context of the sentence. Later in this chapter, you will learn specific vocabulary words that serve as preterite indicators. If you see one of these words in the sentence, you will know the verb is conjugated in the preterite tense.

*Hablar* (to speak) is a regular verb in the preterite, so it will serve as a good example. Table 11-2 is a conjugation chart for the verb *hablar* in the preterite tense. Since the preterite is a past tense, these forms translate to the English past tense form "spoke."

**Table 11-2    Preterite Forms of the Regular –ar Verb Hablar**

| Singular | Plural |
|---|---|
| yo hablé (I spoke) | nosotros/nosotras hablamos (we spoke) |
| tú hablaste (you [familiar] spoke) | vosotros/vosotras hablasteis (you [familiar] spoke) |
| usted habló (you [formal] spoke) | ustedes hablaron (they [formal] spoke) |
| él habló (he spoke) | ellos hablaron (they spoke) |
| ella habló (she spoke) | ellas hablaron (they spoke) |

Table 11-3 shows that the endings for *–er* verbs and *–ir* verbs are the same for regular verbs in the preterite tense.

**Table 11-3  Preterite Endings for Regular *–er* and *–ir* Verbs**

| Singular Pronoun | Ending | Plural Pronoun | Ending |
|---|---|---|---|
| yo | -í | nosotros/nosotras | -imos |
| tú | -iste | vosotros/vosotras | -isteis |
| usted | -ió | ustedes | -ieron |
| él | -ió | ellos | -ieron |
| ella | -ió | ellas | -ieron |

Notice that the *nosotros/nosotras* form of an *–ir* verb looks identical in both the present and preterite tenses, but an *–er* verb has a different *nosotros* form in the preterite. The *nosotros/nosotras* form in the present tense is the only form where *–er* and *–ir* verbs are different.

The verb *comer* (to eat) is a regular *–er* verb in the preterite. Table 11-4, which shows the English past tense form of *ate,* is a good example of regular *–er* verb forms in the preterite tense.

**Table 11-4  Preterite Forms of the Regular *–er* Verb *Comer***

| Singular | Plural |
|---|---|
| yo comí (I ate) | nosotros/nosotras comimos (we ate) |
| tú comiste (you [informal] ate) | vosotros/vosotras comisteis (you [informal] ate) |
| usted comió (you [formal] ate) | ustedes comieron (you [formal] ate) |
| él comió (he ate) | ellos comieron (they ate) |
| ella comió (she ate) | ellas comieron (they ate) |

The verb *escribir* (to write) is a regular *–ir* verb in the preterite. Table 11-5, which shows the English past tense form of *wrote,* is a good example of regular *–ir* verb forms in the preterite tense.

**Table 11-5    Preterite Forms of the Regular –ir Verb Escribir**

| Singular | Plural |
|---|---|
| yo escribí (I wrote) | nosotros/nosotras escribimos (we wrote) |
| tú escribiste (you [informal] wrote) | vosotros/vosotras escribisteis (you [informal] wrote) |
| usted escribió (you [formal] wrote) | ustedes escribieron (you [formal] wrote) |
| él escribió (he wrote) | ellos escribieron (they wrote) |
| ella escribió (she wrote) | ellas escribieron (they wrote) |

# Different Yo Forms in the Preterite Tense

Chapter 1 addressed the spelling and pronunciation rules of Spanish. These rules are extremely consistent, and sometimes a conjugated form of the verb must change its spelling to maintain the correct pronunciation. This happens in the yo form of specific verbs in the preterite tense, because adding –í or –é to the base of the verb messes up the pronunciation of the word. The spelling change is meant to maintain the same basic sound as the infinitive.

## Verbs that end in –gar

Remember that the consonant g is pronounced hard (like the g in good) or soft (like the g in gym) depending on the vowel that follows the g. If a Spanish verb ends in –gar, the infinitive is pronounced with a hard g sound. However, when you remove the –ar infinitive ending and add the yo preterite ending, the hard g is suddenly followed by –é and would be pronounced as a soft g. To maintain the hard g sound of the infinitive, the letter u is added between the g and é. This creates the hard g sound of the infinitive pronunciation.

Whenever you see a verb ending in –gué, you can assume the u is only there to produce the correct hard g sound, and you don't pronounce the u.

To simplify matters, remember that a verb ending in –gar will change g– to gu– in the yo form of the preterite. Table 11-6 is the preterite conjugation chart for the verb pagar (to pay) which serves as a good example. Note that the yo form would be pronounced [pah-GAY].

**Table 11-6 Preterite Forms of the Verb *Pagar***

| Singular | Plural |
|---|---|
| *yo pagué* (I paid) | *nosotros/nosotras pagamos* (we paid) |
| *tú pagaste* (you [informal] paid) | *vosotros/vosotras pagasteis* (you [informal] paid) |
| *usted pagó* (you [formal] paid) | *ustedes pagaron* (you [formal] paid) |
| *él pagó* (he paid) | *ellos pagaron* (they paid) |
| *ella pagó* (she paid) | *ellas pagaron* (they paid) |

The following verbs are all regular *–ar* verbs in the preterite tense. Since they all end in *–gar,* you must change the *g* to *gu* in the *yo* form and then use the regular *yo* ending. All other preterite forms of these verbs are completely regular forms for a regular *–ar* verb in the preterite tense.

| *Infinitive form* | *Preterite* yo *form* |
|---|---|
| *agregar* (to add) | *agregué* |
| *apagar* (to extinguish, to turn off) | *apagué* |
| *cargar* (to load) | *cargué* |
| *encargar* (to put in charge, to entrust) | *encargué* |
| *entregar* (to hand in, to hand over) | *entregué* |
| *jugar* (to play a sport) | *jugué* |
| *llegar* (to arrive) | *llegué* |
| *obligar* (to compel, to force) | *obligué* |
| *pegar* (to beat, to glue) | *pegué* |

## Verbs that end in *–car*

The Spanish letter *c* is a lot like the letter *g*. It has a hard sound (like the English letter *k*) and a soft sound (like the English letter *s*). The *c* is pronounced soft when it's followed by *–i* or *–e*. It is pronounced hard when it's followed by *–o, –a,* or *–u.* Any verb that ends in *–car* will have the hard *c* sound in its infinitive form. This must be maintained in all the conjugated forms, but the preterite *yo* ending causes problems.

When you add *–é* to the base of a verb ending in *–car,* the *c* becomes a soft sound, which is unacceptable. So you must change the letter *c* to *qu* only in the *yo* preterite form. The resulting ending (*–qué*) is pronounced like the English name *Kay*. The combination of letters *–qu* is always pronounced like the English letter *k*, and you never say the *u* sound. It is never pronounced like the English word *queen*.

Table 11-7 is the preterite conjugation chart for the verb *tocar* (to play an instrument, to touch), which is an example for all regular *–ar* verbs in the preterite that end in *–car*.

**Table 11-7   Preterite Forms of the Verb *Tocar***

| *Singular* | *Plural* |
| --- | --- |
| *yo toqué* (I played) | *nosotros/nosotras tocamos* (we played) |
| *tú tocaste* (you [informal] played) | *vosotros/vosotras tocasteis* (you [informal] played) |
| *usted tocó* (you [formal] played) | *ustedes tocaron* (you [formal] played) |
| *él tocó* (he played) | *ellos tocaron* (they played) |
| *ella tocó* (she played) | *ellas tocaron* (they played) |

To simplify the rule: If a verb ends in *–car,* change *c* to *qu* in the *yo* form of the preterite.

Here are some common verbs that end in *–car,* and they are all conjugated like *tocar*.

| *Infinitive form* | *Preterite* yo *form* |
| --- | --- |
| *aplicar* (to apply) | *apliqué* |
| *buscar* (to seek, to look for) | *busqué* |
| *colocar* (to place, to put) | *coloqué* |
| *comunicar* (to communicate) | *comuniqué* |
| *dedicar* (to dedicate) | *dediqué* |
| *educar* (to educate) | *eduqué* |
| *explicar* (to explain) | *expliqué* |
| *fabricar* (to make, to manufacture) | *fabriqué* |
| *indicar* (to indicate) | *indiqué* |
| *marcar* (to mark) | *marqué* |

| | |
|---|---|
| *masticar* (to chew) | *mastiqué* |
| *pescar* (to fish) | *pesqué* |
| *publicar* (to publish) | *publiqué* |
| *sacar* (to take out) | *saqué* |
| *significar* (to mean) | *signifiqué* |

### Verbs that end in *–zar*

In Chapter 1, you learned whenever *z* is followed by *e,* it changes to *c.* This rule becomes important in the preterite tense because the verbs that end in *–zar* will change spelling in the *yo* form. Since the *yo* form has the ending *–é,* the *z* must change to *c.* For example, Table 11-8 shows the preterite conjugation of the verb *cruzar* (to cross).

**Table 11-8   Preterite Forms of the Verb *Cruzar***

| Singular | Plural |
|---|---|
| *yo cucé* (I crossed) | *nosotros/nosotras cruzamos* (we crossed) |
| *tú cruzaste* (you [informal] crossed) | *vosotros/vosotras cruzasteis* (you [informal] crossed) |
| *usted cruzó* (you [formal] crossed) | *ustedes cruzaron* (you [formal] crossed) |
| *él cruzó* (he crossed) | *ellos cruzaron* (they crossed) |
| *ella cruzó* (she crossed) | *ellas cruzaron* (they crossed) |

Here are some common verbs that end in *–zar,* and they are conjugated like *cruzar.*

| Infinitive form | Preterite yo *form* |
|---|---|
| *abrazar* (to embrace, to hug) | *abracé* |
| *alcanzar* (to reach) | *alcancé* |
| *amenazar* (to threaten) | *amenacé* |
| *avanzar* (to advance) | *avancé* |
| *gozar* (to enjoy) | *gocé* |
| *lanzar* (to throw) | *lancé* |

| | |
|---|---|
| *realizar* (to fulfill, to realize [one's dream]) | *realicé* |
| *rezar* (to pray) | *recé* |
| *tropezar* (to stumble, to trip) | *tropecé* |

### *I* to *y*

When the stem of the verb ends in a vowel, some spelling changes are necessary in certain forms in the preterite. This special spelling change only happens in the preterite tense and is not considered a stem changer. If there are three vowels in a row and the middle one is the letter *i*, you must change the *i* to *y*. The preterite endings for *–er* and *–ir* verbs will cause the *i>y* spelling change to happen in the third person forms (*él, ella, usted, ellos, ellas,* and *ustedes*), and an accent will be added to any other letter *–i* in the base of the verb in the conjugation chart.

Table 11-9 is a conjugation chart of the verb *caer* (to fall), which illustrates these changes. Consider the *él* form of the verb. If you simply added the ending *–ió* to the base of the verb *ca–,* the result would be *caió*. Since there are three vowels and the middle one is the letter *i*, it changes to *y* in the chart. Notice this also happens to the third person plural form of the verb.

**Table 11-9   Preterite Forms of the Verb *Caer***

| *Singular* | *Plural* |
|---|---|
| yo *caí* (I fell) | nosotros/nosotras *caímos* (we fell) |
| tú *caíste* (you [informal] fell) | vosotros/vosotras *caísteis* (you [informal] fell) |
| usted *cayó* (you [formal] fell) | ustedes *cayeron* (you [formal] fell) |
| él *cayó* (he fell) | ellos *cayeron* (they fell) |
| ella *cayó* (she fell) | ellas *cayeron* (they fell) |

Other verbs that have a base ending in a vowel are conjugated like *caer*. For example:

| | |
|---|---|
| *creer* | to believe |
| *leer* | to read |
| *oír* | to hear |
| *poseer* | to possess |

Table 11-10 shows the conjugation for the verb *construir*.

**Table 11-10    Preterite Forms of the Verb *Construir***

| Singular | Plural |
|---|---|
| *yo construí* (I built) | *nosotros/nosotras construímos* (we built) |
| *tú construiste* (you [informal] built) | *vosotros/vosotras construisteis* (you [informal] built) |
| *usted construyó* (you [formal] built) | *ustedes construyeron* (you [formal] built) |
| *él construyó* (he built) | *ellos construyeron* (they built) |
| *ella construyó* (she built) | *ellas construyeron* (they built) |

Here are some common *–uir* verbs that are all conjugated like *construir:*

| | |
|---|---|
| *contribuir* | to contribute |
| *distribuir* | to distribute |
| *huir* | to flee, to run away |
| *incluir* | to include |

# Stem Changers in the Preterite Tense

Chapter 4 discussed stem changing verbs in the present tense. If a verb is a stem changer in the present tense, it will not stem change in the preterite unless it is an *–ir* verb. No *–ar* or *–er* verbs will stem change in the preterite.

## Stem-changing verbs ending in *-ir*

An *–ir* verb that stem changes in the present tense will stem change in the preterite but only in the third person forms (*él, ella, usted, ellos, ellas, and ustedes*). Any *–ir* verb that stem changed *o>ue* will stem change *o>u* in the preterite in the third person forms. Table 11-11 demonstrates the preterite patterns for all *–ir* verbs that stem-changes *o>ue* in the present tense. The verb *dormir* (to sleep) is conjugated exactly the same in both tenses.

**Table 11-11 Preterite Forms of *Dormir***

| Singular | Plural |
|---|---|
| *yo dormí* (I slept) | *nosotros/nosotras dormimos* (we slept) |
| *tú dormiste* (you [informal] slept) | *vosotros/vosotras dormisteis* (you [informal] slept) |
| *usted durmió* (you [formal] slept) | *ustedes durmieron* (you [formal] slept) |
| *él durmió* (he slept) | *ellos durmieron* (they slept) |
| *ella durmió* (she slept) | *ellas durmieron* (they slept) |

There are several *–ir* verbs that stem change *e>ie* in the present tense. Any *–ir* verb that stem changes *e>ie* in the present tense, will stem change *e>i* in the preterite but only in the third person forms *(él, ella, usted, ellos, ellas, ustedes)*. Table 11-12, which conjugates the verb *mentir* (to tell a lie), demonstrates the preterite patterns for all *–ir* verbs that stem change *e>ie* in the present tense.

**Table 11-12 Preterite Forms of *Mentir***

| Singular | Plural |
|---|---|
| *yo mentí* (I told a lie) | *nosotros/nosotras mentimos* (we told a lie) |
| *tú mentiste* (you [informal] told a lie) | *vosotros/vosotras mentisteis* (you [informal] told a lie) |
| *usted mintió* (you [formal] told a lie) | *ustedes mintieron* (you [formal] told a lie) |
| *él mintió* (he told a lie) | *ellos mintieron* (they told a lie) |
| *ella mintió* (she told a lie) | *ellas mintieron* (they told a lie) |

Here are some common *–ir* verbs that are all conjugated like *mentir* in the preterite tense:

| | |
|---|---|
| *convertir* | to convert |
| *divertirse* | to enjoy oneself |
| *hervir* | to boil |
| *sentir* | to feel, to regret |
| *preferir* | to prefer |

If an *–ir* verb stem changes *e>i* in the present tense, it will also stem change *e>i* in the preterite, but only in the third person forms (*él, ella, usted, ellos, ellas, ustedes*). Table 11-13, which conjugates the verb *pedir* (to request), demonstrates the preterite patterns for all *-ir* verbs that stem change *e>i* in the present tense.

**Table 11-13   Preterite Forms of *Pedir***

| Singular | Plural |
| --- | --- |
| *yo pedí* (I requested) | *nosotros/nosotras pedimos* (we requested) |
| *tú pediste* (you [informal] requested) | *vosotros/vosotras pedisteis* (you [informal] requested) |
| *usted pidió* (you [formal] requested) | *ustedes pidieron* (you [formal] requested) |
| *él pidió* (he requested) | *ellos pidieron* (they requested) |
| *ella pidió* (she requested) | *ellas pidieron* (they requested) |

Here are some common verbs that are all conjugated like *pedir* in the preterite tense:

| | |
| --- | --- |
| *impedir* | to impede, to prevent |
| *medir* | to measure |
| *repetir* | to repeat |
| *seguir* | to follow |

## Irregulars in the Preterite Tense

Some verbs are truly irregular in the present tense because the stem form of the verb morphs into something unrecognizable. Do not think of these verbs as stem changers because they do not follow the patterns that stem-changing verbs follow. These verbs also do not use the normal preterite endings, but there is a consistent set of endings for all of these irregular verbs.

Some of the most commonly used verbs in the language are irregular in the preterite. This should motivate you to learn these irregular forms. Table 11-14 is a special group of endings that are used for all of the irregular verbs in the following sections. Notice that there are no written accent marks on any of the forms.

**Table 11-14    Endings for Irregular Preterite Verbs**

| Singular pronoun | Ending | Plural pronoun | Ending |
|---|---|---|---|
| yo | -e | nosotros/nosotras | -imos |
| tú | -iste | vosotros/vosotras | -isteis |
| usted | -o | ustedes | -ieron |
| él | -o | ellos | -ieron |
| ella | -o | ellas | -ieron |

## *U*-stem verbs

Several of the irregular verbs have a *u* as part of the stem form of the verb in the preterite even though these verbs do not have a *u* in their infinitive form. The irregular stem that is listed next to the verbs in the following chart is used for every form of the preterite conjugation. All of the following verbs take the endings from Table 11-14 to form their preterite conjugation chart.

| Infinitive form | Stem for all preterite forms |
|---|---|
| *andar* (to walk) | *anduv–* |
| *estar* (to be) | *estuv–* |
| *tener* (to have) | *tuv–* |
| *poner* (to put) | *pus–* |
| *poder* (to be able) | *pud–* |
| *saber* (to know) | *sup–* |
| *caber* (to fit) | *cup–* |

The verb *tener* (to have) is extremely common, so memorize the forms of *tener* in the preterite shown in Table 11-15. They'll help you remember the patterns of all of the *u* stem verbs just presented.

**Table 11-15    Preterite Forms of *Tener***

| Singular | Plural |
|---|---|
| yo tuve (I had) | nosotros/nosotras tuvimos (we had) |
| tú tuviste (you [informal] had) | vosotros/vosotras tuvisteis (you [informal] had) |

*(continued)*

**Table 11-15** *(continued)*

| Singular | Plural |
| --- | --- |
| *usted tuvo* (you [formal] had) | *ustedes tuvieron* (you [formal] had) |
| *él tuvo* (he had) | *ellos tuvieron* (they had) |
| *ella tuvo* (she had) | *ellas tuvieron* (they had) |

### *I*-stem verbs

Certain verbs have an irregular stem with the letter *i* in it. It is extremely important to remember that these verbs are not considered stem changers in the preterite tense although some of them may have been stem changers in the present tense. Just like the *u*-stem verbs, *i*-stem verbs do not follow the rules of a stem-changing verb in the preterite and do not use the normal endings a stem-changing verb uses. The verbs in the following list have a completely different stem that is used for every form of the preterite. Because they are irregular, they use the irregular endings from Table 11-15.

| *Infinitive form* | *Stem for all preterite forms* |
| --- | --- |
| *hacer* (to make, to do) | *hic–* (except in the third person singular forms, which end in *–o,* and that become *hizo*) |
| *querer* (to want, to love) | *quis–* |
| *venir* (to come) | *vin–* |

These *i*-stem verbs are all conjugated like *venir,* in the preterite tense, as shown in Table 11-16.

**Table 11-16** **Preterite Forms of *Venir***

| Singular | Plural |
| --- | --- |
| *yo vine* (I came) | *nosotros/nosotras vinimos* (we came) |
| *tú viniste* (you [informal] came) | *vosotros/vosotras vinisteis* (you [informal] came) |
| *usted vino* (you [formal] came) | *ustedes vinieron* (you [formal] came) |
| *él vino* (he came) | *ellos vinieron* (they came) |
| *ella vino* (she came) | *ellas vinieron* (they came) |

Even though *hacer* uses the same endings as *venir* in the preterite, there's one additional spelling change you have to make on the *él, ella,* and *usted* forms of *hacer* to preserve the soft *c* sound. As you can see in Table 11-17, you must change the *c* to a *z* in front of the *-o* ending.

**Table 11-17   Preterite Forms of *Hacer***

| Singular | Plural |
|---|---|
| *yo hice* (I made) | *nosotros/nosotras hicimos* (we made) |
| *tú hiciste* (you [informal] made) | *vosotros/vosotras hicisteis* (you [informal] made) |
| *usted hizo* (you [formal] made) | *ustedes hicieron* (you [formal] made) |
| *él hizo* (he made) | *ellos hicieron* (they made) |
| *ella hizo* (she made) | *ellas hicieron* (they made) |

## J-stem verbs

The irregular verbs that end in the letter *j* use the same endings as the other irregular preterite verbs with one exception. Notice in Table 11-18 that the third person plural ending of the verb *decir* is *-eron*. Any time the irregular stem ends in *j*, the *ellos, ellas,* and *ustedes* endings will lose the letter *i* and become *-jeron*.

**Table 11-18   Preterite Forms of *Decir***

| Singular | Plural |
|---|---|
| *yo dije* (I said) | *nosotros/nosotras dijimos* (we said) |
| *tú dijiste* (you [informal] said) | *vosotros/vosotras dijisteis* (you [informal] said) |
| *usted dijo* (you [formal] said) | *ustedes dijeron* (you [formal] said) |
| *él dijo* (he said) | *ellos dijeron* (they said) |
| *ella dijo* (she said) | *ellas dijeron* (they said) |

All the verbs that follow are conjugated like *decir:*

| Infinitive form | Stem for all preterite forms |
|---|---|
| *Decir* (to say, to tell) | *dij–* |
| *Traer* (to bring) | *traj–* |
| *Conducir* (to drive, to lead) | *conduj–* |
| *Producir* (to produce) | *produj–* |
| *Traducir* (to translate) | *traduj–* |

## Very irregular preterite verbs

The really irregular verbs in the preterite follow no patterns and simply must be memorized. The verbs *ser* (to be) and *ir* (to go) happen to have identical forms in the preterite. You will be able to tell which verb is being used in the context of a sentence. Table 11-19 is worth learning because it has the preterite forms of two of the most common verbs in the language.

**Table 11-19    Preterite Forms of the Verbs *Ser* and *Ir***

| Singular | Plural |
|---|---|
| yo fui (I was; I went) | nosotros/nosotras fuimos (we were; we went) |
| tú fuiste (you [informal] were; you went) | vosotros/vosotras fuisteis (you [informal] were; you went) |
| usted fue (you [formal] were; you went) | ustedes fueron (you [formal] were; you went) |
| él fue (he was; he went) | ellos fueron (they were; they went) |
| ella fue (she was; she went) | ellas fueron (they were; they went) |

*Ver* (to see) and *dar* (to give) are two verbs that are commonly learned together in the preterite tense because their forms are similar. *Ver* uses the regular endings for a normal –*er* verb in the preterite and is only irregular because it does not have accent marks. What makes *dar* strange is that it is conjugated like *ver* even though it is an –*ar* verb. Notice that there are no accents on any of the forms in Table 11-20 *(ver)* or Table 11-21 *(dar)* and that the forms of *dar* are not the normal forms for an –*ar* verb.

**Table 11-20    Preterite Forms of *Ver***

| Singular | Plural |
|---|---|
| *yo vi* (I saw) | *nosotros/nosotras vimos* (we saw) |
| *tú viste* (you [informal] saw) | *vosotros/vosotras visteis* (you [informal] saw) |
| *usted vio* (you [formal] saw) | *ustedes vieron* (you [formal] saw) |
| *él vio* (he saw) | *ellos vieron* (they saw) |
| *ella vio* (she saw) | *ellas vieron* (they saw) |

**Table 11-21    Preterite Forms of *Dar***

| Singular | Plural |
|---|---|
| *yo di* (I gave) | *nosotros/nosotras dimos* (we gave) |
| *tú diste* (you [informal] gave) | *vosotros/vosotras disteis* (you [informal] gave) |
| *usted dio* (you [formal] gave) | *ustedes dieron* (you [formal] gave) |
| *él dio* (he gave) | *ellos dieron* (they gave) |
| *ella dio* (she gave) | *ellas dieron* (they gave) |

## Preterite Tense Situations

Now that you have mastered conjugating verbs in the preterite tense, you must learn when the preterite tense is appropriate.

There are certain situations in the past that will be stated using the preterite tense. Usually preterite situations have something to do with completed actions that can be placed at a specific point in time. The acronym SAFE will help you remember the types of situations in the past that require you to use the preterite tense. In the English examples below, the verbs in bold would be conjugated in the preterite in Spanish because of the way they are used in the sentence.

Use the preterite tense of the verb when the sentence indicates:

- **S**pecific instance or number of instances

  *Le **llamó** tres veces. El me **llamó** ayer.*
  I **called** him **three** times. He **called** me **yesterday**.

■ Action that interrupts ongoing events

*Ella **llamó** mientras yo trabajaba.*
She **called** while I was working.

■ Focus on beginning or ending of action

***Llovió** a las seis y media en punto.*
It **rained** at exactly 6:30.

■ Enclosed amount of time, or limited and completed time frame

*Los árabes **controlaron** la mayoría de España por más de 700 años.*
The Arabs **controlled** much of Spain for over 700 years.

## Preterite Tense Indicators

While understanding the types of situations that require the preterite is helpful, it is even more useful to learn the specific vocabulary words and expressions that indicate the preterite is probably the appropriate tense to use in the sentence. The following are considered **preterite indicators** because each will require the verb that follows it to be in the preterite tense. This list includes words that automatically require the past tense, and you can be certain the preterite is usually the correct past tense to use if the verb is used in front of or following one of these expressions.

| | |
|---|---|
| *ayer* | yesterday |
| *anoche* | last night |
| *el lunes pasado* | last Monday |
| *la semana pasada* | last week |
| *el fin de semana pasado* | last weekend |
| *el mes pasado* | last month |
| *el año pasado* | last year |
| *la primavera pasada* | last spring |
| *el verano (otoño, invierno) pasado* | last summer (fall, winter) |
| *de repente* | suddenly |

There are other words that serve as preterite indicators only when the sentence is definitely in the past. Something else in the context of the sentence or a previous sentence must indicate that the sentence is in the past, otherwise these indicators may be used with other tenses. However, if you know you need a past tense and you're not sure which of the two, look for one of the following words to indicate that the preterite is the appropriate past tense.

If there's a blank line in front of the indicator, the verb you will be conjugating in the preterite will be in front of, rather than after, the indicator.

| | |
|---|---|
| *esta mañana* | this morning |
| *esta tarde* | this afternoon |
| *esa mañana* | that morning |
| *esa tarde* | that afternoon |
| ____ *a tiempo* | on time |
| ____ *de nuevo* | again |
| *por fin* | finally |
| *en fin* | finally |
| ____ *por primera vez* | for the first time |
| ____ *una vez* | once |

## Chapter Check-Out

Using the verb in parentheses, write the correct form of the verb in the preterite tense for each of the following sentences. Don't forget to consider the subject and use the appropriate form. Each sentence has a preterite indicator. See if you can identify it.

1. *Anoche yo _____ con mi esposo. (bailar)*
2. *Ayer Marta y su padre _____ a la fiesta. (venir)*
3. *El mes pasado Juan y Carla _____ a México (conducir)*
4. *Nosotros _____ a la clase el lunes pasado. (ir)*
5. *Yo _____ al tenis ayer. (jugar)*

**Answers: 1.** *bailé (anoche)* **2.** *vinieron (ayer)* **3.** *condujeron (el mes pasado)* **4.** *fuimos (el lunes pasado)* **5.** *jugué (ayer)*

# Chapter 12

# THE IMPERFECT TENSE

## Chapter Check-In

❏ Conjugating verbs in the imperfect tense

❏ Understanding situations that require the imperfect instead of the preterite

❏ Recognizing indicator words for the imperfect tense

The **imperfect tense** is another past tense aspect in Spanish. There are only three verbs in the entire language are irregular in the imperfect tense. While it is easy to learn how to create the forms of verbs in the imperfect tense, it is more difficult to understand when to use this tense. Usually, the imperfect tense is translated as "was / were doing" something, or "used to do" something.

Since there is only one past tense in English, you will have to learn when to use the imperfect instead of the preterite in Spanish. Chapter 11 discussed situations and indicators for the preterite tense, and this chapter discusses situations where the imperfect tense is appropriate and which special indicators will provide you a clue to use the imperfect tense.

## Regular Verbs in the Imperfect

There are no spelling changes and no stem changes in the imperfect. The –*ar* endings found in Table 12-1 are used for every –*ar* verb in the entire language. There is not a single –*ar* verb that is irregular in the imperfect tense. Notice that the *yo* form is exactly like the *él, ella,* and *usted* forms, so it is important to use the pronoun or noun to specify what the subject is in a specific sentence. Also notice that only the *nosotros/nosotras* form has a written accent mark.

**Table 12-1    Imperfect Tense Endings for All –ar Verbs**

| Singular Pronoun | Ending | Plural Pronoun | Ending |
|---|---|---|---|
| yo | –aba | nosotros/nosotras | –ábamos |
| tú | –abas | vosotros/vosotras | –abais |
| usted | –aba | ustedes | –aban |
| él | –aba | ellos | –aban |
| ella | –aba | ellas | –aban |

A stem-changing verb like *pensar* (to think) will not have any stem change in the imperfect. As you can see in Table 12-2, the verb *pensar* is completely regular in the imperfect tense.

**Table 12-2    Imperfect Tense Forms of the Verb Pensar**

| Singular | Plural |
|---|---|
| yo pensaba (I was thinking, used to think) | nosotros/nosotras pensábamos (we were thinking, used to think) |
| tú pensabas (you [informal] were thinking, used to think) | vosotros/vosotras pensabais (you [informal] were thinking, used to think) |
| usted pensaba (you [formal] were thinking, used to think) | ustedes pensaban (you [formal] were thinking, used to think) |
| él pensaba (he was thinking, used to think) | ellos pensaban (they were thinking, used to think) |
| ella pensaba (she was thinking, used to think) | ellas pensaban (they were thinking, used to think) |

The verb *trabajar* (to work) looks really strange in the imperfect tense, but it also is a good example that all forms of all –ar verbs are regular in the imperfect tense. Read Table 12-3 outloud because it's fun to say the imperfect tense forms of the verb *trabajar*.

**Table 12-3    Imperfect Tense Forms of the Verb Trabajar**

| Singular | Plural |
|---|---|
| yo trabajaba (I was working, used to work) | nosotros/nosotras trabajábamos (we were working, used to work) |

(continued)

**Table 12-3** *(continued)*

| Singular | Plural |
|---|---|
| *tú trabajabas* (you [informal] were working, used to work) | *vosotros/vosotras trabajabais* (you [informal] were working, used to work) |
| *usted trabajaba* you [formal] were working, used to work | *ustedes trabajaban* (you [formal] were working, used to work) |
| *él trabajaba* (he was working, used to work) | *ellos trabajaban* (they were working, used to work) |
| *ella trabajaba* (she was working, used to work) | *ellas trabajaban* (they were working, used to work) |

The endings in Table 12-4 are the regular endings for both *–er* and *–ir* verbs. There are only three irregular verbs in the imperfect tense: *ser, ir,* and *ver* (see "The Three Imperfect Irregulars" later in this chapter). For every other *–er* and *–ir* verb, use the endings in Table 12-4. Notice that all imperfect tense forms of *–er* and *–ir* verbs have a written accent mark on the letter *i.*

**Table 12-4 Imperfect Tense Endings for Regular *–er* and *–ir* Verbs**

| Singular Pronoun | Ending | Plural Pronoun | Ending |
|---|---|---|---|
| yo | -ía | nosotros/nosotras | -íamos |
| tú | -ías | vosotros/vosotras | -íais |
| él | -ía | ellos | -ían |
| ella | -ía | ellas | -ían |
| usted | -ía | ustedes | -ían |

The *–er* verbs use the exact same endings in the imperfect tense as the *–ir* verbs, so look at *perder* as another good example and notice in Table 12-5 that *perder* does not stem change in the imperfect tense.

**Table 12-5 Imperfect Tense Forms of *Perder***

| Singular | Plural |
|---|---|
| *yo perdía* (I was losing, used to lose) | *nosotros/nosotras perdíamos* (we were losing, used to lose) |
| *tú perdías* (you [informal] were losing, used to lose) | *vosotros/vosotras perdíais* (you [informal] were losing, used to lose) |

| Singular | Plural |
|---|---|
| *usted perdía* (you [formal] were losing, used to lose) | *ustedes perdían* (you [formal] were losing, used to lose) |
| *él perdía* (he was losing, used to lose) | *ellos perdían* (they were losing, used to lose) |
| *ella perdía* (she was losing, used to lose) | *ellas perdían* (they were losing, used to lose) |

A regular verb like *vivir* (to live) conjugated in Table 12-6 serves as a good example of an *–ir* verb in the imperfect tense.

**Table 12-6    Imperfect Tense Forms of *Vivir***

| Singular | Plural |
|---|---|
| *yo vivía* (I was living, used to live) | *nosotros/nosotras vivíamos* (we were living, used to live) |
| *tú vivías* (you [informal] were living, used to live) | *vosotros/vosotras vivíamos* (we were living, used to live) |
| *usted vivía* (you [formal] were living, used to live) | *ustedes vivían* (you [formal] were living, used to live) |
| *él vivía* (he was living, used to live) | *ellos vivían* (they were living, used to live) |
| *ella vivía* (she was living, used to live) | *ellas vivían* (they were living, used to live) |

The verb *sentir* (to feel, to regret) is a stem changer in the present tense, but Table 12-7 will remind you that no verbs stem change in the imperfect tense.

**Table 12-7    Imperfect Tense Forms of *Sentir***

| Singular | Plural |
|---|---|
| *yo sentía* (I was feeling, used to feel) | *nosotros/nosotras sentíamos* (we were feeling, used to feel) |
| *tú sentías* (you [informal] were feeling, used to feel) | *vosotros/vosotras sentíais* (you [informal] were feeling, used to feel) |
| *usted sentía* (you [formal] were feeling, used to feel) | *ustedes sentían* (you [formal] were feeling, used to feel) |

*(continued)*

**Table 12-7** *(continued)*

| Singular | Plural |
|---|---|
| *él sentía* (he was feeling, used to feel) | *ellos sentían* (they were feeling, used to feel) |
| *ella sentía* (she was feeling, used to feel) | *ellas sentían* (they were feeling, used to feel) |

## The Three Imperfect Irregulars

The verbs *ser* (to be), *ir* (to go), and *ver* (to see) are completely irregular in the imperfect tense. Tables 12-8 and 12-9 show the complete imperfect tense forms of the verbs *ser* and *ir*, not just the endings. Table 12-10 shows the complete imperfect tense forms for the verb *ver*.

**Table 12-8** Imperfect Tense Forms of *Sentir*

| Singular | Plural |
|---|---|
| *yo era* (I was) | *nosotros/nosotras éramos* (we were) |
| *tú eras* (you [informal] were) | *vosotros/vosotras erais* (you [informal] were) |
| *usted era* (you [formal] were) | *ustedes eran* (you [formal] were) |
| *él era* (he was) | *ellos eran* (they were) |
| *ella era* (she was) | *ellas eran* (they were) |

**Table 12-9** Imperfect Tense Forms of the Verb *Ir*

| Singular | Plural |
|---|---|
| *yo iba* (I was going, used to go) | *nosotros/nosotras íbamos* (we were going, used to go) |
| *tú ibas* (you [informal] were going, used to go) | *vosotros/vosotras ibais* (you [informal] were going, used to go) |
| *usted iba* (you [formal] were going, used to go) | *ustedes iban* (you [formal] were going, used to go) |
| *él iba* (he was going, used to go) | *ellos iban* (they were going, used to go) |
| *ella iba* (she was going, used to go) | *ellas iban* (they were going, used to go) |

Notice in Table 12-10 that *ver* has the regular endings for an *–er* verb. With a normal verb, you remove the entire infinitve (*–er*). What makes *ver* irregular is that all you remove is the *–r* from the infinitive *ver,* and put *ve–* in front of the regular endings. Since all the regular imperfect endings for *–er* and *–ir* verbs have written accent marks, the same is true for *ver.*

**Table 12-10    Imperfect Tense Forms of the Verb *Ver***

| Singular | Plural |
| --- | --- |
| *yo veía* (I was seeing, used to see) | *nosotros/nosotras veíamos* (we were seeing, used to see) |
| *tú veías* (you [informal] were seeing, used to see) | *vosotros/vosotras veíais* (you [informal] were seeing, used to see) |
| *usted veía* (you [formal] were seeing, used to see) | *ustedes veían* (you [formal] were seeing, used to see) |
| *él veía* (he was seeing, used to see) | *ellos veían* (they were seeing, used to see) |
| *ella veía* (she was seeing, used to see) | *ellas veían* (they were seeing, used to see) |

## Imperfect Situations

In grammatical terms, the word "perfect" means completed. The prefix *im–* means "not," so imperfect means not completed. Thus, the imperfect tense is generally used in situations where the completion of the verb is not certain, or at least not the point of the sentence. The acronym WATERS will help you remember that the imperfect is generally used to express ongoing situations that sort of "flow on" and have no specific place in time. Each word that represents a letter in WATERS indicates a situation when an imperfect verb will be used. In the following examples, verbs in the imperfect are in bold.

■ **W**eather

*Llovía.*
It **was raining**.

■ **A**ge

*Cuando **tenía** tres años, **quería** ser bombera.*
When I **was** three, I **wanted** to be a firefighter.

■ **T**ime

***Eran** las cuatro.*
It **was** four o'clock.

■ Emotion

*Estaba* cansada.

I **was** tired.

■ Repetition

Yo **visitaba** a mi abuela de vez en cuando.

I **used to visit** my grandmother from time to time.

■ Setting or description

El sol **brillaba** y la vista **era** bonita.

The sun **was shining** and the view **was** pretty.

Since the English language doesn't have a special tense to indicate repetitive or ongoing actions, there are a number of ways to get across this idea. The expression "used to . . . " in front of a verb, or even using the word "would" in front of the verb can indicate repetitive actions. For example: "I used to study a lot" or "I would cry every day in kindergarten." To show ongoing actions in English, the past progressive tense is often used: "I was studying . . . " Don't try to translate these expressions literally into Spanish, just use the imperfect conjugation of the verb.

## Imperfect Indicators

**Imperfect indicators** are words or phrases that in some way indicate repetitive or habitual actions in the past. Generally, they will be followed by the imperfect tense. Here's a tip to help you remember the indicators: Copy all the imperfect indicators on one color of flash cards and the preterite indicators (see Chapter 11) on a different color. Keep track of which color is preterite and which is imperfect. Then on test day you'll remember the color of the card the expression was written on, and you will know which tense to use if you see one of these expressions. Here is the list of some imperfect indicators:

| | |
|---|---|
| *a menudo* | often |
| *a veces* | sometimes |
| *cada año* | every year |
| *cada día* | each day |
| *cada mes* | each month |

| | |
|---|---|
| *cada verano* | each summer |
| *cuando* | when |
| *cuando ___ era más joven* | when __ was younger |
| *cuando ___ era niño . . . ,*<br>*cuando ___ era niña . . .* | when __ was a little boy/girl |
| *de niño . . . , de niña . . .* | *a*s a child (masculine) . . . , as a little girl |
| *de vez en cuando* | from time to time |
| *día a día* | from day to day |
| *muchas veces* | many times |
| *por lo común* | in general |
| *por lo general* | in general |
| *por regla general* | in general |
| *raras veces* | rarely |
| *siempre* | always |
| *todas las primaveras* | every spring |
| *todas las semanas* | every week |
| *todos los lunes* | every Monday |
| *todos los veranos* | every summer |

## Chapter Check-Out

For the following sentences, identify the imperfect indicator and then conjugate the verb in parenthesis in the imperfect tense to go with the subject of the sentence.

1. *Todos los lunes yo _____ la casa cuando era niño. (limpiar)*
2. *Juan, Marisol y yo _____ a Texas de vez en cuando éramos niños. (ir)*
3. *Beatriz siempre _____ muy activa en el pasado. (ser)*
4. *Por lo general ellos _____ sus libros cuando los necesitaban. (tener)*
5. *Tú _____ en la República Dominicana de niña. (vivir)*

**Answers: 1.** *limpiaba (todos los lunes* and *cuando era niño* are both imperfect indicators) **2.** *íbamos (de vez en cuando* and *cuando niños* are both imperfect indicators) **3.** *era (siempre, en el pasado)* **4.** *tenían (por lo general)* **5.** *vivías (de niña)*

# Chapter 13

# NARRATION IN THE PAST

## Chapter Check-In

❑ Understanding verbs that change meaning in the preterite tense

❑ Using both past tenses in one sentence

❑ Creating past tense sentences using *hace* expressions

When you read or hear a Spanish sentence about the past, you will have no trouble understanding the sentence even if you do not stop to consider the tense(s) of the verb(s) in the past. However, you will begin to understand the Spanish past tenses better if you stop to analyze which tense is used by a native speaker and why they used it. It's quite common to use both tenses in one sentence as the focus of the sentence shifts from description to action or from what was ongoing to what happened at a specific instant.

For a Spanish speaker, the use of the two past tenses happens without much thought. The speaker knows whether the intent of the sentence is focusing on background information or the action of the sentence and uses the imperfect or preterite accordingly. When learners of the language agonize over determining which tense would be correct in a given situation, most of the time they agonize in vain because the sentence will be understood regardless of whether the imperfect or preterite is used. Often the slight difference in meaning between the preterite and imperfect is unimportant.

There are, however, certain cases where the meaning of the sentence changes greatly depending on which past tense is used. This chapter discusses how some verbs that are generally used in the imperfect will have a completely different meaning when used in the preterite, and how certain idiomatic expressions are created by using both tenses in one sentence.

# Verbs That Change Meaning in the Preterite

There are certain verbs in Spanish that change meaning when used in the preterite.

*Conocer* in its infinitive form means "to be acquainted with" or "to know a person or place." If used in the imperfect, it means "used to know" or "knew someone or someplace" in the past. However the point in time the person or place was first known is a very specific instance, and therefore will be expressed using the preterite tense. In English, the first moment you knew someone is expressed by saying you "met" someone. The preterite forms of *conocer* are used to indicate the equivalent Spanish concept of "met." Here are examples of *conocer* in the imperfect and preterite tenses:

■ **Imperfect:** *conocer* = knew, was acquainted with

   *Yo conocía a Sergio de niño.*
   I knew Sergio as a child.

   *Tú conocías bien la ciudad de México.*
   You were well acquainted with Mexico City.

■ **Preterite:** *conocer* = met, became acquainted with

   *Laura conoció a Manolo el 14 de febrero.*
   Laura met Manolo on February 14th.

   *Mis estudiantes conocieron Madrid durante nuestro viaje educativo a España.*
   My students became acquainted with Madrid during our Educational trip to Spain.

*Saber* means "to know a fact." In the imperfect, it simply means "used to know" or "knew a fact" because knowledge of a fact was ongoing. When the moment the fact was first known is the focus of the sentence, it is stated in English as the instance when something was "found out." The preterite forms of *saber* are the Spanish way of expressing the English idiomatic expression "found out." Here are examples of *saber* in the imperfect and preterite tenses:

■ **Imperfect:** *saber* = knew (some fact)

*Él sabía la dirección de memoria.*
He knew the address by heart.

■ **Preterite:** *saber* = found out (some fact)

*Él supo la dirección y fue a su casa.*
He found out the address and went to her house.

*Poder* is translated "to be able." It is always followed by a verb in its infinitive form. This concept is often expressed idiomatically in English as "can (is able to) do something" in the present tense or "could (was able to) do something" in the past.

The imperfect forms of *poder* express an ongoing ability to do something in the past. In a negative sentence, the imperfect tense of *poder* indicates an ongoing lack of ability to do something that was assumed or obvious. Used negatively in the imperfect, the indication is that one never specifically tried to do something but, rather, assumed the inability was ongoing.

*Poder* is used in the preterite tense to indicate a specific time when an ability to do something was not normally the case. In English a speaker says "I managed to do it" when something isn't typically do-able.

In a negative sentence, the preterite of *poder* means that one could not do something at a specific time. In order for there to have been a specific time when one could not do something, the idea is that one tried and failed. Here are some examples of *poder* in the imperfect and preterite tenses in affirmative and negative situations:

■ **Imperfect affirmative:** *poder* = was able, could do something

*Constanza podía cantar como un pájaro.*
Constanza could (was able to) sing like a bird.

■ **Preterite affirmative:** *poder* = managed to do something

*Esteban pudo subir la montaña.*
Esteban managed to climb the mountain.

■ **Imperfect negative:** *poder* = wasn't able, couldn't do something (assumed)

*Nadie podía cambiar la ley.*
Nobody could change the law.

- **Preterite negative:** *poder* = could not do something (tried and failed)

  *El atleta no pudo seguir.*

  The athlete could not continue.

*Querer* in the imperfect means "wanted or loved in an ongoing manner." However, in the preterite, *querer* indicates that the wanting was to no avail. Used in the preterite negatively, *querer* is understood to mean that one not only didn't want to do something, but refused to. Here are some examples of *querer* in the imperfect and preterite tenses in affirmative and negative situations:

- **Imperfect affirmative:** *querer* = wanted something or wanted to do something (ongoing)

  *Benito siempre quería un barco.*

  Benito always wanted a boat.

- **Preterite affirmative:** *querer* = wanted something or to do something (at a specific moment in time)

  *Yo quise llorar cuando recibí la mala noticia.*

  I wanted to cry when I received the bad news.

- **Imperfect negative:** *querer* = didn't want something or to do something (ongoing)

  *Él no quería estudiar álgebra.*

  He didn't want to study algebra.

- **Preterite negative:** *querer* = refused to do something (at a specific time)

  *Mi padre no quiso conducir.*

  My father refused to drive.

# Preterite-Imperfect Formulas

The preterite and imperfect tenses are often used together in the same sentence. There are a few typical sentence-structure formulas that are easy to learn. Two vocabulary words that are necessary to join two past tense verbs in the same sentence are *mientras* (while) and *cuando* (when). Notice that *cuando* does not have an accent mark because it is not being used as a question word.

## Joining verbs with *mientras*

The conjunction *mientras* can be used to join two verbs in the imperfect, or it can be used in sentences where one verb is in the preterite and the other is in the imperfect. The sentence will change meaning depending on the tense of the verbs joined by *mientras*. Read the explanations carefully and then analyze the examples after each formula. Visual cues are provided in both the formula and example: A verb in the imperfect tense is underlined, and a verb in the preterite is in bold.

To indicate that two actions are occurring simultaneously and are assumed to be ongoing, the conjunction word *mientras* is used between two verbs, and both verbs will be conjugated in the imperfect tense. It is necessary that neither action interrupt the other for both verbs to be conjugated in the imperfect tense.

Sentence structure formula: <u>Imperfect</u> *mientras* <u>imperfect</u>

*Ellos <u>secaban</u> los platos mientras yo los <u>lavaba</u>.*
They <u>were drying</u> the dishes while I <u>was washing</u> them.

When the verb following *mientras* is in the imperfect and the other verb is in the preterite, the action of the verb in the preterite interrupts the ongoing action of the verb in the imperfect.

Sentence structure formula: **Preterite** *mientras* <u>imperfect</u>

*Samuel **llamó** mientras tú <u>estudiabas</u>.*
Samuel called while you were studying.

Both in Spanish and English, the previous sample sentence could be switched around. It is acceptable to have *mientras* in between the two verbs, or *mientras* may begin the sentence followed by a verb in the imperfect, a comma, and a verb in the preterite. Regardless of the order of the sentence, the ongoing action will be in the imperfect, and the interrupting verb will be in the preterite. This is a very common sentence structure in the past. For example, when *mientras* and the ongoing action is stated first, there will be a comma before the interrupting verb (in the preterite):

Sentence structure formula: *Mientras* <u>imperfect</u>, **preterite**

*Mientras tú <u>estudiabas</u>, Samuel **llamó**.*
While you were studying, Samuel called.


## Joining verbs with *cuando*

The conjunction *cuando* is almost always followed by the preterite tense because it indicates the specific moment of the action of the verb that follows it. The other verb in the sentence may be an ongoing action that is interrupted by the preterite verb. In such cases, the ongoing verb is in the imperfect tense.

Sentence structure formula: <u>Imperfect</u> *cuando* **preterite**

*Alicia <u>trabajaba</u> cuando yo **entré** en la oficina.*
Alicia was working when I entered the office.

Just like sentences using *mientras,* the sentence order can be switched around, but the verb following *cuando* will be conjugated in the preterite tense, regardless of where it is placed in the sentence.

Sentence structure formula: *Cuando* **preterite**, <u>imperfect</u>

*Cuando yo **entré** en la oficina, Alicia <u>trabajaba</u>.*
When I entered the office, Alicia was working.

As you can see in the previous example, when *cuando* is used at the beginning of the sentence, it will be followed by the preterite and a comma. After the comma, the next verb will be in the imperfect.

In some sentences, the conjunction *cuando* is used to join two preterite verbs. This sentence structure indicates that the action of both verbs was completed at the same time or that one was the result of the other.

Sentence structure formula: **Preterite** *cuando* **preterite**

*Carlos me **llamó** cuando él **llegó**.*
Carlos called me when he arrived.

*Yo **grité** cuando **vi** al fantasma.*
I screamed when I saw the ghost.

Sometimes the same basic construction is reversed. Whenever the conjunction *cuando* is the first word of the sentence, a comma is placed between the two preterite verbs.

Sentence structure formula: *Cuando* **preterite, preterite**

*Cuando él **llegó,** Carlos me **llamó***
When he arrived, Carlos called me.

*Cuando **vi** al fantasma, yo **grité.***
When I saw the ghost, I screamed.

# Expressions of Time

The verb *hacer* (to make or to do) is often used along with the preterite or imperfect to create idiomatic expressions of time. In such sentences, *hacer* is always in the third person singular *(él, ellos, usted)* form. In the formulas explained in this section, the *él* form of *hacer* is followed by an amount of time, the conjunction *que* and a verb in one of the past tenses.

The tense in which *hacer* is conjugated affects the entire meaning of the sentence and influences whether the imperfect or preterite tense is appropriate for the other verb in the sentence. *Hace* formulas are used in Spanish to indicate how long something happened, or how long ago something had been happening.

*Hace* formula sentences are called "idiomatic" because they use a specific formula of verbs and tenses to create a meaning that is not exactly word for word the way the sentence is written in English. Pay close attention to the examples for each formula because the English sentences are written very differently. In some cases, a literal translation of the Spanish sentence is included in parentheses just to show how strange these sentences would sound if translated word for word to English.

The question created in the following formula is used to ask how long ago something occurred:

Question structure formula: *Cuánto tiempo hace + que +* **preterite**

*¿Cuánto tiempo hace que **conociste** a Berto?*
How long ago did you meet Berto?

The formula used to state how long ago something occurred is similar to the formula used to ask the question. The verb following *que* is in the preterite tense because it happened at a specific time. This idiomatic expression indicates how long ago the verb in the preterite was done.

Sentence structure formula: *Hace* + time + que + **preterite**

*Hace dos años que **conocí** a Berto.*
I met Berto two years ago. (It "makes" two years that I met Berto.)

*Hace un mes que Carmen **llegó**.*
Carmen arrived a month ago. (It "makes" a month that Carmen arrived.)

To ask a question about how long something had been going on, use the following question formula:

Question structure formula: *¿Cuánto tiempo hacía que* + <u>imperfect</u>?

*¿Cuánto tiempo <u>hacía</u> que tú y Mario <u>trabajaban</u> juntos?*
How long had you and Mario been working together?

When *hacer* is used in the imperfect with an amount of time, *que,* and another verb in the imperfect tense, this expression indicates how long something had been going on in the past and that continued in the past until something else happened. Here is the formula:

Sentence structure formula: <u>*Hacía*</u> + time + que + <u>imperfect</u>

*Hacía una semana que visitaba a mis primos.*
I had been visiting my cousins for a week. (It "made" a week that I had been visiting my cousins)

<u>*Hacía* ochos días que no <u>dormía</u>.</u>
I hadn't been sleeping for eight days. (It "made" eight days that I wasn't sleeping.)

When the imperfect tense is used with *desde hace,* the expression is the same as the formula with the imperfect and *hacía*. These sentences indicate how long something had been going on.

Sentence structure formula: <u>imperfect</u> + *desde hace* + time

*Bailaban desde hace una hora.*
They had been dancing for an hour (and it is still going on).

The following type of question formula is used to elicit a response using *desde hace.* Questions using this formula ask how long something had been going on.

Question structure formula: *Desde cuándo* + <u>imperfect</u>

*¿Desde cuándo bailaban?*
How long had they been dancing?

## Chapter Check-Out

For the following sentences, use the imperfect or preterite tense according to the formulas.

1. *Hacía un mes que ellos _____ español. (estudiar)*
2. *Tú _____ desde hace una semana. (conducir)*
3. *Hace cinco meses que yo _____ de la casa de mi familia. (salir)*
4. *¿Desde cuándo _____ María en McDonald's? (trabajar)*
5. *Hace mucho tiempo que el chico _____ su chaqueta. (perder)*

**Answers: 1.** *estudiaban* **2.** *conducías* **3.** *salí* **4.** *trabajaba* **5.** *perdió*

# Chapter 14
# PREPOSITIONS

## Chapter Check-In

❑ Using prepositions correctly

❑ Determining whether to use *por* or *para*

❑ Understanding how verbs and prepositions are used together

❑ Learning the pronouns that follow prepositions

**P**repositions join words together and show the relationship between the different parts of a sentence. These little words can cause you big problems because they do not necessarily translate well between English and Spanish. This chapter will help you understand when each preposition is appropriate because you cannot simply replace the Spanish preposition with an English equivalent.

## Simple Prepositions

Since prepositions are used differently in Spanish than they are in English, it is important to know when to use each Spanish preposition. They're called **simple prepositions** because they are only one word.

Some simple prepositions can be translated to a simple English equivalent. The most common ones are listed here:

| | |
|---|---|
| *ante* | before, in the presence of |
| *bajo* | under (figuratively); *bajo control*, for example |
| *contra* | against |
| *desde* | from (as in since) |
| *después de* | after |

| | |
|---|---|
| *durante* | during |
| *entre* | among |
| *entre* | between |
| *excepto* | except |
| *hacia* | toward |
| *hasta* | as far as, even up to |
| *hasta* | until |
| *mediante* | by means of |
| *menos* | except |
| *salvo* | except |
| *según* | according to |
| *sin* | without |
| *sobre* | about, concerning (topic) |
| *sobre* | above, on, over, on top of (physically) |
| *tras* | after |
| *tras* | after (figuratively); *día tras día,* for example |

However, the most commonly used simple prepositions are *a, en, de, con, para,* and *por.* After reading the explanation of these prepositions in the following sections, you will realize that there is nothing "simple" about them. It is impossible to ascertain a simple English translation for any of the following simple prepositions because you have to understand the situations in which you use each one.

## Preposition: *a*

The preposition *a* has several uses. It's used to indicate motion toward a place or thing, and as "the personal *a*" to introduce the clarification of indirect and direct objects. It's used between two verbs idiomatically. It's also used to indicate how something is done and when in time something occurred or will occur. Finally, it's used when a contraction must occur.

### Motion toward a place or thing

The most common use for the preposition *a* is to indicate motion toward a place or thing. In such circumstances, it means *to, toward,* or *at.*

*Vamos a la ciudad.*
We go to the city.

*Ignacio llegó a la oficina muy temprano.*
Ignacio arrived at the office very early.

*Llegué a Lima anoche.*
I arrived in Lima last night.

*José regresó a casa esta mañana.*
José returned home this morning.

## Use with direct and indirect objects

The preposition *a* is used to label a direct object when it refers to a person, an animal, or a personified idea. Chapter 10 addressed how to identify the direct object of the sentence and that you must use the personal *a* in front of the direct object if it is a person. Since this usage doesn't have an English equivalent, it will not appear in the English translation of the following examples.

*Quiero invitar a Lidia también.*
I want to invite Lydia also.

*¿A quiénes llamas tú?*
Whom are you calling?

*A* is also used in front of an indirect object to clarify to whom the indirect object refers. Chapter 10 can help you review how to use the preposition *a* to clarify exactly who or what the indirect object pronoun represents as well as how to use it with verbs like *gustar*. Consider the following examples:

*A Daniel le gustan las películas románticas.*
Daniel likes romantic movies.

*Eva le compró a su madre un regalo.*
Eva bought her mother a gift.

If there is no indirect object pronoun in front of the verb of the sentence, the preposition *para* may be used instead of *a* to introduce the recipient of the direct object. Compare the following examples:

*Silvia le compra la blusa (a su madre).*
Silvia buys her mother the blouse.

*Silvia compra la blusa para su madre.*
Silvia buys the blouse for her mother.

### Purpose between two verbs

The preposition *a* is used to convey the idea of purpose between a conjugated verb of motion and the infinitive that follows. The most common usage of this is with a conjugated form of the verb *ir* (to go) + *a* + infinitive. Notice in the following examples that the English version usually is stated as "someone is going to do something." In Spanish, however, the present tense of *ir* is used, so the sentence is really saying "someone is going to do something" or "will do something." These sentences in both languages indicate that something happens in the future without using the future tense.

*Victoria va a estudiar medicina.*
Victoria is going to study medicine.

*César y Mariana van a casarse.*
Cesar and Mariana are going to get married.

### How something is done

The preposition *a* can be used to indicate the manner in which something is done and is followed by a noun.

*Viajamos a caballo por el desierto.*
We traveled by horse through the desert.

*Es necesario llegar a pie.*
It's necessary to arrive on foot.

*Los estudiantes escriben a lápiz durante un examen.*
The students write in pencil during a test.

Not all expressions about manner will use *a*. Idiomatic expressions that indicate manner can use the prepositions *en* or *de* and must be learned individually.

### Location on a timeline

The preposition *a* can be used to identify a location on a timeline. To indicate what time something occurred or will occur, *a* is used with the definite article *las,* followed by the time. When the time is one o'clock (plus or minus any amount of minutes), *a la* is used in front of the feminine article *una.*

> *Voy a llegar a las ocho y veinte.*
> I am going to arrive at eight-twenty.

> *Ellos regresaron a la una y media.*
> They returned at one-thirty.

With practice over time, you will learn when to use *a* and when to use *en* in certain expressions. For example, Spanish uses *en casa* to express "at home," not *a*, since the preposition *en* can mean "in" or "at" in English. (See "Preposition: *en*" later in this chapter.)

### Contraction with *a*

There are two contractions in Spanish that are required: *a + el* and *de + el.* Any time the pronoun *a* is followed by the definite article *el*, the contraction *al* must be used. (For more on *de + el*, see "Preposition: *de*" later in this chapter.) This contraction does not occur with the other definite articles, as you can see in the following examples:

> *a el lago* (to the lake) must contract to *al lago* (to the lake).
> *a la pizarra* (to the chalkboard) does not contract.
> *a los partidos* (to the games) does not contract.
> *a las montañas* (to the mountains) does not contract.

## Preposition: *de*

The preposition *de* is one of the most frequently used prepositions in Spanish. It has several English translations: of, from, by, and belonging to. The only way to know when the preposition *de* is appropriate is to understand the situations when it's used.

## Origin

One use of *de* is to indicate origin. Here are a couple examples:

> *Soy de Nicaragua.*
> I am from Nicaragua.

> *El libro viene de la biblioteca.*
> The book comes from the library.

## Possession

There are no apostrophes in Spanish. Possession is indicated by using the preposition *de*. The item that is possessed is followed by *de* and the person who owns it. For example, the only way to say "Mark's car" is "*El coche de Marco.*" Here's another example:

> *Los libros de Diana son interesantes.*
> Diana's books are interesting.

To inquire about the possessor, you must use *de* in front of the question word *quién*. *De quién* is equivalent to the English question word "whose." Check out these examples:

> *¿De quién es la casa?*
> Whose house is it?

> *Es la casa de Natalia.*
> It's Natalia's house.

## Motion away from something

There are certain verbs in Spanish that are typically followed by *de*, such as *venir* (to come), *salir* (to leave), and *llegar* (to arrive). With these verbs, *de* is used to indicate motion away from a place.

> *No quiero salir de mi patria.*
> I don't want to leave my homeland.

> *Lola llega de Virginia hoy.*
> Lola arrives from Virginia today.

## Made of

To indicate the contents or the material that something is made of, use *de*. The Spanish equivalent of the word "made" *(hecho)* is often not necessary, as you can see in the examples. Notice that when used, *hecho* reflects the number and gender of the subject (that which is "made of . . .")

*La ropa (hecha) de algodón es muy suave.*
The clothing (made) of cotton is very soft.

*El traje es de poliéster.*
The suit is (made) of polyester.

## Modify a noun

*De* is used to create a phrase in which a noun modifies another noun. In English, it is acceptable to use a noun as an adjective by simply placing one noun in front of another. For example, "a baseball game" uses the noun "baseball" to modify the noun "game." This is not permitted in Spanish. The noun being described is first, followed by the preposition *de* and the noun that is being used to describe it. *Un partido de béisbol* is literally translated "a game of baseball" but must be used to mean "a baseball game." Here are a couple more examples:

*Olvidé mi libro de álgebra.*
I forgot my algebra book.

*Los niños tienen clases de natación.*
The children have swimming classes.

## Contraction with *de*

Whenever the pronoun *de* is followed by the definite article *el*, the contraction *del* must be used. For example:

*de el norte* (from the north) must contract to: <u>*del*</u> *norte* (from the north).

*de la luna* (from the Moon) does not contract.

*de los libros* (from the books) does not contract.

*de las novelas* (from the novels) does not contract.

The contractions of *al* and *del* do not occur if it is the pronoun *él* rather than the definite article *el* preceded by *a* or *de*.

## Preposition: *en*

The preposition *en* is mistakenly considered a cognate for the English preposition "in" or sometimes "on." While there will be times when *en* is used like "in" or "on," there are many uses of *en* that are translated to a different English pronoun. The only way to place this preposition correctly is to learn the specific reasons for using *en*.

### Location

The preposition *en* has many uses in Spanish, but the most difficult for English speakers to remember is that *en* is used to indicate location, such as "at home" *(en casa)* (except for the few reasons listed previously with the rules for *a*). Most of the time an English speaker uses the preposition "at" when indicating where someone is undertaking some activity. The Spanish uses are more literal. A person works in a restaurant, not at a restaurant, so the Spanish use the preposition *en* to indicate this concept. Here are some examples:

> *Mis amigos trabajan en McDonald's.*
> My friends work at McDonald's.

> *Lo conocí en el centro comercial.*
> I met him at the mall.

There are some circumstances where the Spanish pronoun *en* is translated as the English preposition "on," as in this example:

> *Ellos pusieron los libros en la mesa.*
> They put the books on the table.

### Amount of time

*En* is used to express an amount of time necessary for completing something. This usage of *en* is similar to a familiar English preposition "in."

> *Terminó la tarea en diez minutos.*
> She finished the task in ten minutes.

> *Volvimos en unos minutos.*
> We returned in a few minutes.

## Price exchange and how something is done

The preposition *en* is used in many places that could just as easily use the preposition *por*. For example, to indicate the price of exchange or the means by which something is done. Either preposition is acceptable in such cases. Also, *en* can be used instead of *por* to indicate the price of exchange. For example:

> *Te lo dejo en diez pesos.*
> I'll let you have it for ten pesos.

In some specific expressions, *en* is used to indicate the means by which something is done (for more expressions, see Appendix C).

> *Le dije ese cuento en broma.*
> I told you that story jokingly.

> *Belita siempre habla en serio.*
> Belita always speaks seriously.

## Common error with *en*

A common error with *en* is to use it when referring to days of the week, however, that is not the case in Spanish. To state that something occurs "on Monday" would be stated in Spanish with the definite article "*el lunes.*" The definite article is also used in the plural to indicate "on Mondays" in general: *los lunes* would indicate "every Monday." To state that something generally occurs "on weekends" use *los fines de semanas.*

> *Siempre vamos a la playa los sábados.*
> We always go to the beach on Saturdays.

> *Uds. tienen una prueba el miércoles.*
> You guys have a quiz on Wednesday.

## Preposition: *con*

The preposition *con* is pretty consistently translated as the English preposition "with." It is used to indicate accompaniment, contents, and means of accomplishment.

## Accompaniment

The preposition *con* indicates accompaniment.

> *Benito llega con flores cada vez que viene.*
> Benito arrives with flowers each time he comes.

> *Ella sale con su novio.*
> She leaves with her boyfriend.

> *Me gusta el té con limón.*
> I like tea with lemon.

## How something is done

*Con* is one of the prepositions that can indicate the means by which something is done. *Con* may be followed by a noun or a verb in its infinitive form.

> *Abre la puerta con la llave.*
> He opens the door with a key.

> *Ella siempre gana con llorar.*
> She always wins by crying.

## How something has been accomplished

When *con* is used to express a contrast between what has been accomplished given the circumstances, it should be translated to the English expression "in spite of . . ."

> *Con todos sus problemas, ella todavía es feliz.*
> With (in spite of) all her problems, she still is happy.

## Contents

*Con* can be used instead of *de* to indicate the contents of a container.

> *Tengo una bolsa con comestibles.*
> I have a bag of groceries.

> *El cesto con ropa es para lavar.*
> The basket of clothing is for washing.

# *Para* and *Por*

There are two prepositions that must be explained together because they are most commonly confused by English speakers. The prepositions *para* and *por* both have a number of English translations, but the word that you would use in English does not determine which of the two prepositions to use in Spanish. You must consider what relationship is being expressed, and use the appropriate preposition.

## Preposition: *para*

The reasons for using *para* can easily be remembered with the acronym PRODDS. Each word below represents one of the reasons, and they're all explained in detail in the following sections.

- **P**urpose
- **R**ecipient
- **O**pinion
- **D**estination
- **D**eadline
- **S**tandard

### Purpose

*Para* is used with an infinitive to express the purpose of doing something. Sometimes in English, purpose is stated using the preposition "for." The phrase "in order to" is sometimes used in front of an infinitive to indicate purpose, but in English it is not necessary to use anything at all in such expressions. In Spanish, the preposition *para* is required even if the English equivalent is understood rather than stated. The following examples show the use of *para* when the speaker is stating a purpose:

*Trabajamos para ganar dinero.*
We work to earn money.

*Viajo para entender otras culturas.*
I travel in order to understand other cultures.

*Coma las legumbres para la salud.*
Eat vegetables for health / to be healthy.

In some cases the English sentence will use the preposition "for" followed by a gerund. Remember that a verb that immediately follows a preposition will always be in its infinitive form in Spanish.

> *Esta agua es para beber.*
> This water is for drinking.

### Recipient

The intended recipient of an object is indicated with the preposition *para*.

> *Yo traje la comida para mi abuela.*
> I brought the meal for my grandmother.

An exception to this rule is when you want to express the recipient of an emotion, which is done with *por*.

> *Siento mucho amor por mi abuela.*
> I feel much love for my grandmother.

### Opinion

*Para* is also used to indicate a personal opinion.

> *Para mí los derechos humanos son importantes.*
> In my opinion, human rights are important.

> *Las compañías grandes son importantes para el líder.*
> The big companies are important to the leader.

### Destination

*Para* is used to indicate the destination of something in a real, physical sense or in a figurative, metaphorical sense.

> *Las toallas son para el baño.*
> The towels are for the bathroom.

> *Salimos para las islas del Caribe mañana.*
> We leave for the Caribbean Islands tomorrow.

## Deadline

*Para* is used to indicate a deadline or due date.

> *El proyecto es para el veinte de mayo.*
> The project is due the 20th of May.

> *Es necesario terminar el programa para las dos.*
> It's necessary to finish the program by two o'clock.

## Standard

The standard is what is considered "normal." To express that something strays from the norm in English, the preposition "for" is used in an expression like, "She's very cool for a teacher." In other words, she isn't all that cool, it's just that she's cooler than the standard that is considered typical for a teacher. In Spanish, this expression of something that is contrary to the established or understood standard is stated using *para*.

> *Su hijo sabe mucho para su edad.*
> His son knows a lot for his age.

> *Para ser extranjera, ella habla inglés bien.*
> For being a foreigner, she speaks English well.

## Preposition: *por*

The reasons for using *por* can easily be remembered with the acronym DEEMMMS. Each word below represents one of the reasons, and they're all explained in detail in the following sections.

- **D**uration
- **E**motions
- **E**xchange
- **M**otivation
- **M**eans
- **M**ovement
- **S**ubstitution

## Duration

*Por* is used to express the duration of time or the length of time that something lasts.

> *Vivimos en Puerto Rico por dos años.*
> We lived in Puerto Rico for two years.

## Emotion

The recipient of an emotion is expressed with the preposition *por*. Don't forget that *para* is used for the recipient of everything other than emotions.

> *Su amor no es por mí.*
> His/her love is not for me.

## Exchange

When one thing is exchanged for another, *por* is used to express "for," as in when money is exchanged for something.

> *Talia pagó veinte dólares por los zapatos.*
> Talia paid twenty dollars for the shoes.

> *Quiero darte mi coche por tu coche.*
> I want to give you my car (in exchange) for your car.

Whether or not you realize it, when you thank someone, you are exchanging your words of gratitude for something that has been done for you or given to you. For this reason, *por* is used after *gracias* or the verb *agradecer* (to thank).

> *En España, los niños les agradecen a los Reyes Magos por los regalos.*
> In Spain, the children thank the Three Wise Men for the gifts.

> *Te doy las gracias por tu ayuda.*
> I give you thanks for your help.

## Motivation

It is difficult to differentiate between motivation (which is expressed with *por*) and purpose (which is expressed with *para*). Motivation is the equivalent to the English expression "due to." If you could replace the Spanish preposition with "due to," then the Spanish preposition should be *por*.

Motivation is the cause behind it rather than the goal in front of it. The following examples show the different uses of *por* and *para*:

> *Tengo muchas muestras de champú por el viaje de negocios.*
> I have many samples of shampoo due to the business trip.

> *Tengo muchas muestras de champú para el viaje.*
> I have many samples of shampoo for the trip.

There are also a few verbs that are consistently followed by the preposition *por* to indicate motivations. *Andar* (to walk), *caminar* (to walk), *ir* (to go), *regresar* (to return), *volver* (to return), *enviar* (to send), and similar verbs will be followed by *por* when the purpose or motive is being provided.

> *Ellos van a la tienda por la leche.*
> They go to the store for milk.

> *Raul regresó por la comida de su madre.*
> Raul returned for his mother's food.

### Means (of communication or transportation)

When you want to indicate a means of communication or transportation, *por* is used. Here are some typical expressions with *por* indicating means of communication and transportation:

| | |
|---|---|
| *por autobús* | by bus |
| *por avión* | by plane |
| *por barco* | by boat |
| *por computadora* | by computer |
| *por correo* | by mail |
| *por correo electrónico* | by e-mail |
| *por escrito* | in writing |
| *por fax* | by fax |
| *por ferrocarril* | by train |
| *por medio de* | by means of |
| *por teléfono* | by phone |

## Movement (in an area)

While it's misleading to translate an English preposition to a Spanish preposition, you should use *por* anytime the idea expresses "through," "by," or "along." *Por* indicates movement within an area.

> *Viajamos por los pueblos blancos de la Costa del Sol*
> We traveled through the whitewashed villages of the Costa del Sol.

> *Caminamos por las orillas del río.*
> We walked by the bank of the river.

> *Ella sigue por la calle principal.*
> She continues along the main street.

## Substitution

The best way to know that the preposition is indicating substitution is to try the English expression "in place of" or "instead of." If these expressions sound appropriate, the preposition is indicating a substitution, which requires the use of *por.* Compare the following pairs of sentences:

> *Isabel compra el regalo por su madre. Su madre está enferma y no puede ir de compras.*
> Isabel buys the gift for (in place of) her mother. Her mother's ill and can't go to the store.

> *Isabel compra el regalo para su madre. Es el cumpleaños de su madre.*
> Isabel buys the gift for her mother. It's her mother's birthday.

> *Marta canta para Yolanda. A Yolanda le gusta la música.*
> Marta sings for Yolanda. Yolanda likes music.

> *Marta canta por Yolanda. Yolanda no puede cantar porque tiene laringitis.*
> Marta sings in place of Yolanda. Yolanda can't sing because she has laryngitis.

## Idiomatic expressions

There are certain verbs that use the preposition *por* to create an idiomatic expression and certain verbs that are used with *para.* These do not logically follow any of the rules for using *por* and *para,* because that is what an **idiomatic expression** is: a group of words that have a specific meaning when used together but don't make sense if you try to translate them separately into English. See Appendix C for a list of idiomatic expressions. There are many that include either *por* or *para*.

To avoid confusing the *por* and *para* rules, learn the idiomatic expressions with *por* and *para* separately. It may help you learn them if you put all the idiomatic expressions that include the preposition *por* on one color of flashcard and the expressions using *para* on another color, so that the color can help you remember the appropriate preposition. When you quiz yourself, rewrite both sets of idiomatic expressions on all white cards to see if you can remember whether to use *por* or *para* with each expression, as well as to see if you understand what the expression means.

# Compound Prepositions

A **compound preposition** is formed with more than one word, but it is exactly like a simple preposition. The last word of a compound preposition is always one of the simple prepositions, so it will be easy to recognize compound prepositions. You will notice that many of the following compound prepositions are formed with a directional word and the simple preposition *de*. Remember that if a directional word is used without *de*, it is no longer considered a preposition. The most common compound prepositions indicate location. The following are some compound prepositions of location. Other compound prepositions are more idiomatic and can be found in Appendix C.

| | |
|---|---|
| *a espaldas de* | behind the back of |
| *a fines de* | at the end |
| *a lo largo de* | along |
| *a partir de* | from (time or date) on, starting . . . |
| *a través de* | through |
| *abajo de* | underneath |
| *adentro de* | inside |
| *afuera de* | outside (of) |
| *al lado de* | next to |
| *alrededor de* | around |
| *antes de* | before |

| | |
|---|---|
| *enfrente de* | in front of |
| *frente a* | opposite, facing |
| *fuera de* | outside of (prep) |
| *junto a* | close to, next to |
| *lejos de* | far from |

# Preposition Use with Verbs

Verbs and prepositions are used together in both English and Spanish, but not always in the same way.

## Verbs with prepositions

There are certain Spanish verbs that require a specific preposition to be used after them. These prepositions must follow the verb form to join them to an infinitive, but they are usually not translated into English.

The following verbs are followed by a preposition and then another verb in its infinitive form (to help you remember which are stem changes, the stem change is indicated in parentheses). Note with the exceptions, however, that most of the time these verbs are followed by nouns; therefore, either another preposition is used or no preposition at all.

| | |
|---|---|
| *acabar de* + infinitive | to have just ___ed BUT: *acabo la tarea* |
| *acertar (e>ie) a* + infinitive | to happen to, to succeed in . . . |
| *aprender a* + infinitive | to learn to . . . BUT: *aprendo español* |
| *ayudar a* + infinitive | to help to . . . |
| *comenzar (e>ie) a* + infinitive | to begin to . . . BUT: *comienzo la tarea* |
| *consentir (e>ie) en* + infinitive | to consent to . . . |
| *decidirse a* + infinitive | to decide to . . . BUT: *decido la hora* |
| *dejar de* + infinitive | to stop ___ing BUT: *dejo mi país* |
| *empezar (e>ie) a* + infinitive | to begin to . . . BUT: *empiezo la tarea* |
| *enseñar a* + infinitive | to teach to . . . BUT: *enseño español* |
| *forzar (o>ue) a* + infinitive | to force to . . . |
| *inspirar a* + infinitive | to inspire to . . . BUT: *inspiro miedo* |

| | |
|---|---|
| *molestarse en* + infinitive | to take the trouble to . . . BUT: *molesto a mis amigos* |
| *negarse (e>ie) a* + infinitive | to refuse to . . . BUT: *niego el delito* |
| *parar de* + infinitive | to stop ____ing BUT: *paro el carro* |
| *probar (o>ue) a* + infinitive | to try to . . . BUT: *pruebo de todo* |
| *tratar de* + infinitive | to try to . . . BUT: *trato enfermos* |

To use one of the verbs from the previous list in a Spanish sentence, the first verb is conjugated, and the verb after the preposition is in the infinitive form regardless of how the English equivalent is stated. In English, the second verb will often be in its infinitive form, just like Spanish. However, sometimes in English, the second verb is in its gerund form: "–ing."

The following verbs are followed by a preposition and then a noun or pronoun:

| | |
|---|---|
| *asistir a* | to attend (a function) |
| *avergonzarse (o>ue) de* | to be ashamed of |
| *casarse con* | to marry |
| *contar (o>ue) con* | to count on |
| *convertirse (e>ie) en* | to become, change into |
| *cuidar a* | to care for, take care of (someone) |
| *cuidar de* | to take care of (something) |
| *encontrarse (o>ue) con* | to meet up with, run into |
| *enfadarse con* | to get angry at |
| *enojarse con* | to get angry at |
| *equivocarse con* | to be mistaken about |
| *equivocarse en* | to make a mistake about |
| *gozar de* | to enjoy |
| *marcharse de* | to leave / go away |
| *montar en* | to ride |
| *morir (o>ue) de* | to die of (literally) |
| *morirse (o>ue) de* | to die of (not literally) |

| | |
|---|---|
| *parar(se) en* | to stop at, to stay in |
| *pensar (e>ie) de* | to have an opinion of |
| *pensar (e>ie) en* | to think of |
| *preocuparse con* | to worry about |
| *probar (o>ue) de* | to sample, to try out |
| *salir con* | to go out with, to date |
| *salir de* | to go away from (somewhere), to leave from |
| *servir de* | to be useful as |
| *sonar (o>ue) a* | to sound like (something) |
| *subir a* | to climb, go up or get on (something) |
| *trabajar en* | to work on, to work at |

Following are some sample sentences using the expressions from the previous list:

> *El vino se convirtió en vinagre.*
> The wine turned into vinegar.

> *La bebe goza de su botella de leche.*
> The baby enjoys her bottle of milk.

> *Raquel se marchó de la clase.*
> Raquel left the class.

## Verbs with prepositions in English but not Spanish

There are expressions in English that require a verb followed by a preposition. You may think you need to provide a Spanish equivalent when you translate these expressions, but no preposition is required. For the following expressions, there is a Spanish verb that is not followed by any preposition.

| | |
|---|---|
| *agradecer* | to be grateful for |
| *apagar* | to turn off |
| *bajar* | to go down |

| | |
|---|---|
| *buscar* | to look for |
| *caerse* | to fall down |
| *calentar (e>ie)* | to heat up |
| *colgar (o>ue)* | to hang up |
| *conocer* | to be acquainted with |
| *cortar* | to cut off, out |
| *entregar* | to hand over |
| *envolver (o>ue)* | to wrap up |
| *escuchar* | to listen to |
| *esperar* | to wait for, to hope for |
| *mirar* | to look at |
| *pagar* | to pay for |
| *quitar* | to take off |
| *saber* | to know how to |
| *sacar* | to take out |
| *salir* | to go out |

## Verbs after prepositions

Whenever a preposition is immediately followed by a verb, that verb will be in its infinitive form. This is not always true in English, so there will be times when it will not "sound right" to use an infinitive, but there are no exceptions to this Spanish rule: A verb must be in its infinitive form if it immediately follows a preposition.

*El joven aprende a cocinar.*

The young man learns to cook.

*Yo estoy cansada de escribir.*

I am tired of writing.

*Es imposible tener éxito sin trabajar.*

It's impossible to have success without working.

## Chapter Check-Out

For the following sentences, decide if a preposition is necessary for the blank. If it is, write the correct preposition; if it isn't, write a line in the blank.

1. *La familia aprende _____ esquíar en las montañas suizas.*

2. *Esa compañía me notifica _____ escrito.*

3. *La polícia busca _____ una muñeca perdida.*

4. *Después de la lucha, ellos se marcharon _____la casa*

5. *Ella es muy inteligente _____ ser bebé.*

**Answers: 1.** *a* **2.** *por* **3.** —— **4.** *de* **5.** *para*

# Chapter 15

# MORE PRONOUNS: REFLEXIVE, PREPOSITIONAL, AND DEMONSTRATIVE

## Chapter Check-In

❏ Understanding reflexive verbs and using reflexive pronouns

❏ Learning the pronouns that follow prepositions

❏ Using demonstrative pronouns

This chapter starts by building on what you've already learned about pronouns in earlier chapters—subject pronouns and pronoun cases (Chapter 3) and direct and indirect object pronouns (Chapter 10). So, you already have a head start on understanding reflexive pronouns. Reflexive pronouns are used when the subject or doer and the recipient of the actions in the sentence are the same. Then you'll learn about prepositional pronouns, which adds to what you just learned about prepositions in Chapter 14. To round this chapter out, demonstrative pronouns are covered to follow up with demonstrative adjectives that were addressed in Chapter 8.

## Reflexivity

If a verb in its infinitive form ends with –se, it is called a **reflexive verb.** Some verbs are always reflexive, but almost any verb you have already learned can be used as a reflexive verb. The term **reflexive** indicates that the subject of the sentence both causes and receives the action of the verb. The verb *lavar* means to wash (something or someone else), the reflexive verb *lavarse* means to wash oneself.

## Reflexive pronouns

In Spanish, a reflexive verb has an extra pronoun used with or without the subject pronoun that reflects the subject. The **reflexive pronoun** is placed in the sentence in exactly the same position as a direct or indirect object pronoun. If a reflexive pronoun is used in conjunction with a direct or indirect object pronoun (never with both at the same time), the reflexive pronoun is always first. The order of pronouns in a sentence is easily remembered with the acronym SRID:

- **S**ubject

- **R**eflexive

- **I**ndirect object

- **D**irect object

Although all four pronouns are never used together, whatever pronouns appear in a sentence will follow the order SRID. The subject of a sentence may be understood, but if there is a subject pronoun, it will precede all other pronouns. In the following examples, the reflexive pronouns are in bold, indirect pronouns are underlined, and direct objects are both underlined and in bold.

The sentence may have a **reflexive** and indirect object pronoun:

> *Se me acaba la disputa.* (The argument is over for me.)

The sentence may have a **reflexive** and **direct object** pronoun:

> *Yo **Me** lavo la cara antes de dormir. **Me** la lavo cada noche.*

The sentence may have an indirect and **direct object** pronoun:

> *Es necesario comprar mucha medicina. Mis padres me la compran cuando estoy enfermo.*

Notice in all of these examples that the order of the pronouns is consistent. Regardless of how many pronouns are used, they will always be in the SRID order: subject, reflexive, indirect object, and then direct object—all before the conjugated verb form.

When a reflexive verb is conjugated in any tense, the *–se* is removed from the infinitive form, and the appropriate reflexive pronoun is used to reflect the subject of the sentence. Notice in Table 15-1 that the reflexive pronouns are similar to direct and indirect object pronouns but are even easier to learn because the third person form of the reflexive pronoun is always *se*. The reflexive pronouns are listed with the subject pronouns that they reflect. Sometimes the subject pronoun is not used, but if a verb is being used reflexively, the reflexive pronoun is required.

**Table 15-1   Subject Pronouns and Corresponding Reflexive Pronouns**

| Singular Subject Pronoun | Singular Reflexive Pronoun | Plural Subject Pronoun | Plural Reflexive Pronoun |
|---|---|---|---|
| *yo* (I) | *me* (myself) | *nosotros/nosotras* (we) | *nos* (ourselves) |
| *tú* (you, familiar) | *te* (yourself) | *vosotros/vosotras* (you, familiar) | *os* (youselves) |
| *usted* (you, formal) | *se* (yourself) | *ustedes* (you, formal) | *se* (yourselves) |
| *él* (he) | *se* (himself) | *ellos* (they) | *se* (themselves) |
| *ella* (she) | *se* (herself) | *ellas* (they) | *se* (themselves) |

Table 15-2 demonstrates how to conjugate a reflexive verb in the present tense.

**Table 15-2   The Present Tense Conjugation of the Reflexive Verb *Lavarse***

| Singular | Plural |
|---|---|
| *yo me lavo* (I wash myself) | *nosotros/nosotras nos lavamos* (we wash ourselves) |
| *tú te lavas* (you wash yourself) | *vosotros/vosotras os laváis* (you wash yourself) |
| *usted se lava* (you wash yourself) | *ustedes se lavan* (you wash yourself) |
| *él se lava* (he washes himself) | *ellos se lavan* (they wash themselves) |
| *ella se lava* (she washes herself) | *ellas se lavan* (they wash themselves) |

## Reciprocity

When plural subjects have reflexive pronouns, there are actually two possible interpretations. Reflexive pronouns can indicate that the action of the verb falls back on the subject, or reciprocity. That means the people represented by the plural subject do the action of the verb to each other.

Sometimes it is obvious that the reflexive pronoun is being used to indicate reciprocity. For example:

> *Ellos se casaron el 21 de mayo.*
> They married (each other) on May 21st.

Technically, the sentence could be stating that they married themselves, but logic allows us to assume that reciprocity is indicated. The other use of the reflexive can be assumed in a sentence, such as:

> *Nosotros nos bañamos cada mañana.*
> We bathe ourselves each morning.

It is possible, but not probable, that we bathe each other. When a reflexive verb has a plural subject, there will be two possible translations, but the context of the sentence should give away the correct interpretation. This problem does not occur when the subject is singular because it is impossible to have reciprocity with only one person.

## Reflexive verbs

The section on reflexive verbs is included here because reflexive pronouns are used if the verb of the sentence being conjugated is a reflexive verb. It is difficult to understand when to use a reflexive pronoun unless you understand the most common verbs that are always reflexive and how a verb that is not normally reflexive can be used in a "reflexive way" that requires a reflexive pronoun. A verb that is reflexive is not irregular. It has the same conjugation as a non-reflexive verb except that an extra pronoun is used with it.

The closest equivalent in English would be using myself, yourself, himself, herself, ourselves, or themselves after the verb. Another use of the reflexive is to indicate that the members of a plural subject do something to each other.

Many reflexive verbs refer to doing something to one's own body. Because the reflexive pronoun already indicates that the subject of the sentence is doing the action of the verb to him/herself, it is considered repetitive to use a possessive adjective in front of the body parts in question. The appropriate definite article is used in front of the body part instead of a possessive adjective.

> *Yo <u>me</u> peino (<u>el</u> pelo) dos veces al día.*
> I comb <u>my</u> hair twice a day.

*Lupe <u>se</u> lava <u>las</u> manos antes de comer.*

Lupe washes <u>her</u> hands before eating.

Verbs like *caer* or *dormir* are used reflexively to indicate that the action of the verb happened without the subject of the verb's voluntary cooperation.

*El estudiante, aburrido, se durmió durante la lección.*

The bored student fell asleep during the lesson.

*Yo me caí en frente de la clase.*

I fell down in front of the class.

## Common reflexive verbs

Many of the verbs below are always reflexive, and some of the verbs you have seen before without the *–se*. When these verbs are indicating that the subject is doing the action of the verb to itself, they become reflexive verbs and require the reflexive pronoun.

| | |
|---|---|
| *acostarse (o>ue)* | to go to bed |
| *bañarse* | to bathe oneself, to take a bath |
| *caerse* | to fall down |
| *cepillarse* | to brush (one's own hair) |
| *desayunarse* | to eat breakfast |
| *despedirse (e>i)* | to say goodbye, to take leave |
| *despertarse (e>ie)* | to wake up |
| *divertirse (e>ie)* | to enjoy oneself, to have a good time |
| *dormirse (o>ue)* | to fall asleep |
| *ducharse* | to take a shower |
| *irse* | to leave, to go away |
| *lavarse* | to wash oneself |
| *levantarse* | to get up, to stand (oneself) up |
| *llamarse* | to call oneself, to be |
| *marcharse* | to leave, to go away |

| | |
|---|---|
| *peinarse* | to comb (one's own hair) |
| *ponerse* | to put something on oneself |
| *quedarse* | to stay, to remain |
| *quitarse* | to take something off of oneself |
| *sentarse (e>ie)* | to sit oneself down |
| *vestirse (e>i)* | to dress oneself, to get dressed |

# Prepositional Pronouns

There is a special case of pronouns you must use to replace a noun that is the object of a preposition. Notice in Table 15-3 that the prepositional pronouns are exactly like subject pronouns with the exception of *mí* and *ti*. Also notice that *mí* has an accent mark and *ti* does not.

**Table 15-3    Object of a Preposition Pronouns**

| Person | Singular | Plural |
|---|---|---|
| First person | *mí* (me) | *nosotros/nosotras* (us) |
| Second person | *ti* (you) | *vosotros/vosotras* (you) |
| Second person (formal you) | *usted* (you) | *ustedes* (you) |
| Third person (masculine) | *él* (him) | *ellos* (them) |
| Third person (feminine) | *ella* (her) | *ellas* (them) |

As you can see in the examples that follow, these pronouns sound strange in sentences because the pronouns used after a preposition sound like direct and indirect object pronouns in English and sound like subject pronouns in Spanish (except for *mí* and *ti*). The sentence "I sing for him" translates to "*Yo canto para él.*" The pronoun *él* in this sentence translates as "him" instead of "he."

> *Mi hermana trabaja por <u>mí</u> porque estoy enferma.*
> My sister works for <u>me</u> because I'm sick.

> *Yo no compré esta comida para <u>ti</u>.*
> I didn't buy this meal for <u>you</u>.

*Ese libro romántico es el mejor para <u>ella</u>.*
That romantic book is the best for <u>her</u>.

*Queremos viajar con <u>él</u> porque él conoce bien la ciudad.*
We want to travel with <u>him</u> because he knows the city well.

*Ella no nos invita a <u>nosotros</u> porque no somos buenos amigos.*
She doesn't invite <u>us</u> because we are not good friends.

*Catalina no baila con <u>ellos</u> cuando ponen música lenta.*
Catalina doesn't dance with <u>them</u> when they play slow music.

When the preposition *con* (with) is followed by the pronoun *mí*, it becomes a single word: *conmigo*. Notice that the accent mark disappears when *–go* is added. *Conmigo* is translated as "with me" and must be used whenever *con* is followed by *mí*. The same thing happens when *con* is followed by *ti*. *Contigo* means "with you" and must be used whenever the preposition *con* is followed by *ti*. Here are some examples:

*Tú debes comer <u>conmigo</u> porque yo sé cuáles son los mejores restaurantes.*
You should eat <u>with me</u> because I know which are the best restaurants.

*Ella no quiere bailar <u>contigo</u>. Ella quiere bailar <u>con él</u>.*
She doesn't want to dance <u>with you</u>. She wants to dance <u>with him</u>.

# Demonstrative Pronouns

Chapter 8 discussed how demonstrative adjectives are placed in front of a noun to indicate the proximity of the noun to the speaker. A **demonstrative pronoun** is used to replace a noun if the noun is understood. In English, it is common to say "this one" or "these ones." Technically, the word "this" or "these" should be used alone to replace a noun, and the word "one(s)" is unnecessary and incorrect. In Spanish, the appropriate demonstrative pronoun is used alone to replace a noun.

In Table 15-4, demonstrative pronouns are identical to the demonstrative adjectives. However, you may see an accent on the stressed syllable to distinguish the demonstrative pronoun from the demonstrative adjective. The accents are optional for the demonstrative pronouns.

**Table 15-4    Demonstrative Pronouns**

| Singular | Masculine | Feminine | Plural | Masculine | Feminine |
|---|---|---|---|---|---|
| this | *éste* | *ésta* | these | *éstos* | *éstas* |
| that | *ése* | *ésa* | those | *ésos* | *ésas* |
| that (way over there) | *aquél* | *aquélla* | those (way over there) | *aquéllos* | *aquéllas* |

When a demonstrative pronoun refers to an idea, situation, or concept, the appropriate **neutral demonstrative pronoun** is used. Since neutral demonstrative pronouns do not replace a specific noun, but rather refer to general ideas or concepts, they do not need to represent any gender and there is only one form. Notice in Table 15-5 that the neutral pronouns never have accent marks.

**Table 15-5    Neutral Demonstrative Pronouns**

| | |
|---|---|
| this | *esto* |
| that | *eso* |
| that (far away/long ago) | *aquello* |

Here are some examples:

> *Eso es lo que te dije.*
> That is what I told you.

> *Mi niñez (Aquello que me pasó me trae tantos recuerdos.)*
> My childhood (That which happened to me brings back so many memories.)

## Chapter Check-Out

For numbers 1 and 2, conjugate the reflexive verb in parentheses to go with the subject. Be sure to use the appropriate reflexive pronoun.

**1.** *Los novios _____ este sábado. (casarse)*

**2.** *Yo siempre _____ con pantalones. (vestirse)*

For numbers 3 and 4, write the appropriate pronoun after the preposition for the second sentence.

3. *María no puede ir de compras. Su esposo va de compras por _____.* *(María)*

4. *Mis primos vienen a visitarme. Quiero cocinar la comida favorita de _____. (mis primos)*

For numbers 5 and 6, write the appropriate form of the demonstrative pronoun in the blank for the second sentence.

5. *La comida en el restaurante ayer fue mejor. Debemos comer en _____ otra vez. (ese/ése)*

6. *No me gustan esas canciones viejas, me gustan _____ más modernas. (estas/éstas)*

**Answers: 1.** *se casan* **2.** *me visto* **3.** *ella* **4.** *ellos* **5.** *ese/ése* **6.** *estas/éstas*

# Chapter 16
# COMMANDS

## Chapter Check-In

❏ Understanding commands
❏ Learning the different forms of commands
❏ Using reflexive pronouns with commands

If you want to tell someone to do something, you must give a **command.** Since a command is addressed directly to someone, the understood recipient of the command is "you." Or, if you are included in the recipient group, it can be "us." The "you" is almost never stated when an English command is given—as in "take out the trash"—but it is common in Spanish to use the subject pronoun for "you" (*tú, usted, ustedes, vosotros/as*) after the command form of the verb. Since there are four different ways to say "you" in Spanish, there are also four different types of commands, plus one extra form for the affirmative *tú* (informal) command. The command form of the verb that you use depends on whom you are addressing.

## *Tú* Commands

In the case of a *tú* command, different forms are used for affirmative commands and negative commands. There is also a special set of commands for the *vosotros/vosotras* form of *tú*.

### Regular affirmative *tú* commands

The form used when an affirmative command is given to someone you would address as *tú* is the most unusually formed, so it's best to start with these. It may seem strange, but the form of the verb used for an affirmative *tú* command almost always looks like the present tense *él* form of the verb. For this reason, it is common to use the pronoun *tú* after the command so you can tell the difference between "he does something" and "you, do something." For example:

> *Baila todos los días*
> He dances every day.

> *¡Baila tú todos los días!*
> Dance every day! (addressed to you singular)

You may notice the inverted exclamation points (¡) that are used before writing a command in Spanish. These will also help indicate that the statement is an imperative, or a command form and, as a result, your voice would indicate this if it were a spoken command.

As long as you remember how to create the present tense *él* form of the verb, you can create the affirmative *tú* command form because they are almost always the same. This includes the stem-changing verbs. If a verb stem changes in the present tense, the command form will have the same stem change.

Don't forget that this form is only used when the command is stated affirmatively. If you tell someone whom you address as *tú* not to do something, it is a negative command, and there is a different form you must use. But first there are, of course, some verbs that have an irregular form for affirmative *tú* commands.

## Irregular affirmative *tú* commands

There are very few irregular affirmative *tú* commands that are not identical to the present tense *él* form of the verb. Table 16-1 lists the eight most commonly used verbs with irregular affirmative *tú* commands as well as the equivalent English command.

**Table 16-1  Irregular Affirmative *Tú* Command Forms**

| *Infinitive* | *Affirmative* Tú *Command* | *English Command* |
|---|---|---|
| decir | di | say or tell |
| hacer | haz | make or do |
| ir | ve | go |
| poner | pon | put |
| salir | sal | leave |

*(continued)*

**Table 16-1** *(continued)*

| Infinitive | Affirmative Tú Command | English Command |
|---|---|---|
| ser | sé | be |
| tener | ten | have |
| venir | ven | come |

Notice that the *tú* command for *ser* is the same as the present tense *yo* form of the verb *saber*. Sometimes the context of the sentence will make it clear which of the two is intended; however, placing the subject pronoun after the command further clarifies the meaning. Notice in the following examples how using a subject pronoun will clarify these identical twins.

> *Sé tú un buen niño mientras tu madre va de compras.*
>
> Be a good boy while your mother goes shopping. (affirmative *tú* command, *ser*)

> *Yo sé la respuesta.*
>
> I know the answer. (present tense *yo* form, *saber*)

## Negative *tú* commands

The present tense *yo* form is the base for creating a negative *tú* command. Most verbs that stem change in the present tense stem change in the *yo* form, so this will also occur in the negative *tú* command. In the present tense, the *yo* form almost always ends in –*o*. To create a negative *tú* command, remember this mantra: form of *yo*, drop the –*o*, add the opposite ending. Adding the opposite ending means if a verb has an infinitive that ends in –*ar*, the present tense *tú* ending for an –*er*/–*ir* verb is used to create the negative *tú* command. If a verb ends in –*er* or –*ir*, the present tense *tú* ending for –*ar* verbs is used to create the negative *tú* command.

So, once you remember the *yo* form, drop the –*o* ending and use the endings for negative *tú* commands listed in Table 16-2.

**Table 16-2   Endings for Negative *Tú* Commands**

| Infinitive Ending | Negative Tú Command Ending |
|---|---|
| –ar | no –es |
| –er | no –as |
| –ir | no –as |

Here are a few examples:

| | |
|---|---|
| *¡No comas dulces!* | Don't eat sweets! |
| *¡No llegues tarde!* | Don't arrive late! |
| *¡No digas mentiras!* | Don't tell lies! |

Be sure to notice that even though an affirmative *tú* command is like the *él* form of the verb, a negative *tú* command uses *tú* endings, but they use the *tú* ending of the opposite kind of verb.

### *Vosotros* commands

A *vosotros* command is used to order a group of people whom you would address in the *tú* form. The *vosotros* command forms are unusual because it is much safer to use the *ustedes* commands with any group (see "*Usted* and *Ustedes* Commands" later in this chapter).

To create an affirmative *vosotros* command, replace the –*r* at the end of the infinitive with a –*d*. If a verb is reflexive, and the pronoun *os* is attached, the –*d* is dropped. Table 16-3 shows a few examples.

**Table 16-3    Affirmative *Vosotros* Command Forms**

| *Infinitive* | *Affirmative Command* |
|---|---|
| *bañarse* (to bathe, reflexive) | *bañaos* |
| *beber* (to drink) | *bebed* |
| *contestar* (to answer) | *contestad* |
| *servir* (to serve) | *servid* |

A negative *vosotros* command is based on the *yo* form of the verb. Think of the present tense *yo* form of the verb you want to make into a negative *vosotros* command, then drop the –*o* ending and add the *vosotros/vosotras* ending normally used for the opposite kind of verb. The endings are shown in Table 16-4.

**Table 16-4    Endings for Negative *Vosotros* Commands**

| *Infinitive Ending* | *Negative* Vosotros *Command Ending* |
|---|---|
| –*ar* | *no –éis* |
| –*er* | *no –áis* |
| –*ir* | *no –áis* |

Following are a few of the verbs commonly used with negative *vosotros* commands. The infinitive is listed first followed by an example with the verb conjugated in the negative *vosotros* command form. Notice that when the subject pronoun *vosotros* is used, it follows the verb.

| | | |
|---|---|---|
| *bailar* | *¡No bailéis vosotros!* | Don't (you) dance! |
| *comer* | *¡No comáis la torta!* | Don't (you) eat the cake! |
| *hacer* | *¡No hagáis la tarea!* | Don't (you) perform the task! |
| *pedir* | *¡No pidáis comida muy cara en este restaurante!* | Don't (you [plural]) order a very expensive meal at this restaurant! |

## *Usted* and *Ustedes* Commands

Since the pronoun *usted* is specifically used to demonstrate respect, it's especially important to remember to use the correct form if you wish to command someone whom you would address using *usted*.

*Usted* and *ustedes* commands are created like negative *tú* commands and are used for both affirmative and negative commands.

To create an *usted* command, remember the mantra: form of *yo*, drop the −*o*, add the opposite ending. Think of the present tense *yo* form of the verb you want to make into an *usted* command, then drop the −*o* ending and add the *él, ella,* or *usted* ending normally used for the opposite kind of verb. For an −*ar* verb, use −*e*, and for an −*er* or −*ir* verb, use −*a*. Table 16-5 shows the endings for *usted* and *ustedes* commands.

**Table 16-5   Endings for Affirmative and Negative *Usted* and *Ustedes* Commands**

| Infinitive Ending | Usted *Affirmative/ Negative Endings* | Ustedes *Affirmative/ Negative Endings* |
|---|---|---|
| −*ar* | −*e* | −*en* |
| −*er* | −*a* | −*an* |
| −*ir* | −*a* | −*an* |

# Command Forms of Verbs

The tables in this section use affirmative and negative command forms of *tú*, *usted*, and *ustedes* with regular and irregular *–ar*, *–er*, and *–ir* verbs so that you can compare the endings for each.

Table 16-6 uses actual verbs to demonstrate the endings from Tables 16-2 and 16-5. Pay close attention to stem-changing verbs in all the different forms. The *vosotros/vosotras* command forms that were explained earlier are so unusual that they're not included in the following charts. You can always use the *ustedes* command form when you are speaking to a group of people. Since the *ustedes* form relays an attitude of respect and is easier to form, you can't go wrong. It is important to review the explanation of *vosotros* command forms so that you can recognize what is being said if someone gives you a command in this form, but keep things simple and use the *ustedes* command forms when you are speaking to a group.

Chapter 6 presented a list of verbs that end in *–go* in the *yo* form of the present tense. It's important to review those verbs because each type of command form is affected by this irregularity. A verb that ends in *–go* in the *yo* form will keep the *g* when you drop the *–o* to form *usted*, *ustedes*, and the negative *tú* command forms. In addition, they generally have irregular affirmative *tú* command forms as you may have noticed earlier in Table 16-1. Table 16-7 includes all of the command forms for the most common *–go* verbs.

Several verbs that end in *–zco* in the *yo* form of the present tense were presented in Chapter 6. Review those verbs, and then take a look at Table 16-8 to see how the command forms are affected.

Chapter 11 introduced the concept of changing the spelling of a verb to maintain the correct pronunciation. You learned a list of common verbs that end in *–car*, *–gar*, or *–zar* because when you conjugate verbs in the preterit tense, the *yo* form has an ending that requires you to change the spelling of any verb that ends in *–car*, *–gar*, or *–zar*.

That same spelling change is necessary when you add the "opposite endings" to create a command form. If a verb ends in *–car*, change *c* to *qu* in all command forms except the *tú* affirmative. If a verb ends in *–gar*, change *g* to *gu* in all command forms except the *tú* affirmative. If a verb ends in *–zar*, change *z* to *c* in all command forms except the *tú* affirmative.

**Table 16-6   Regular and Stem–Changing Verbs in All Command Forms**

| Infinitive | Usted Affirmative | Usted Negative | Ustedes Affirmative | Ustedes Negative | Tú Affirmative | Tú Negative |
|---|---|---|---|---|---|---|
| almorzar (to eat lunch) | almuerce | no almuerce | almuercen | no almuercen | almuerza | no almuerces |
| comer (to eat) | coma | no coma | coman | no coman | come | no comas |
| escribir (to write) | escriba | no escriba | escriban | no escriban | escribe | no escribas |
| hablar (to walk) | hable | no hable | hablen | no hablen | habla | no hables |
| jugar (to play) | juegue | no juegue | jueguen | no jueguen | juega | no juegues |
| mentir (to lie) | mienta | no mienta | mientan | no mientan | miente | no mientas |
| pedir (to order) | pida | no pida | pidan | no pidan | pide | no pidas |
| tocar (to touch) | toque | no toque | toquen | no toquen | toca | no toques |

**Table 16-7  Command Forms of Common –go Verbs**

| Infinitive | Yo Form | Usted Affirmative | Usted Negative | Ustedes Affirmative | Ustedes Negative | Tú Affirmative | Tú Negative |
|---|---|---|---|---|---|---|---|
| decir (to say, tell) | digo | diga | no diga | digan | no digan | di | no digas |
| hacer (to do, make) | hago | haga | no haga | hagan | no hagan | haz | no hagas |
| poner (to put) | pongo | ponga | no ponga | pongan | no pongan | pon | no pongas |
| salir (to leave) | salgo | salga | no salga | salgan | no salgan | sal | no salgas |
| tener (to have) | tengo | tenga | no tenga | tengan | no tengan | ten | no tengas |
| venir (to come) | vengo | venga | no venga | vengan | no vengan | ven | no vengas |

**Table 16-8  Command Forms of Common –zco Verbs**

| Infinitive | Yo Form | Usted Affirmative | Usted Negative | Ustedes Affirmative | Ustedes Negative | Tú Affirmative | Tú Negative |
|---|---|---|---|---|---|---|---|
| conocer (to know a person) | conozco | conozca | no conozca | conozcan | no conozcan | conoce | no conozcas |
| desaparecer (to disappear) | desaparezco | desaparezca | no desaparezca | desaparezcan | no desaparezcan | desaparece | no desaparezcas |
| obedecer (to obey) | obedezco | obedezca | no obedezca | obedezcan | no obedezcan | obedece | no obedezcas |
| ofrecer (to offer) | ofrezco | ofrezca | no ofrezca | ofrezcan | no ofrezcan | ofrece | no ofrezcas |

A comprehensive list of the command forms of common verbs with spelling changes is provided in Table 16-9. Some of these verbs are also stem changers, so look carefully at every form.

If a verb has a truly irregular *yo* form in the present tense, all of the command forms will also be completely irregular. Table 16-10 is a list of all the truly irregular command forms.

## Command Forms with Reflexive Pronouns

When dealing with the command forms of reflexive verbs, the reflexive pronouns must be attached to the end of an affirmative command and placed in front of a negative command. If you attach even one pronoun to the end of the command form, you must add an accent mark to maintain the correct stress. The written accent mark must be added to the next-to-last syllable before you attach any pronoun. Table 16-11 provides the command forms of several reflexive verbs. Notice where the reflexive pronoun is placed in each negative and affirmative form, and pay close attention to written accent marks.

**Table 16-9    Command Forms of Common Verbs with Spelling Changes**

| Infinitive | Yo Form | Usted Affirmative | Usted Negative | Ustedes Affirmative | Ustedes Negative | Tú Affirmative | Tú Negative |
|---|---|---|---|---|---|---|---|
| abrazar (to hug) | abrazo | abrace | no abrace | abracen | no abracen | abraza | no abraces |
| buscar (to search for) | busco | busque | no busque | busquen | no busquen | busca | no busques |
| cargar (to load) | cargo | cargue | no cargue | carguen | no carguen | carga | no cargues |
| comenzar (to begin) | comienzo | comience | no comience | comiencen | no comiencen | comienza | no comiences |
| explicar (to explain) | explico | explique | no explique | expliquen | no expliquen | explica | no expliques |
| jugar (to play) | juego | juegue | no juegue | jueguen | no jueguen | juega | no juegues |
| llegar (to arrive) | llego | llegue | no llegue | lleguen | no lleguen | llega | no llegues |
| sacar (to take [out]) | saco | saque | no saque | saquen | no saquen | saca | no saques |
| tocar (to touch, to play [music]) | toco | toque | no toque | toquen | no toquen | toca | no toques |

**Table 16-10  Truly Irregular Command Forms**

| Infinitive | Yo Form | Usted Affirmative | Usted Negative | Ustedes Affirmative | Ustedes Negative | Tú Affirmative | Tú Negative |
|---|---|---|---|---|---|---|---|
| dar (to give) | doy | dé | no dé | den | no den | da | no des |
| estar (to be) | estoy | esté | no esté | estén | no estén | está | no estés |
| ir (to go) | voy | vaya | no vaya | vayan | no vayan | ve | no vayas |
| saber (to know) | sé | sepa | no sepa | sepan | no sepan | sabe | no sepas |
| ser (to be) | soy | sea | no sea | sean | no sean | sé | no seas |

**Table 16-11  Command Forms with Reflexive Pronouns**

| Infinitive | Usted Affirmative | Usted Negative | Ustedes Affirmative | Ustedes Negative | Tú Affirmative | Tú Negative |
|---|---|---|---|---|---|---|
| caerse (to fall down) | caígase | no se caiga | caíganse | no se caigan | cáete | no te caigas |
| dormirse (to fall asleep) | duérmase | no se duerma | duérmanse | no se duerman | duérmete | no te duermas |
| lavarse (to wash oneself) | lávese | no se lave | lávense | no se laven | lávate | no te laves |
| sentarse (to sit down) | siéntese | no se siente | siéntense | no se sienten | siéntate | no te sientes |

## Chapter Check-Out

For the following five verbs, write the command forms in the following order: affirmative *usted,* negative *usted,* affirmative *ustedes,* negative *ustedes,* affirmative *tú,* and negative *tú.* Don't forget that the affirmative *tú* command is the strangest form.

1. *comenzar*
2. *dormirse*
3. *vestirse*
4. *tener*
5. *ser*

For the next five verbs, write both the negative and affirmative *vosotros/ vosotras* command forms. Be careful with placement of the reflexive pronoun.

6. *beber*
7. *bailar*
8. *pedir*
9. *sentarse*
10. *hacer*

**Answers: 1.** *comience, no comience, comiencen, no comiencen, comienza, no comiences* **2.** *duérmase, no se duerma, duérmanse, no se duerman, duérmete, no te duermas* **3.** *vístase, no se vista, vístanse, no se vistan, vístete, no te vistas* **4.** *tenga, no tenga, tengan, no tengan, ten, no tengas* **5.** *sea, no sea, sean, no sean, sé, no seas* **6.** *bebed, no bebáis* **7.** *bailad, no bailéis* **8.** *pedid, no pidáis* **9.** *sentaos, no os sentéis* **10.** *haced, no hagáis*

# Chapter 17
# NEGATIVES

## Chapter Check-In

❑ Learning negative expressions

❑ Writing negative sentences

❑ Differentiating between *sino* and *pero*

To make a sentence negative, there are some special issues that you must understand. You cannot simply translate the words of a negative English sentence and create an idiomatically correct and understandable negative sentence in Spanish. If you think it sounds a bit silly when a new English speaker says, "He no studies nothing," you will want to learn how to avoid the equivalent mistake as you learn Spanish.

English speakers seem to use mathematic logic in their sentence structure, which means that two negatives make a positive. The Spanish simply do not see the need to apply a math concept to language structure. In the Spanish perspective, a sentence that is negative should be completely negative. Instead of avoiding a double negative, Spanish sentences use all the negative words possible when a sentence is negative.

## Negative Words and Expressions

It's a lot easier to learn about negative Spanish sentences if you have already learned the important vocabulary typically used in negative sentences and their affirmative counterparts.

Table 17-1 is a list of affirmative words that have negative counterparts. It is important to learn these words and understand that a negative sentence will never use the affirmative versions even though the English equivalent might.

**Table 17-1   Affirmative and Negative Words**

| Affirmative | Negative |
|---|---|
| *sí* (yes) | *no* (no, not) |
| *algo* (something) | *nada* (nothing) |
| *alguien* (someone, somebody) | *nadie* (no one, nobody) |
| *alguno/-a/-os/-as* (any, some) | *ninguno/-a* (no, no one, not any, none)* |
| *o . . . o* (either . . . or) | *ni . . . ni* (neither . . . nor, not . . . nor) |
| *siempre* (always) | *nunca, jamás* (never, not ever) |
| *también* (also) | *tampoco* (not either, neither) |

*Note that the word "no" cannot negate a noun in Spanish as it does in English. You must use a form of the word *ninguno* to do this. (For example, *no tengo ningún dinero.*)

Some negative expressions are created by using a group of words with a specific meaning separate from their word-for-word translations. It is important to learn these expressions exactly as they are written because the significance of idiomatic expressions usually depends on the exact order of the words, and they cannot be looked up in most dictionaries. Following is a list of the most common negative idiomatic expressions:

| | |
|---|---|
| *ahora no* | not now |
| *apenas* | scarcely/hardly |
| *de ninguna manera* | no way, by no means |
| *de ningún modo* | no way, by no means |
| *en ninguna parte* | nowhere |
| *por ninguna parte* | nowhere |
| *en/por ningún lado/sitio/lugar* | nowhere |
| *ni hablar* | no way |
| *ni (ella) tampoco* | nor she either |
| *ni siquiera* | not even |
| *(no) en absoluto* | absolutely not |
| *no más de* (number) | no more than (amount) |
| *no más que* (action) | only (action) |

| | |
|---|---|
| *no solo . . . sino también . . .* | not only . . . but also . . . |
| *(Nunca, no) en mi vida* | never in my life |
| *nunca jamás* | never ever (emphatically) |
| *nunca más* | never again |
| *todavía no* | still not, not yet |
| *sin novedad* | nothing new |
| *ya no* | no longer |

## Negative Sentences

One of the main differences between English and Spanish negative sentences is that the Spanish create a simple negative sentence by placing *no* in front of the conjugated verb.

> *Él habla español.*  *Él no habla español.*
> He speaks Spanish.  He no speaks Spanish.

> *Nosotros bailamos.*  *Nosotros no bailamos.*
> We dance.  We no dance

If you translate the Spanish negative sentences word for word, it sounds funny because an English sentence uses a helping verb to make a sentence negative even though the affirmative sentence has no helping verb.

> He speaks Spanish. He <u>does</u> not speak Spanish.
> We dance. We <u>do</u> not dance.

You probably never even considered the word <u>do</u> or <u>does</u> as part of a negative sentence in English, but you must remember that Spanish does not use any helping verbs to make a sentence negative. They simply place a *no* in front of the verb. Don't try to translate the word "do" or "does" to any Spanish sentence.

The best way to create a simple negative sentence is to consider the affirmative sentence and put a *no* in font of the verb. If you want to write the negative sentence, "Marco doesn't play soccer," first create the sentence, "Marco plays soccer." Once you have the verb conjugated correctly in the affirmative sentence, add *no* in front of the verb and you have the Spanish equivalent to "Marco doesn't play soccer." See the following example:

*Marco juega al fútbol.*
Marco plays soccer.

*Marco <u>no</u> juega al fútbol.*
Marco <u>doesn't</u> play soccer.

It's common to hear that Spanish sentences use "double negatives." In reality, not every negative sentence has more than one negative word, and some negative sentences have three or four. There are certain words that have affirmative and negative versions (as in Table 17-1). When a Spanish sentence is negative, there will always be a negative word in front of the verb, and any other word in the sentence that has a negative version will be in the negative even though equivalent English negative sentences often use affirmative words.

There are two ways to write a negative sentence: either with the word *no* followed by the conjugated verb of the sentence or with another negative word (from Table 17-1) followed by the conjugated verb of the sentence. If the word *no* is used prior to the conjugated verb of the sentence, then if necessary one of the words from Table 17-1 directly follows the conjugated verb. See the following examples:

*Alguien trabaja aquí.*
Somebody works here.

*No trabaja nadie aquí.* or *Nadie trabaja aquí.*
Nobody works here.

*José tiene algo en la mano.*
José has something in his hand.

*José no tiene nada en la mano.* or *Nada tiene José en la mano.*
José doesn't have anything in his hand.

*Siempre estudiamos antes de un examen.*
We always study before a test.

*Nunca estudiamos antes de un examen.* or *No estudiamos nunca antes de un examen.*
We never study before a test.

*Me gusta la pizza también.*
I like pizza, too.

*No me gusta la pizza tampoco.* or *Tampoco me gusta la pizza.*
I don't like pizza either.

# Negatives and Other Parts of Speech

Different parts of speech, such as pronouns, adjectives, and conjunctions change forms when used in negative sentences.

## Pronouns

If there are any reflexive or direct or indirect object pronouns, they will come between the *no* and the verb. The only pronoun that precedes the *no* is the subject pronoun if it's used.

*Me compré alguna ropa.*
I bought myself some clothes.

*No me compré ninguna ropa.* or *Ninguna ropa me compré.*
I don't buy myself any clothes.

You probably noticed that *alguno* and *ninguno* can change endings to become feminine and/or plural, as in the case of *alguno*. These words can be adjectives or pronouns, and the gender of their ending matches the gender of the noun it replaces or modifies.

In the following examples, the words *algunas* and *ninguna* are used as adjectives. They precede the noun they modify and must match that noun's gender and number. Keep in mind that negative words have no plural because they indicate that there is none of something, and hence the plural does not apply when there is not even a singular instance to speak of.

*Tenemos algunas mascotas.*
We have some pets.

*No tenemos ninguna mascota.* or *Ninguna mascota tenemos.*
We don't have any pets.

When used as a pronoun, the noun being replaced must already be established so that the correct gender and number can be used.

> *Tenemos algunas.*
> We have some.

> *No tenemos ninguna.*
> We don't have any.

The previous examples use *algunas* and *ninguna* as pronouns replacing the understood noun *mascotas*. Sometimes the pronoun is used with an adjective describing it:

> *¿Compraste algunas flores?*
> Did you buy any flowers? (*algunas* is an adjective modifying *flores*)

> *Compré algunas bonitas.*
> I bought some pretty ones. (*algunas* is a pronoun replacing *flores*)

> *Compré algunas.*
> I bought some. (*algunas* is a pronoun replacing *flores*)

> *No compré ninguna flor bonita* or *Ninguna flor bonita compré.*
> I didn't buy any pretty flowers. (*ninguna* is an adjective modifying *flores*)

> *No compré ninguna.*
> I didn't buy any. (*ninguna* is a pronoun replacing *flores*)

Consider the following examples, and focus on the nouns that the adjectives *alguna* and *ninguna* modify and the pronouns that they replace:

> *Necesito alguna ayuda*
> I need some help. (*alguna* is an adjective modifying *ayuda*)

> *Ahorita, necesito alguna.*
> I need some right now. (*alguna* is a pronoun replacing *ayuda*)

> *Tú no necesitas ninguna ayuda.*
> You don't need any help. (*ninguna* is an adjective modifying *ayuda*)

*A veces no necesito ninguna pero ahora necesito alguna.*

Sometimes I don't need any (I need none), but now I need some. (*alguna* and *ninguna* both are pronouns replacing the word *ayuda*)

## Adjectives

Technically, the words *alguno* and *ninguno* are only used as pronouns. If used as an adjective, the *–o* is dropped, and they change to *algún* and *ningún* when followed by a singular masculine noun.

For example, *alguno* and *ninguno* drop the *–o* and are used as adjectives here:

*Tú tienes algún dinero. Yo no tengo ningún dinero.*

You have some money. I don't have any money.

Now, here is an example of *alguno* and *ninguno* being used as pronouns:

*Tú tienes dinero y yo quiero alguno. Mi otro amigo no tiene ninguno.*

You have lots of money and I want some. My other friend doesn't have any.

## Conjunctions: *sino* and *pero*

It's important to understand the differences between the conjunctions *sino* and *pero* because they can both be translated as "but."

*Sino* is used when the first clause of the sentence is negative and the second clause contradicts it. It expresses the concept that in English is stated, "not this but rather that." *Sino* is usually translated as "but rather."

*No quiero el coche blanco, sino el coche rojo.*

I don't want the white car, but rather the red car.

*No nos gusta el cine, sino los deportes.*

We don't like movies, but rather sports.

Notice in the following sentences that the conjunction *pero* is used when the concept is continued rather than contrasted, even if the first sentence is negative.

*Yo no quiero ir, pero necesito ir.*

I don't want to go, but I need to.

*Ellos tienen dinero pero no son felices.*

They have money, but they are not happy.

Another use of *sino* is in the expression "*no solo . . . sino tambien . . . .*" It is equivalent to the English "not only . . . but also . . . ."

*No solo tenemos comida, sino también refrescos.*

We not only have food, but also beverages.

## Chapter Check-Out

Write a negative version of each of the following sentences:

1. *Alguien tiene algún dinero.*
2. *Alguien siempre tiene algo.*
3. *Siempre necesitamos una chaqueta o un suéter.*
4. *Le gusta bailar también.*
5. *Mi amiga necesita algo.*

**Answers: 1.** *Nadie tiene ningún dinero.* **2.** *Nadie nunca tiene nada.* **3.** *Nunca necesitamos ni chaquetas ni suéteres.* **4.** *No le gusta bailar tampoco.* **5.** *Mi amiga no necesita nada.*

# REVIEW QUESTIONS

Use these review questions to reinforce and practice what you've learned in this book. After you work through them, you're well on your way to understanding the Spanish language.

## Chapter 1

1. If a word ends in the letter *-n* or *-s* or ends in any vowel, the natural stress is on the

   a. last syllable
   b. next-to-last syllable
   c. first syllable

2. True or False: The Spanish language never uses the letters *ph* to produce the *f* sound.

3. True or false: The letters *b* and *v* sound the same in Spanish.

4. What word has the same *c* sound as the word *cima*.

   a. *cantar*
   b. *centro*
   c. *comer*

## Chapter 2

5. Write the appropriate definite article to indicate the gender and number for the nouns \_\_\_\_\_ *ciudad* and \_\_\_\_\_ *naciones*.

6. Write the appropriate indefinite article to indicate the gender and number for the nouns \_\_\_\_\_ *perro* and \_\_\_\_\_ *playas*.

7. Write the plural form of the noun *el autobús* \_\_\_\_\_.

## Chapter 3

8. Write the subject pronoun that would be used to replace the subject of the following sentence:

   *Marco y yo trabajamos en la tienda.* \_\_\_\_\_ *trabajamos en la tienda.*

9. List three Spanish subject pronouns that mean "you."

10. List the Spanish subject pronouns for the following:

    a. first person singular

    b. second person singular

    c. first person plural

    d. third person plural (feminine)

## Chapter 4

11. Write the appropriate present tense form of the verb for the following sentence:

    *Tú _____ la canción muy bien. (cantar)*

12. Create a conjugation chart with the present tense forms of the verb *trabajar*.

13. Translate to Spanish: Maria and Sara hope to travel.

## Chapter 5

14. Translate to Spanish: Jaime or Ana cooks, but I clean.

15. True or false: With numbers, the Spanish use a comma as a decimal point and use a period where the English number would have a comma.

## Chapter 6

16. Select the correct verb for the context of the sentence, and conjugate it in the present tense to go with the subject of the sentence.

    *Ella _____ en la biblioteca. (ser, estar)*

17. Select the correct verb for the context of the sentence, and conjugate it in the present tense to go with the subject of the sentence.

    *Yo no _____ a su hermana. (saber, conocer)*

18. Write the correct present tense form of the stem-changing verb in parentheses.

    *Ella _____ una hamburguesa. (pedir)*

19. True or false: In the present tense, the *nosotros/nosotras* form of a stem-changing verb does not stem change.

## Chapter 7

**20.** Translate these question words to Spanish: Who? What? When? Where? How? Why?

**21.** Translate to Spanish: Do they write letters?

## Chapter 8

**22.** Create the form of the possessive adjective in parentheses to match the noun it modifies.

*No tenemos _____ lápices. (nuestro)*

**23.** Write the appropriate form of the demonstrative adjective in parentheses.

*Recomendamos _____ libros. (eso)*

**24.** True or false: An adjective that indicates number, quantity, or amount is placed in front of the noun it modifies.

**25.** True or false: If a noun is plural, all adjectives that modify the noun must also be in a plural form.

## Chapter 9

**26.** Create an adverb from the adjective *completo*.

**27.** True or false: An adverb created from an adjective that has a written accent mark will not have the written accent.

**28.** True or false: When two or more adverbs end in *–mente,* the suffix *–mente* is used only with the last adverb, and all preceding adverbs lose the *–mente* and keep the singular feminine form of the adjective.

**29.** Write the Spanish word for the following adverbs: much (a lot), little (a little), too much, so much, more, and less.

## Chapter 10

**30.** Rewrite the following sentence using object pronouns to replace the direct and indirect objects: *El maestro les da buenas lecciones a los alumnos.*

**31.** True or false: There is always a conjugated verb in every sentence, so you can always put both object pronouns in front of the conjugated form of the verb.

**32.** Translate the following sentence to Spanish: My father buys our grandmother a house.

**33.** Select the appropriate pronoun for the following sentence: *A Juan _____ gustan los coches rápidos.*

    **a.** *lo*

    **b.** *le*

    **c.** *les*

    **d.** *las*

## Chapter 11

**34.** Consider the subject of the sample sentence and write the appropriate preterite tense form of the verb *estar:*

*Nosotros _____ en el restaurante ayer.*

**35.** Consider the subject of the sentence and write the appropriate preterite tense form of the verb *cerrar:*

*Samuel no _____ la puerta anoche.*

**36.** True or false: Any verb that stem changes in the present tense will stem change exactly the same way in the preterite.

**37.** True or false: The preterite *yo* form of a verb that ends in *–gar* will have the letter *u* before the *–é* ending.

## Chapter 12

**38.** Write the correct imperfect tense form of the verb *tener:*

*El museo _____ muchas estatuas.*

**39.** Write the correct imperfect tense form of the verb *ser:*

*Los niños _____ muy simpáticos.*

**40.** Identify the imperfect indicator in the sentence:

*Yo veía las vistas de la Costa del Sol cada verano.*

**41.** True or false: There are no irregular verbs in the imperfect tense.

**42.** True or false: The imperfect tense is used to focus on a completed action or a specific instance.

## Chapter 13

**43.** Read the following sentence and decide whether to use the preterite or imperfect tense of the verb *conocer*. Then conjugate the verb to go with the subject in the correct tense.

*Ayer yo _____ a una amiga de mi hermano.*

**44.** Translate the following sentence to Spanish, using a formula with *hacer*: The class ended a month ago.

**45.** True or false: When the verb *querer* is used negatively in the preterite, the meaning of the expression is "refused."

**46.** True or false: If one verb in the sentence is in the preterite tense, all verbs will be in the preterite.

## Chapter 14

**47.** Write the appropriate preposition:

*Él me llamó _____ teléfono.*

**48.** Write the appropriate preposition:

*Vamos _____ esquiar en las montañas.*

**49.** Write the appropriate preposition:

*Trabajo _____ un restaurante mexicano.*

**50.** Write the appropriate preposition:

*No tengo mi libro. Este es el libro _____ Miguel.*

**51.** Write the appropriate preposition:

*Mi madre se enfada _____ mis primos cuando gritan.*

## Chapter 15

**52.** Conjugate the reflexive verb in the present tense to go with the subject. Be sure to use the correct reflexive pronoun.

*Nosotros _____ la ropa antes de dormir. (quitarse)*

**53.** Conjugate the reflexive verb in the present tense to go with the subject. Be sure to use the correct reflexive pronoun.

*Ellos _____ muy temprano cada mañana. (desayunarse)*

**54.** Translate to Spanish: I stay in the house when I am sick.

**55.** Translate to Spanish: The parents love each other.

## Chapter 16

For each of the following infinitives, write the correct command forms:

| | |
|---|---|
| *Usted* affirmative | *Usted* negative |
| *Ustedes* affirmative | *Ustedes* negative |
| *Tú* affirmative | *Tú* negative |

**56.** *empezar*

**57.** *ir*

**58.** *dormir*

**59.** *jugar*

**60.** *venir*

## Chapter 17

**61.** Change the following sentence to the negative: *Alguien trabaja aquí.*

**62.** Change the following sentence to the negative: *José tiene algo en su mano.*

**63.** Change the following sentence to the negative: *Siempre lees algún libro.*

**64.** Change the following sentence to the negative: *Me gustan los deportes también.*

## Answers

**1.** b **2.** True **3.** True **4.** b **5.** *la, las* **6.** *un, unas* **7.** *los autobuses* **8.** *Nosotros*
**9.** *tú, usted (Ud.) / ustedes (Uds.), vosotros/vosotras* **10. a.** *yo* **b.** *tú* **c.** *nosotros/
nosotras* **d.** *ellas* **11.** cantas **12.** *yo trabajo, tú trabajas, él/ella/usted trabaja,
nosotros/nosotras trabajamos, vosotros trabajáis, ellos/ellas/ustedes trabajan*
**13.** *María y Sara esperan viajar.* **14.** *Jaime o Ana cocina pero yo limpio.*
**15.** True **16.** *está* **17.** *conozco* **18.** *pide* **19.** True **20.** *¿Quién?, ¿Qué?* or
*¿Cuál?, ¿Cuándo?, ¿Dónde?, ¿Cómo?, ¿Por qué?* **21.** *¿Escriben ellos cartas?*
**22.** *nuestros* **23.** *esos* **24.** True **25.** True **26.** *completamente* **27.** False
**28.** True **29.** *mucho, poco, demasiado, tanto, más, menos* **30.** *El maestro se
las da.* **31.** True **32.** *Mi padre le compra una casa a/para nuestra abuela.*
**33.** b **34.** *estuvimos* **35.** *cerró* **36.** False **37.** True **38.** *tenía* **39.** *eran*
**40.** *cada verano* **41.** False **42.** False **43.** *conocí* **44.** *La clase terminó hace un
mes.* **45.** True **46.** False **47.** *por* **48.** *a* **49.** *en* **50.** *de (para is aceptable)*
**51.** *con* **52.** *nos quitamos* **53.** *se desayunan* **54.** *Yo me quedo en casa cuando
estoy enfermo(−a).* **55.** *Los padres se aman.* **56.** *empiece, no empiece, empiecen, no empiecen, empieza, no empieces* **57.** *vaya, no vaya, vayan, no vayan,
ve, no vayas* **58.** *duerma, no duerma, duerman, no duerman, duerme, no
duermas* **59.** *juegue, no juegue, jueguen, no jueguen, juega, no juegues*
**60.** *venga, no venga, vengan, no vengan, ven, no vengas* **61.** *Nadie trabaja
aquí* or *No trabaja nadie aquí.* **62.** *José no tiene nada en su mano* or
*Nada tiene José en su mano.* **63.** *Nunca lees ningún libro* or *No lees nunca
ningún libro.* **64.** *No me gustan los deportes tampoco* or *Tampoco me gustan
los deportes.*

# RESOURCE CENTER

This Resource Center offers the best resources available in print and online to help you study and review the core concepts of Spanish. You can find additional resources, plus study tips and tools to help test your knowledge, at www.cliffsnotes.com.

## Books

This CliffsNotes book is one of many great books about Spanish language concepts. If you want some additional resources, check out these other books:

*The Big Red Book of Spanish Idioms* provides a comprehensive listing and explanations of common idiomatic expressions in Spanish. This book is extremely useful because the meanings of idioms cannot be determined simply by looking up each individual word in the dictionary. McGraw-Hill, $12.95.

*The Concise American Heritage Larousse Spanish Dictionary* provides the clearest and most detailed entries and includes many idiomatic expressions. Houghton Mifflin Harcourt, $26.00.

*501 Spanish Verbs,* by Christopher Kendris and Theodore Kendris, is as important as a dictionary if you want to produce written or spoken sentences in Spanish. This book charts all the forms of all the tenses of the 501 most common verbs in an easy-to-understand format. There is also a clear explanation of all the forms and tenses at the beginning of the book. Barron's Educational Services, $16.99.

*1001 Spanish Pitfalls,* by Marion Peter Holt and Julianne Deuber, helps you avoid making the most commonly made errors as a typical English speaker learning to speak, read, and write Spanish. You'll learn about tricky vocabulary, idoms, and technical terms as well as rules of grammar. Barron's Educational Services, $11.99.

*Spanish For Dummies,* by Susan Wald, is designed to get you speaking Spanish quickly. This easy-to-understand book teaches the basics of Spanish with practical lessons, cultural facts, fun, and handy references including a Spanish-English mini-dictionary, common verb lists, and more. Wiley Publishing, Inc., $24.99.

*Velázquez World Wide Spanish English Dictionary* provides comprehensive Spanish-English and English-Spanish translation, a complete listing of Spanish verb conjugations, and an abundance of idiomatic phrases, among other useful features. Velázquez Press, $12.95.

## Internet

Visit the following websites for more information about Spanish language concepts (since websites constantly change, try a search on any Web browser by typing "Spanish Language"):

**Learn-Spanish-Language**—www.learnSpanish.com—is a great all-around site for newcomers to the Spanish language.

**AllExperts**—www.allexperts.com/getExpert.asp?Category=1551—is the site to use when you have a question about the Spanish language. There are all different sorts of experts willing to help you translate, prepare an individualized study plan, or help you with your Spanish homework.

**Lingolex**—www.lingolex.com/spanish.htm—is a very interesting site for learning basic Spanish. There is a chatroom where you can practice your Spanish, and fun activities will help you master some of the challenging grammatical concepts and improve your vocabulary.

**Spanish Unlimited**—www.spanishunlimited.com—is "The right place to learn Spanish and meet new friends." There are popular games, weekly lessons, Spanish jokes, and even a verb conjugator to help you use the correct form of any verb.

# GLOSSARY

**acronym** A word formed by the first letters of a set of specific phrases or series of words used to help you remember the details of the information.

**adjective** A word that describes (modifies) a noun or pronoun. A Spanish adjective usually follows the noun or pronoun it modifies and matches its gender and number.

**adverb** An adverb can be used to modify a verb, an adjective, or another adverb. Adverbs generally tell how, when, or where something happened.

**agreement** There are many situations where the number and gender of a word must "match" another word. If a noun is singular and feminine, any word that modifies that noun must be in a singular, feminine form. Another aspect of agreement is the necessity to use the correct form of a conjugated verb to match the subject that is responsible for the action of the verb.

**apocopated adjectives** If placed in front of a singular, masculine noun, some adjectives must be in a shortened form. These are called apocopated adjectives.

**–ar verbs** Verbs in the infinitive form ending with the letters –ar. The other two types of verbs in Spanish are verbs ending in –er and –ir.

**clarification** The indirect object pronouns are very vague. When it is unclear what noun an indirect object is replacing, a clarification is written using the preposition *a* plus a noun or pronoun.

**cognate** A word that is similar in both Spanish and English. A cognate will either look similar or sound similar but not both.

**command** When you tell someone to do something, you use a form of the verb called a command. In Spanish there are different command forms depending on whether you are addressing someone as *tú, vosotros, nosotros,* or *ustedes.*

**compound preposition** A compound preposition is an expression made up of two or more words, the last one being a simple preposition.

**compound word** A word that is composed of a verb in its *él* form and a plural noun combined in that order. Compound nouns are always masculine and can be singular even though they end in *–s.*

**conjugation chart** To indicate what form of the verb is used with each subject pronoun, there is a conjugation chart for each tense of the verb. A verb conjugation chart has the pronouns in a specific order and the correct form of the verb to use with that subject in that tense.

**conjunction** A word used to join two words or phrases such as "and" *(y),* "but" *(pero),* and "or" *(o).*

**consonant** In both Spanish and English, the consonants are all the letters of the alphabet except *a, e, i, o,* and *u.*

**definite articles** The four specific words used in front of a noun to indicate a specific person or thing are *el, la, los,* and *las.* The Spanish definite article must match the gender and number of the noun it modifies; it is equivalent to the English word "the."

**Demonstrative adjective** An adjective or pronoun that points out the relative distance of an object or person. "This" and "that" are singular demonstratives in English, and "these" and "those" are plurals. In Spanish, these are *este, esta, estos, estas* (for *this* and *these*) and *ese, esa, esos, esas* (for *that* and *those*).

**diphthongs** A combination of two vowels that form one syllable. This is caused either by a strong vowel *(a, e, o)* combined with a weak vowel *(i, u)* or the combination of two weak vowels.

**direct object** The noun or pronoun that receives the action of the verb.

**–er verbs** Verbs in the infinitive form ending with the letters *–er.* The other two types of verbs in Spanish are verbs ending in *–ar* and *–ir.*

**first person** Indicates that the subject of the verb is the singular I *(yo)* or the plural we *(nosotros/nosotras).*

**formal** The forms of pronouns and verbs used when addressing someone in a respectful manner are called formal. In Spanish these are *Usted* (singular) and *Ustedes* (plural).

**gender** All nouns in Spanish have gender. Each noun is either masculine or feminine, and all words that modify a

noun will be in a form that matches the gender of the noun.

**gerund** (also called the present participle) is the *–ing* form of the verb. It is almost always used with an auxiliary verb (like *estar*). Unlike English, gerunds cannot be nouns and cannot be used after prepositions.

**idiomatic expression** A group of words that have a specific meaning different from the translation of each individual word making up the expression.

**imperfect indicators** are triggers words that indicate the past action is ongoing *(muchas veces, a menudo, los sábados).*

**imperfect tense** The imperfect tense is one of the two past tenses in Spanish and is used to describe and narrate ongoing or repetitive actions in the past.

**indefinite articles** There are four specific words that are used in front of a noun to indicate that it refers to an indefinite person or thing. The singular forms *un* and *una* are equivalent to the English word "a." The plural forms *unos* and *unas* are equivalent to the English word "some." Spanish indefinite articles must match the noun they modify.

**indirect object** Tells for whom (what) or to whom (what) something is done. Like direct object pronouns, indirect object pronouns always go just before the verb of which they are the object.

**infinitive** The form of the verb that has not been conjugated ending in *–ar, –er,* or *–ir.* This is called the infinitive form of the verb and is what you find when you look up a verb in the dictionary. In English, infinitives are introduced by the word "to" (to eat, to write). In Spanish, the infinitive can be used as a noun *(Nadar es buen ejercicio)*.

**informal** When addressing someone in a friendly manner, informal forms of pronouns and verbs are used. In Spanish, *tú* is used to address one person, and in Spain, *vosotros* is used to address "you" plural.

**intensifier** A word, usually an adverb, that has little meaning in itself but provides force, intensity, or emphasis to another word. The most common intensifier in English is "very." Its equivalent in Spanish is *muy*, which also is quite common.

**interrogative pronouns** A question word (such as who?, what?, where?, and when?) is called an interrogative pronoun. In Spanish, these include *¿Quién?*, *¿Qué?*, *¿Dónde?*, and *¿Cuándo?*

**–ir verbs** are verbs in the infinitive form ending with the letters *–ir*. The other two types of verbs in Spanish are verbs ending in *–ar* and *–er*.

**irregular verbs** A verb that does not follow the normal patterns of conjugated forms is called irregular.

**mnemonic devices** Techniques that help you remember something. *See also* **acronym.**

**modifier** A word that describes or provides more information about another word modifies that word. An adjective modifies a noun, and an adverb modifies a verb, an adjective, or another adverb.

**natural stress** *See* stress.

**neutral demonstrative pronoun** The pronoun *lo* is used either to represent a generality or abstract concept that does not have gender or when the antecedent is unclear.

**noun** A word that names a person, place, thing, animal or idea.

**number** Reference to whether something is singular or plural. You must consider number with Spanish nouns, pronouns, adjectives, and verbs.

**object of a preposition** The noun or pronoun that follows a preposition is called the object of a preposition.

**objective case** The pronouns used as the direct object, indirect object, and object of a preposition are all the same in English. They are called the objective case pronouns.

**past participle** The past participle form of the verb generally ends in *–ado* or *–ido* unless it is irregular. It can be changed into an adjective or used with a helping verb.

**person** The pronoun and form of verb that indicates the person involved. *See also* **first person; second person; third person.**

**personal *a*** The preposition *a* is placed in front of any word that refers to a person or people and serves as the direct object of the sentence.

**possessive** An adjective or pronoun that shows ownership.

**preposition** Prepositions are words that are used in front of nouns, pronouns, or the infinitives of verbs to form phrases that typically describe a relationship of time or space.

**preposition pronoun** In Spanish there is a specific group of pronouns that must be used to replace a noun after a preposition. Any pronoun that you use immediately following a preposition must be an object of the preposition.

**present progressive** The present tense of the verb *estar* (to be) is used with the present participle *(–iendo, –ando, –yendo)* form of the verb to indicate an ongoing action in the present, or an action that is in progress.

**preterite indicators** To determine which of the two Spanish tenses is appropriate in a sentence, look for specific words *(una vez, anoche, el año pasado)* called preterite indicators that indicate that the preterite should be used.

**preterite** The preterite is used in Spanish to focus on a specific instance, a single occurrence, or the beginning or completion of an action in the past.

**pronoun** A word that takes the place of a noun. A pronoun functions as the same part of speech and has the same person, number, and gender as the noun it replaces.

**reflexive** Indicates that the subject and the recipient of the action of the sentence are the same.

**reflexive pronoun** Specific pronouns used with reflexive verbs to indicate that the subject and the recipient of the action are the same.

**reflexive verb** A verb that has a reflexive pronoun used with it either to indicate that the subject and the recipient of the action of the verb are the same or to indicate reciprocity between members of the subject.

**second person** Indicates that the subject of the verb is *you (tú* or *usted). Tú* is used to address someone informally (first-name basis), and *Usted* is used to address someone formally (or who is older).

**simple prepositions** Single-word prepositions such as *a, en, de,* and *sin.*

**stem** The stem of a verb is what is left when you remove the *–ar, –er,* or *–ir* from the infinitive form. This is also called the base of the verb.

**stem-changing verbs** A verb that changes the stem from *e>ie, o>ue,* or *e>i* in all forms except *nosotros/nosotras* and *vosotros/vosotras.* Stem-changing verbs must be memorized. There is no way to know otherwise whether a verb requires a stem change or not.

**stress** There are very specific rules that govern the syllable that is pronounced most strongly in any given word. This is called the natural stress of a word. A written accent mark indicates a vowel that is stressed but that would not be according to the rules that govern the natural stress of a word.

**subject case** Pronouns are grouped in cases. The pronouns used to replace a noun that is the subject of the sentence must come from the subject case.

**subject pronoun** To replace a noun that is the subject of the sentence with a pronoun, you must use one of the pronouns from the subject pronoun case.

**subject** The person, place, or thing responsible for the action of the verb.

**superlative** The extreme form of an adjective in English often ends in *–est.* Or they can be irregular: the most, least, best, worst. In Spanish there are also a few irregulars, but most superlatives are either created with the suffix

–*ísimo* or created by using an idiomatic expression.

**tense** The time indicated by the verb of a sentence, for example, past, present, future, and conditional.

**third person** The third person form of the verb in Spanish is used with the singular pronouns *él* (he), *ella* (she), or *usted* (you, formal, singular), and the plural pronouns *ellos* (they, masculine), *ellas* (they, feminine), and *ustedes* (you, formal, plural).

**tilde** A mark (˜) over the letter *ñ,* which indicates the pronunciation is like the "ny" in the English word "canyon."

**transitive verbs** A verb that accepts a direct object is called transitive.

**umlaut** A symbol over the letter *ü* that indicates the *u* is pronounced in situations when it normally would not be pronounced.

**verb** A word expressing an action or a state of being.

**verb conjugation** The categorizing of verbs according to the forms used for each subject and in each tense.

**verb conjugation** To inflect a verb in its forms for distinctions such as number, person, voice, mood, and tense; to break the infinitive form down into one of the six verb forms to match the appropriate subject of the sentence.

**vowel** In both Spanish and English, the vowels are the letters *a, e, i, o, u,* and, sometimes, *y.*

# Appendix A
# THEMATIC VOCABULARY

**A** good way to improve your vocabulary is to make flashcards for the following lists and study them.

The definite article is included with each noun, so be sure to learn the gender as you learn the noun. It may help to put the feminine words on pink flashcards and the masculine nouns on blue flashcards. Some lists also include other parts of speech such as adjectives and verbs. Remember that verbs end in *–ar, –er,* or *–ir* in Spanish. If an adjective ends in *–o,* remember that it quite likely has four forms (for example, *bueno = buena, buenos, buenas*).

## Animals

| | | | |
|---|---|---|---|
| *el animal* | animal | *el león* | lion |
| *el burro* | donkey | *el pájaro* | bird |
| *el caballo* | horse | *el perro* | dog |
| *el elefante* | elephant | *el tiburón* | shark |
| *la gallina* | hen | *el tigre* | tiger |
| *el gallo* | rooster | *la vaca* | cow |
| *el gato* | cat | | |

## Body and Health

| | | | |
|---|---|---|---|
| *la barba* | beard | *el cabello, el pelo* | hair |
| *la barbilla* | chin | *la cabeza* | head |
| *el bigote* | mustache | *el cáncer* | cancer |
| *la boca* | mouth | *la cara, el rostro* | face |
| *el brazo* | arm | *la ceja* | eyebrow |

| | | | |
|---|---|---|---|
| *el cerebro* | brain | *el pecho, el seno* | chest, breast |
| *la cintura* | waist | *el pie* | foot |
| *el codo* | elbow | *la piel* | skin |
| *el cuello* | neck | *la pierna* | leg |
| *la cura* | cure | *el pulgar* | thumb |
| *el dedo* | finger | *el pulmón* | lung |
| *los dientes* | teeth | *el puño* | fist |
| *el dolor* | pain, ache | *la receta* | prescription |
| *la enfermedad* | illness | *el resfriado* | cold (illness) |
| *la enfermera* | nurse | *la rodilla* | knee |
| *la espalda* | back | *la salud* | health |
| *el esqueleto* | skeleton | *la sangre* | blood |
| *la fiebre* | fever | *el tobillo* | ankle |
| *la frente* | forehead | *la uña* | fingernail |
| *la garganta* | throat | **Verbs** | |
| *el hígado* | liver | *cuidar* | to care for |
| *el hombro* | shoulder | *doler* | to ache, hurt |
| *el hueso* | bone | *ejercer* | to practice a profession, to exert |
| *la lengua* | tongue | | |
| *la mano* | hand | *ejercitar* | to exercise, to practice |
| *la medicina* | medicine | | |
| *la mejilla* | cheek | *empeorar* | to get worse |
| *la muñeca* | wrist | *enfermarse* | to get sick |
| *el músculo* | muscle | *estornudar* | to sneeze |
| *la nariz* | nose | *mejorarse* | to get better |
| *el oído* | inner ear | *padecer, sufrir* | to suffer |
| *la oreja* | outer ear | *recuperar* | to recuperate |
| *los ojos* | eyes | *toser* | to cough |
| *las pastillas* | pills | | |

# Clothing

| | | | |
|---|---|---|---|
| el abrigo | coat | el guante | glove |
| el anillo, la sortija | ring | la manga | sleeve |
| los anteojos, las gafas, los lentes | eyeglasses | la media | stocking, hose |
| | | la moda | fashion |
| los aretes, los pendientes | earrings | los pantalones | pants |
| | | los pantalones cortos | shorts |
| el atavío | attire | el pañuelo | handkerchief, tissue |
| la blusa | blouse | | |
| la bolsa, el bolso | purse, handbag | el pijama | pajamas |
| el bolsillo | pocket | la pulsera | bracelet |
| el botón | button | el saco | blazer |
| los calcetines, las medias | socks | el sombrero | hat |
| | | el traje | suit |
| la camisa | shirt | el traje de baño | bathing suit |
| la camiseta | T-shirt | el uniforme | uniform |
| el camisón | nightgown | el vestido | dress |
| la cartera | wallet, purse | los zapatos | shoes |
| el calzado | footwear | **Verbs** | |
| el collar | necklace | coser | to sew |
| la corbata | tie, necktie | llevar | to wear |
| el chaleco | vest | ponerse | to put on |
| la chaqueta | jacket | probarse | to try on |
| el cinturón | belt | quedarle, caber | to fit |
| el diseño | design | quitarse | to take off |
| el estilo | style | vestirse | to get dressed |
| la falda | skirt | | |
| la gorra | (baseball) cap | | |

# Days of the Week

(are not capitalized in Spanish)

| | | | |
|---|---|---|---|
| *domingo* | Sunday | *jueves* | Thursday |
| *lunes* | Monday | *viernes* | Friday |
| *martes* | Tuesday | *sábado* | Saturday |
| *miércoles* | Wednesday | | |

# Family

| | | | |
|---|---|---|---|
| *la abuela* | grandmother | *la nieta* | granddaughter |
| *el abuelo* | grandfather | *el nieto* | grandson |
| *la esposa* | wife | *el padre* | father |
| *el esposo* | husband | *los padres* | parents |
| *la familia* | family | *el papá* | dad |
| *la hermana* | sister | *los parientes* | relatives |
| *el hermano* | brother | *la prima* | cousin (female) |
| *la hija* | daughter | *el primo* | cousin (male) |
| *el hijo* | son | *la sobrina* | niece |
| *la madre* | mother | *el sobrino* | nephew |
| *la mamá* | mom | *la tía* | aunt |
| *el marido* | husband | *el tío* | uncle |

# Foods

| | | | |
|---|---|---|---|
| *el agua* | water | *el chocolate* | chocolate |
| *el alimento* | food | *la ensalada* | salad |
| *el azúcar* | sugar | *la fruta* | fruit |
| *el café* | coffee | *la gaseosa* | soda pop |
| *la carne* | meat | *el helado* | ice cream |
| *la cereza* | cherry | *el huevo* | egg |

| | | | |
|---|---|---|---|
| *la leche* | milk | *el pollo* | chicken |
| *la legumbre* | vegetable | *el postre* | dessert |
| *el limón* | lemon/lime | *el queso* | cheese |
| *la mantequilla* | butter | *el refresco* | beverage |
| *la manzana* | apple | *la sal* | salt |
| *la naranja* | orange | *la sopa* | soup |
| *el pan* | bread | *el té* | tea |
| *el pastel* | pastry, pie | *el vino* | wine |
| *la papa* | potato | **Verbs** | |
| *la patata* | potato | *beber* | to drink |
| *la pera* | pear | *comer* | to eat |
| *el pescado* | fish | *tomar* | to take, to drink |
| *la pimienta* | pepper | | |

## Home

| | | | |
|---|---|---|---|
| *la acera* | sidewalk | *la batidora* | blender |
| *la alcoba,* *el cuarto,* *el dormitorio* | bedroom | *la buhardilla,* *el desván* | attic |
| | | *la butaca, el sillón* | armchair |
| *la alfombra* | rug, carpet | *la cacerola,* *cazuela* | pan |
| *el apartamento,* *el departamento* | apartment | | |
| | | *la cama* | bed |
| *el armario* | closet | *la casa* | house |
| *el ascensor* | elevator | *el césped* | lawn |
| *la aspiradora* | vacuum cleaner | *el cesto, la canasta* | basket |
| *el azulejo* | tile | *la chimenea* | fireplace |
| *el balcón* | balcony | *la colcha* | bedspread |
| *el baño* | bathroom | *la cocina* | kitchen |
| *el barrio,* *el vecindario* | neighborhood | *el colchón* | mattress |

| | | | |
|---|---|---|---|
| *el comedor* | dining room | *la lavadora* | washer |
| *la cómoda* | dresser | *la manta* | blanket |
| *las cortinas* | curtains | *la mecedora* | rocking chair |
| *los cubiertos* | silverware | *la mesa* | table |
| *el cuarto* | (bed)room | *el (horno de) microondas* | microwave |
| *el cubo, el balde* | pail | | |
| *la cuna* | cradle | *los muebles* | the furniture |
| *el despacho* | office | *la nevera* | refrigerator |
| *el domicilio* | residence | *la pared* | wall |
| *el edificio* | the building | *el patio* | courtyard |
| *el enchufe* | socket, electrical outlet | *la piscina* | swimming pool |
| *la escalera* | stairs | *el piso* | floor (level) |
| *el escritorio* | desk | *el polvo* | dust |
| *el estante* | bookshelf, bookcase | *el rincón* | corner |
| | | *la sábana* | sheet |
| *la estufa* | stove | *la sala* | living room |
| *el fregadero* | kitchen sink | *la secadora* | dryer |
| *la funda* | pillowcase | *la silla* | chair |
| *el gabinete* | cabinet, library room, closet | *el sofá* | sofa |
| | | *el sótano* | basement |
| *la gaveta, el cajón* | drawer | *el suelo* | floor |
| *el grifo, la llave* | faucet | *el techo* | roof |
| *la habitación* | room | *el timbre* | doorbell |
| *la hierba, el césped* | grass | *la tubería* | plumbing |
| *el horno* | oven | *el vecino* | the neighbor |
| *la lámpara* | lamp | *la ventana* | the window |

# Months of the Year

(are not capitalized in Spanish)

| | | | |
|---|---|---|---|
| *enero* | January | *julio* | July |
| *febrero* | February | *agosto* | August |
| *marzo* | March | *septiembre* | September |
| *abril* | April | *octubre* | October |
| *mayo* | May | *noviembre* | November |
| *junio* | June | *diciembre* | December |

# Nature

| | | | |
|---|---|---|---|
| *el aire* | air | *la montaña* | mountain |
| *el árbol* | tree | *el monte* | hill, mountain, woodland |
| *el bosque* | forest | *el mundo* | world (Earth) |
| *el campo* | countryside | *la naturaleza* | nature |
| *el cielo* | sky | *la nube* | cloud |
| *la estrella* | star | *la planta* | plant |
| *la flor* | flower | *la playa* | beach |
| *la hierba* | grass | *el río* | river |
| *la hoja* | leaf | *el sol* | sun |
| *el jardín* | garden | *la tierra* | land, earth, dirt |
| *la luna* | moon | | |

# Neighborhood and Buildings

| | | | |
|---|---|---|---|
| *el aeropuerto* | airport | *el barrio* | neighborhood |
| *la aldea* | the village | *la biblioteca* | library |
| *el almacén* | store | *la bodega, la tienda* | grocery store |
| *la autopista, la carretera* | highway | *el buzón* | mailbox |
| *el banco* | bank, bench | *la calle* | street |

| | | | |
|---|---|---|---|
| *la cárcel* | prison | *la manzana* | city block |
| *la carnicería* | butcher shop, meat market | *el mercado* | market |
| | | *el museo* | museum |
| *la casa (oficina) de correos* | post office | *el palacio* | palace |
| *la catedral* | cathedral | *la panadería* | bakery |
| *el centro* | downtown | *la parada* | bus stop |
| *la cuadra* | block | *el parque* | park |
| *el edificio* | building | *la plaza* | town square |
| *la estación* | station | *el puente* | bridge |
| *el estadio* | stadium | *el supermercado* | supermarket |
| *la farmacia* | drug store | *el templo* | temple |
| *el hospital* | hospital | *la tienda* | store |
| *el hotel* | hotel | *la zapatería* | shoe store |
| *la iglesia* | church | | |

## School

| | | | |
|---|---|---|---|
| *la alumna* | pupil (female) | *la clase* | class |
| *el alumno* | pupil (male) | *el colegio* | private school |
| *la asignatura, la materia* | subject, course | *el conocimiento* | knowledge |
| | | *el cuaderno* | notebook |
| *el aula, la sala de clase* | classroom | *el curso* | course (of study) |
| *el bachillerato* | high school | | |
| *la beca* | scholarship | *la tarea* | homework |
| *el borrador* | eraser, draft | *el decano* | dean |
| *las calificaciones, las notas* | grades | *el director* | principal |
| | | *la enseñanza* | teaching |
| *la carrera* | career | *el error* | mistake |
| *la ciudad universitaria* | college (university) campus | *la escuela de artes y oficios* | vocational school |

| | | | |
|---|---|---|---|
| *la escuela de comercio* | business school | *la matrícula* | registration |
| *la escuela pública* | public school | *la mochila, el morral* | bookbag, backpack |
| *la escuela secundaria* | middle school, high school | *el nivel* | level |
| *la escuela técnica* | technical school | *la nota* | mark (grade) |
| | | *la página* | page |
| *la especialización* | major (course of study) | *la palabra* | word |
| | | *el papel* | paper |
| *el estudiante* | student (male) | *el párrafo* | paragraph |
| *la estudiante* | student (female) | *el pensamiento* | thought |
| *el examen* | test | *la pizarra, el pizarrón* | chalkboard |
| *la facultad* | professional school (within the university system) | *el bolígrafo* | pen |
| | | *la (escuela) primaria* | elementary school |
| *la frase* | sentence | *el profesor* | teacher |
| *la habilidad/ destreza* | skill | *la profesora* | teacher (female) |
| *el horario* | schedule | *el profesorado* | faculty |
| *el jardín de infantes, el kinder* | kindergarten | *la prueba* | quiz/test |
| | | *el puntaje* | score |
| | | *el pupitre* | student's desk |
| *el lápiz* | pencil | *el requisito* | requirement |
| *la lección* | lesson | *la residencia estudiantil* | dormitory |
| *el libro* | book | | |
| *la licenciatura* | university degree, masters degree | *el semestre* | semester |
| | | *la sabiduría* | wisdom |
| *la maestra* | teacher (female) | *la (escuela) secundaria, superior* | high school |
| *el maestro* | teacher (male) | | |

| | | | |
|---|---|---|---|
| *el título* | diploma | *matricularse* | to register |
| *el vocabulario* | vocabulary | *poner/prestar atención* | to pay attention |
| *las vacaciones escolares* | school breaks | *preguntar* | to ask a question |

**Verbs**

| | | | |
|---|---|---|---|
| *aprender* | to learn | *realizar* | to fulfill, to make real |
| *aprobar* | to pass | *reprobar, suspender (una asignatura)* | to fail a course |
| *asistir a* | to attend | | |
| *comportarse bien* | to behave | *responder* | to answer |
| *contestar* | to answer | *solicitar* | to apply, to ask for |
| *enseñar* | to teach | | |
| *entrenarse* | to train | *tomar apuntes* | to take notes |
| *escoger* | to choose | | |

**Adjectives**

| | | | |
|---|---|---|---|
| *explicar* | to explain | *aplicado, trabajador* | hard working |
| *faltar* | to miss, to skip | *cotidiano* | daily |
| *graduarse* | to graduate | *exigente* | demanding |
| *ingresar* | to enroll | *optativo* | elective |
| *licenciarse* | to graduate with a professional degree | | |

## Sports, Diversions, and Amusements

| | | | |
|---|---|---|---|
| *el baloncesto, el basquetbol* | basketball | *las diversiones* | amusements |
| | | *el fútbol* | football |
| *el béisbol* | baseball | *la lucha libre* | wrestling |
| *la canción* | song | *la música* | music |
| *el cine* | movie theater (the movies) | *la natación* | swimming |
| | | *la película* | film |
| *el concierto* | concert | *el programa* | program |
| *el disco compacto* | CD | | |

| | | | |
|---|---|---|---|
| *la radio* | the radio broadcast | *el vólibol* | volleyball |
| | | **Verbs** | |
| *el teatro* | theater (live acting) | *bailar* | to dance |
| | | *cantar* | to sing |
| *la televisión* | television (industry, medium) | *jugar (u>ue)* | to play a sport or game |
| *el televisor* | television set | *nadar* | to swim |
| *el tenis* | tennis | *patinar* | to skate |
| *el tocadiscos* | CD player | *tocar* | to play (an instrument) |
| *el video* | video | | |

## Travel

| | | | |
|---|---|---|---|
| *el autobús* | bus | *el este* | east |
| *el automóvil, el carro, el coche* | car | *el norte* | north |
| | | *el oeste* | west |
| *el avión* | plane | *el sur* | south |
| *el baúl* | trunk | *el ferrocarril* | train |
| *la bicicleta* | bicycle | *la maleta* | suitcase |
| *el billete, el pasaje* | ticket | *el tren* | train |
| *el camino* | road, path | *el viaje* | trip, voyage |

## Weather and Seasons

| | | | |
|---|---|---|---|
| *la estación* | season | *la nieve* | snow |
| *la primavera* | spring | *el tiempo* | weather |
| *el verano* | summer | **Weather Expressions** | |
| *el otoño* | autumn | *Hace calor.* | It's hot. |
| *el invierno* | winter | *Hace fresco.* | It's cool |

| | | | |
|---|---|---|---|
| *Hace frío.* | It's cold. | **Verbs** | |
| *Hace viento.* | It's windy. | *llover (o>ue)* | to rain |
| *Hace sol.* | It's sunny. | *nevar (e>ie)* | to snow |

## Work

| | | | |
|---|---|---|---|
| *el abogado* | lawyer | *el criado* | servant |
| *el actor* | actor | *el cura, el padre,* | priest |
| *la actriz* | actress | *el sacerdote,* | |
| *el agricultor,* | farmer | *el párroco* | |
| *el campesino,* | | *el chófer* | chauffeur |
| *el granjero* | | *el, la dentista* | dentist |
| *el ama de casa* | housewife | *el dependiente* | sales clerk |
| *el artesano* | craftsman | *el doctor, el médico* | doctor |
| *el, la atleta* | athlete | *el dueño,* | owner |
| *el bailarín* | dancer | *el propietario* | |
| *el barbero* | barber | *el empleo,* | job, work |
| *el bibliotecario* | librarian | *el trabajo* | |
| *el bombero* | firefighter | *la enfermera* | nurse |
| *el cajero* | bank teller | *la entrevista* | interview |
| *el carnicero* | butcher | *la fábrica* | factory |
| *el carpintero* | carpenter | *el farmacéutico* | druggist, pharmacist |
| *el científico* | scientist | *el fontanero,* | plumber |
| *el cirujano* | surgeon | *el plomero* | |
| *el cocinero* | cook | *el gerente* | manager |
| *el, la comerciante* | merchant, businessman (woman) | *el ingeniero* | engineer |
| | | *el jardinero* | gardener |
| | | *el jefe* | boss |
| *la compañía,* | company | *el, la juez* | judge |
| *la empresa* | | *el locutor* | announcer |
| *el contador* | accountant | | |

| | | | |
|---|---|---|---|
| *el maestro* | teacher | *la solicitud* | application |
| *el marinero* | sailor | *el sueldo* | salary (pay) |
| *el mecánico* | mechanic | *el taller* | shop |
| *el ministro* | minister | *el traductor* | translator |
| *el modisto* | dressmaker, fashion designer | *el abastecedor* | provider, caterer, grocer |

**Verbs**

| | | | |
|---|---|---|---|
| *el negocio* | business | *aprovecharse de* | to take advantage of |
| *la niñera* | babysitter | | |
| *el, la oculista* | eye doctor | *avanzar* | to advance |
| *el obrero* | worker | *conseguir* | to get |
| *el oficio* | occupation | *contratar* | to hire |
| *el panadero* | baker | *despedir* | to fire |
| *el peluquero* | hairdresser | *entrevistar* | to interview |
| *el, la periodista* | journalist, newspaperman | *llenar* | to fill |
| | | *lograr* | to achieve |
| *el policía* | the policeman | *negociar* | to negotiate |
| *el redactor* | editor | *obtener* | to obtain |
| *el reportero* | reporter | *rechazar* | to reject |
| *el sastre* | tailor | *rellenar* | to fill out |
| *la secretaria* | secretary | *trabajar* | to work |
| *el soldado* | soldier | | |

# APPENDIX B
# VERB CHARTS

This book covers the verb tenses and forms presented in the first two years of foreign language study. Because each tense is taught separately, it is difficult to visualize how the forms for any given verb compare in the different tenses. This appendix provides the charts for the most common verbs in the forms and tenses presented in this book.

## The Verb *Hablar*

The verb *hablar* is a regular *–ar* verb in all forms and tenses.

> *hablar* = to speak
> gerund form = *hablando*
> past participle = *hablado*

## Present tense

| | |
|---|---|
| *yo hablo* | *nosotros/nosotras hablamos* |
| *tú hablas* | *vosotros/vosotras habláis* |
| *él habla* | *ellos hablan* |
| *ella habla* | *ellas hablan* |
| *usted habla* | *ustedes hablan* |

## Preterite tense

| | |
|---|---|
| *yo hablé* | *nosotros/nosotras hablamos* |
| *tú hablaste* | *vosotros/vosotras hablasteis* |
| *él habló* | *ellos hablaron* |
| *ella habló* | *ellas hablaron* |
| *usted habló* | *ustedes hablaron* |

## Imperfect tense

| | |
|---|---|
| yo hablaba | nosotros/nosotras hablábamos |
| tú hablabas | vosotros/vosotras hablabais |
| él hablaba | ellos hablaban |
| ella hablaba | ellas hablaban |
| usted hablaba | ustedes hablaban |

## Command forms

| Infinitive | Usted Affirmative | Usted Negative | Ustedes Affirmative | Ustedes Negative | Tú Affirmative | Tú Negative |
|---|---|---|---|---|---|---|
| hablar | hable | no hable | hablen | no hablen | habla | no hables |

# The Verb *Comer*

The verb *comer* is a regular –*er* verb in all forms and tenses.

> *comer* = to eat
> gerund form = *comiendo*
> past participle = *comido*

## Present tense

| | |
|---|---|
| yo como | nosotros/nosotras comemos |
| tú comes | vosotros/vosotras coméis |
| él come | ellos comen |
| ella come | ellas comen |
| usted come | ustedes comen |

## Preterite tense

| | |
|---|---|
| yo comí | nosotros/nosotras comimos |
| tú comiste | vosotros/vosotras comisteis |
| él comió | ellos comieron |
| ella comió | ellas comieron |
| usted comió | ustedes comieron |

## Imperfect tense

| | |
|---|---|
| yo comía | nosotros/nosotras comíamos |
| tú comías | vosotros/vosotras comíais |
| él comía | ellos comían |
| ella comía | ellas comían |
| usted comía | ustedes comían |

## Command forms

| Infinitive | Usted Affirmative | Usted Negative | Ustedes Affirmative | Ustedes Negative | Tú Affirmative | Tú Negative |
|---|---|---|---|---|---|---|
| comer | coma | no coma | coman | no coman | come | no comas |

# The Verb *Escribir*

The verb *escribir* is a regular *–ir* verb in all forms and tenses.

> *escribir* = to write
> gerund form = *escribiendo*
> past participle = *escrito*

## Present tense

| | |
|---|---|
| yo escribo | nosotros/nosotras escribimos |
| tú escribes | vosotros/vosotras escribís |
| él escribe | ellos escriben |
| ella escribe | ellas escriben |
| usted escribe | ustedes escriben |

## Preterite tense

| | |
|---|---|
| yo escribí | nosotros/nosotras escribimos |
| tú escribiste | vosotros/vosotras escribisteis |
| él escribió | ellos escribieron |
| ella escribió | ellas escribieron |
| usted escribió | ustedes escribieron |

## Imperfect tense

| | |
|---|---|
| *yo escribía* | *nosotros/nosotras escribíamos* |
| *tú escribías* | *vosotros/vosotras escribíais* |
| *él escribía* | *ellos escribían* |
| *ella escribía* | *ellas escribían* |
| *usted escribía* | *ustedes escribían* |

## Command forms

| *Infinitive* | Usted *Affirmative* | Usted *Negative* | Ustedes *Affirmative* | Ustedes *Negative* | Tú *Affirmative* | Tú *Negative* |
|---|---|---|---|---|---|---|
| *escribir* | *escriba* | *no escriba* | *escriban* | *no escriban* | *escribe* | *no escribas* |

# The Verb *Ir*

The verb *ir* is irregular in almost all forms and tenses.

> *ir* = to go
> gerund form = *yendo*
> past participle = *ido*

## Present tense

| | |
|---|---|
| *yo voy* | *nosotros/nosotras vamos* |
| *tú vas* | *vosotros/vosotras vais* |
| *él va* | *ellos van* |
| *ella va* | *ellas van* |
| *usted va* | *ustedes van* |

## Preterite tense

| | |
|---|---|
| *yo fui* | *nosotros/nosotras fuimos* |
| *tú fuiste* | *vosotros/vosotras fuisteis* |
| *él fue* | *ellos fueron* |
| *ella fue* | *ellas fueron* |
| *usted fue* | *ustedes fueron* |

## Imperfect tense

| | |
|---|---|
| *yo iba* | *nosotros/nosotras íbamos* |
| *tú ibas* | *vosotros/vosotras ibais* |
| *él iba* | *ellos iban* |
| *ella iba* | *ellas iban* |
| *usted iba* | *ustedes iban* |

## Command forms

| *Infinitive* | Usted *Affirmative* | Usted *Negative* | Ustedes *Affirmative* | Ustedes *Negative* | Tú *Affirmative* | Tú *Negative* |
|---|---|---|---|---|---|---|
| *ir* | *vaya* | *no vaya* | *vayan* | *no vayan* | *ve* | *no vayas* |

# The Verb *Ser*

The verb *ser* is irregular in almost all forms and tenses.

> *ser* = to be
> gerund form = *siendo*
> past participle = *sido*

## Present tense

| | |
|---|---|
| *yo soy* | *nosotros/nosotras somos* |
| *tú eres* | *vosotros/vosotras sois* |
| *él es* | *ellos son* |
| *ella es* | *ellas son* |
| *usted es* | *ustedes son* |

## Preterite tense

| | |
|---|---|
| *yo fui* | *nosotros/nosotras fuimos* |
| *tú fuiste* | *vosotros/vosotras fuisteis* |
| *él fue* | *ellos fueron* |
| *ella fue* | *ellas fueron* |
| *usted fue* | *ustedes fueron* |

## Imperfect tense

| | |
|---|---|
| *yo era* | *nosotros/nosotras éramos* |
| *tú eras* | *vosotros/vosotras erais* |
| *él era* | *ellos eran* |
| *ella era* | *ellas eran* |
| *usted era* | *ustedes eran* |

## Command forms

| *Infinitive* | Usted *Affirmative* | Usted *Negative* | Ustedes *Affirmative* | Ustedes *Negative* | Tú *Affirmative* | Tú *Negative* |
|---|---|---|---|---|---|---|
| *ser* | *sea* | *no sea* | *sean* | *no sean* | *sé* | *no seas* |

# The Verb *Dar*

The verb *dar* is irregular in some forms and tenses.

> *dar* = to give
> gerund form = *dando*
> past participle = *dado*

## Present tense

| | |
|---|---|
| *yo doy* | *nosotros/nosotras damos* |
| *tú das* | *vosotros/vosotras dais* |
| *él da* | *ellos dan* |
| *ella da* | *ellas dan* |
| *usted da* | *ustedes dan* |

## Preterite tense

| | |
|---|---|
| *yo di* | *nosotros/nosotras dimos* |
| *tú diste* | *vosotros/vosotras disteis* |
| *él dio* | *ellos dieron* |
| *ella dio* | *ellas dieron* |
| *usted dio* | *ustedes dieron* |

## Imperfect tense

| | |
|---|---|
| *yo daba* | *nosotros/nosotras dábamos* |
| *tú dabas* | *vosotros/vosotras dabais* |
| *él daba* | *ellos daban* |
| *ella daba* | *ellas daban* |
| *usted daba* | *ustedes daban* |

## Command forms

| *Infinitive* | Usted<br>*Affirmative* | Usted<br>*Negative* | Ustedes<br>*Affirmative* | Ustedes<br>*Negative* | Tú<br>*Affirmative* | Tú<br>*Negative* |
|---|---|---|---|---|---|---|
| *dar* | *dé* | *no dé* | *den* | *no den* | *da* | *no des* |

# The Verb *Estar*

The verb *estar* is irregular in some forms and tenses.

> *estar* = to be
> gerund form = *estando*
> past participle = *estado*

## Present tense

| | |
|---|---|
| *yo estoy* | *nosotros/nosotras estamos* |
| *tú estás* | *vosotros/vosotras estáis* |
| *él está* | *ellos están* |
| *ella está* | *ellas están* |
| *usted está* | *ustedes están* |

## Preterite tense

| | |
|---|---|
| *yo estuve* | *nosotros/nosotras estuvimos* |
| *tú estuviste* | *vosotros/vosotras estuvisteis* |
| *él estuvo* | *ellos estuvieron* |
| *ella estuvo* | *ellas estuvieron* |
| *usted estuvo* | *ustedes estuvieron* |

## Imperfect tense

| | |
|---|---|
| yo estaba | nosotros/nosotras estábamos |
| tú estabas | vosotros/vosotras estabais |
| él estaba | ellos estaban |
| ella estaba | ellas estaban |
| usted estaba | ustedes estaban |

## Command forms

| Infinitive | Usted Affirmative | Usted Negative | Ustedes Affirmative | Ustedes Negative | Tú Affirmative | Tú Negative |
|---|---|---|---|---|---|---|
| estar | esté | no esté | estén | no estén | está | no estés |

# The Verb *Hacer*

The verb *hacer* is irregular in some forms and tenses.

  *hacer* = to make or to do
  gerund form = *haciendo*
  past participle = *hecho*

## Present tense

| | |
|---|---|
| yo hago | nosotros/nosotras hacemos |
| tú haces | vosotros/vosotras hacéis |
| él hace | ellos hacen |
| ella hace | ellas hacen |
| usted hace | ustedes hacen |

## Preterite tense

| | |
|---|---|
| yo hice | nosotros/nosotras hicimos |
| tú hiciste | vosotros/vosotras hicisteis |
| él hizo | ellos hicieron |
| ella hizo | ellas hicieron |
| usted hizo | ustedes hicieron |

## Imperfect tense

| | |
|---|---|
| *yo hacía* | *nosotros/nosotras hacíamos* |
| *tú hacías* | *vosotros/vosotras hacíais* |
| *él hacía* | *ellos hacían* |
| *ella hacía* | *ellas hacían* |
| *usted hacía* | *ustedes hacían* |

## Command forms

| *Infinitive* | Usted *Affirmative* | Usted *Negative* | Ustedes *Affirmative* | Ustedes *Negative* | Tú *Affirmative* | Tú *Negative* |
|---|---|---|---|---|---|---|
| *hacer* | *haga* | *no haga* | *hagan* | *no hagan* | *haz* | *no hagas* |

# The Verb *Poner*

The verb *poner* is irregular in some forms and tenses.

> *poner* = to put
> gerund form = *poniendo*
> past participle = *puesto*

## Present tense

| | |
|---|---|
| *yo pongo* | *nosotros/nosotras ponemos* |
| *tú pones* | *vosotros/vosotras ponéis* |
| *él pone* | *ellos ponen* |
| *ella pone* | *ellas ponen* |
| *usted pone* | *ustedes ponen* |

## Preterite tense

| | |
|---|---|
| *yo puse* | *nosotros/nosotras pusimos* |
| *tú pusiste* | *vosotros/vosotras pusisteis* |
| *él puso* | *ellos pusieron* |
| *ella puso* | *ellas pusieron* |
| *usted puso* | *ustedes pusieron* |

## Imperfect tense

| | |
|---|---|
| *yo ponía* | *nosotros/nosotras poníamos* |
| *tú ponías* | *vosotros/vosotras poníais* |
| *él ponía* | *ellos ponían* |
| *ella ponía* | *ellas ponían* |
| *usted ponía* | *ustedes ponían* |

## Command forms

| *Infinitive* | Usted *Affirmative* | Usted *Negative* | Ustedes *Affirmative* | Ustedes *Negative* | Tú *Affirmative* | Tú *Negative* |
|---|---|---|---|---|---|---|
| *poner* | *ponga* | *no ponga* | *pongan* | *no pongan* | *pon* | *no pongas* |

# The Verb *Salir*

The verb *salir* is irregular only in the *yo* form of the present tense (and command forms).

> *salir* = to leave
> gerund form = *saliendo*
> past participle = *salido*

## Present tense

| | |
|---|---|
| *yo salgo* | *nosotros/nosotras salimos* |
| *tú sales* | *vosotros/vosotras salís* |
| *él sale* | *ellos salen* |
| *ella sale* | *ellas salen* |
| *usted sale* | *ustedes salen* |

## Preterite tense

| | |
|---|---|
| *yo salí* | *nosotros/nosotras salimos* |
| *tú saliste* | *vosotros/vosotras salisteis* |

él salió                          ellos salieron

ella salió                        ellas salieron

usted salió                       ustedes salieron

## Imperfect tense

yo salía                          nosotros/nosotras salíamos

tú salías                         vosotros/vosotras salíais

él salía                          ellos salían

ella salía                        ellas salían

usted salía                       ustedes salían

## Command forms

| Infinitive | Usted Affirmative | Usted Negative | Ustedes Affirmative | Ustedes Negative | Tú Affirmative | Tú Negative |
|---|---|---|---|---|---|---|
| salir | salga | no salga | salgan | no salgan | sal | no salgas |

# The Verb *Ver*

The verb *ver* has several irregular forms including the past participle.

> *ver* = to see
>
> gerund form = *viendo*
>
> past participle = *visto*

## Present tense

yo veo                            nosotros/nosotras vemos

tú ves                            vosotros/vosotras veis

él ve                             ellos ven

ella ve                           ellas ven

usted ve                          ustedes ven

## Preterite tense

| | |
|---|---|
| *yo vi* | *nosotros/nosotras vimos* |
| *tú viste* | *vosotros/vosotras visteis* |
| *él vio* | *ellos vieron* |
| *ella vio* | *ellas vieron* |
| *usted vio* | *ustedes vieron* |

## Imperfect tense

| | |
|---|---|
| *yo veía* | *nosotros/nosotras veíamos* |
| *tú veías* | *vosotros/vosotras veíais* |
| *él veía* | *ellos veían* |
| *ella veía* | *ellas veían* |
| *usted veía* | *ustedes veían* |

## Command forms

| Infinitive | Usted Affirmative | Usted Negative | Ustedes Affirmative | Ustedes Negative | Tú Affirmative | Tú Negative |
|---|---|---|---|---|---|---|
| *ver* | *vea* | *no vea* | *vean* | *no vean* | *ve* | *no veas* |

# The Verb *Saber*

The verb *saber* has issues in all tenses except the imperfect tense.

> *saber* = to know a fact
> gerund form = *sabiendo*
> past participle = *sabido*

## Present tense

| | |
|---|---|
| *yo sé* | *nosotros/nosotras sabemos* |
| *tú sabes* | *vosotros/vosotras sabéis* |
| *él sabe* | *ellos saben* |

| | |
|---|---|
| ella sabe | ellas saben |
| usted sabe | ustedes saben |

## Preterite tense

| | |
|---|---|
| yo supe | nosotros/nosotras supimos |
| tú supiste | vosotros/vosotras supisteis |
| él supo | ellos supieron |
| ella supo | ellas supieron |
| usted supo | ustedes supieron |

## Imperfect tense

| | |
|---|---|
| yo sabía | nosotros/nosotras sabíamos |
| tú sabías | vosotros/vosotras sabíais |
| él sabía | ellos sabían |
| ella sabía | ellas sabían |
| usted sabía | ustedes sabían |

## Command forms

| Infinitive | Usted Affirmative | Usted Negative | Ustedes Affirmative | Ustedes Negative | Tú Affirmative | Tú Negative |
|---|---|---|---|---|---|---|
| saber | sepa | no sepa | sepan | no sepan | sabe | no sepas |

# The Verb *Caer*

The verb *caer* looks strange in all its forms, and it has regular forms only in the imperfect tense.

> *caer* = to fall
> gerund form = *cayendo*
> past participle = *caído*

## Present tense

| | |
|---|---|
| *yo caigo* | *nosotros/nosotras caemos* |
| *tú caes* | *vosotros/vosotras caéis* |
| *él cae* | *ellos caen* |
| *ella cae* | *ellas caen* |
| *usted cae* | *ustedes caen* |

## Preterite tense

| | |
|---|---|
| *yo caí* | *nosotros/nosotras caímos* |
| *tú caíste* | *vosotros/vosotras caísteis* |
| *él cayó* | *ellos cayeron* |
| *ella cayó* | *ellas cayeron* |
| *usted cayó* | *ustedes cayeron* |

## Imperfect tense

| | |
|---|---|
| *yo caía* | *nosotros/nosotras caíamos* |
| *tú caías* | *vosotros/vosotras caíais* |
| *él caía* | *ellos caían* |
| *ella caía* | *ellas caían* |
| *usted caía* | *ustedes caían* |

## Command forms

| Infinitive | Usted Affirmative | Usted Negative | Ustedes Affirmative | Ustedes Negative | Tú Affirmative | Tú Negative |
|---|---|---|---|---|---|---|
| *caer* | *caiga* | *no caiga* | *caigan* | *no caigan* | *cae* | *no caigas* |

# The Verb *Traer*

The forms of the verb *traer* are like all the forms in the verb *caer* except the preterite.

*traer* = to bring
gerund form = *trayendo*
past participle = *traído*

## Present tense

| | |
|---|---|
| *yo traigo* | *nosotros/nosotras traemos* |
| *tú traes* | *vosotros/vosotras traéis* |
| *él trae* | *ellos traen* |
| *ella trae* | *ellas traen* |
| *usted trae* | *ustedes traen* |

## Preterite tense

| | |
|---|---|
| *yo traje* | *nosotros/nosotras trajimos* |
| *tú trajiste* | *vosotros/vosotras trajisteis* |
| *él trajo* | *ellos trajeron* |
| *ella trajo* | *ellas trajeron* |
| *usted trajo* | *ustedes trajeron* |

## Imperfect tense

| | |
|---|---|
| *yo traía* | *nosotros/nosotras traíamos* |
| *tú traías* | *vosotros/vosotras traíais* |
| *él traía* | *ellos traían* |
| *ella traía* | *ellas traían* |
| *usted traía* | *ustedes traían* |

## Command forms

| Infinitive | Usted Affirmative | Usted Negative | Ustedes Affirmative | Ustedes Negative | Tú Affirmative | Tú Negative |
|---|---|---|---|---|---|---|
| *traer* | *traiga* | *no traiga* | *traigan* | *no traigan* | *trae* | *no traigas* |

# The Verb *Pensar*

*Pensar* is a typical *–ar* verb with an *e>ie* stem change. All forms have regular endings, and they follow normal stem-changing patterns.

> *pensar* = to think
> gerund form = *pensando*
> past participle = *pensado*

## Present tense

| | |
|---|---|
| *yo pienso* | *nosotros/nosotras pensamos* |
| *tú piensas* | *vosotros/vosotras pensáis* |
| *él piensa* | *ellos piensan* |
| *ella piensa* | *ellas piensan* |
| *usted piensa* | *ustedes piensan* |

## Preterite tense

| | |
|---|---|
| *yo pensé* | *nosotros/nosotras pensamos* |
| *tú pensaste* | *vosotros/vosotras pensasteis* |
| *él pensó* | *ellos pensaron* |
| *ella pensó* | *ellas pensaron* |
| *usted pensó* | *ustedes pensaron* |

## Imperfect tense

| | |
|---|---|
| *yo pensaba* | *nosotros/nosotras pensábamos* |
| *tú pensabas* | *vosotros/vosotras pensabais* |
| *él pensaba* | *ellos pensaban* |
| *ella pensaba* | *ellas pensaban* |
| *usted pensaba* | *ustedes pensaban* |

## Command forms

| Infinitive | Usted Affirmative | Usted Negative | Ustedes Affirmative | Ustedes Negative | Tú Affirmative | Tú Negative |
|---|---|---|---|---|---|---|
| pensar | piense | no piense | piensen | no piensen | piensa | no pienses |

# The Verb *Mentir*

The verb *mentir* is a typical *–ir* verb with an *e>ie* stem change. All forms have regular endings, and they follow normal stem-changing patterns. Note that it follows a different stem-changing pattern in the preterite.

> *mentir* = to lie (to tell an untruth)
> gerund form = *mintiendo*
> past participle = *mentido*

## Present tense

| | |
|---|---|
| *yo miento* | *nosotros/nosotras mentimos* |
| *tú mientes* | *vosotros/vosotras mentís* |
| *él miente* | *ellos mienten* |
| *ella miente* | *ellas mienten* |
| *usted miente* | *ustedes mienten* |

## Preterite tense

| | |
|---|---|
| *yo mentí* | *nosotros/nosotras mentimos* |
| *tú mentiste* | *vosotros/vosotras mentisteis* |
| *él mintió* | *ellos mintieron* |
| *ella mintió* | *ellas mintieron* |
| *usted mintió* | *ustedes mintieron* |

## Imperfect tense

| | |
|---|---|
| *yo mentía* | *nosotros/nosotras mentíamos* |
| *tú mentías* | *vosotros/vosotras mentíais* |

| | |
|---|---|
| *él mentía* | *ellos mentían* |
| *ella mentía* | *ellas mentían* |
| *usted mentía* | *ustedes mentían* |

## Command forms

| Infinitive | Usted Affirmative | Usted Negative | Ustedes Affirmative | Ustedes Negative | Tú Affirmative | Tú Negative |
|---|---|---|---|---|---|---|
| *mentir* | *mienta* | *no mienta* | *mientan* | *no mientan* | *miente* | *no mientas* |

# The Verb *Tener*

The verb *tener* is very irregular in the Preterite but also is a stem changer. An irregular *yo* form in the present tense affects the command forms.

> *tener* = to have (possession)
> gerund form = *teniendo*
> past participle = *tenido*

## Present tense

| | |
|---|---|
| *yo tengo* | *nosotros/nosotras tenemos* |
| *tú tienes* | *vosotros/vosotras tenéis* |
| *él tiene* | *ellos tienen* |
| *ella tiene* | *ellas tienen* |
| *usted tiene* | *ustedes tienen* |

## Preterite tense

| | |
|---|---|
| *yo tuve* | *nosotros/nosotras tuvimos* |
| *tú tuviste* | *vosotros/vosotras tuvisteis* |
| *él tuvo* | *ellos tuvieron* |
| *ella tuvo* | *ellas tuvieron* |
| *usted tuvo* | *ustedes tuvieron* |

## Imperfect tense

yo tenía

tú tenías

él tenía

ella tenía

usted tenía

nosotros/nosotras teníamos

vosotros/vosotras teníais

ellos tenían

ellas tenían

ustedes tenían

## Command forms

| Infinitive | Usted Affirmative | Usted Negative | Ustedes Affirmative | Ustedes Negative | Tú Affirmative | Tú Negative |
|---|---|---|---|---|---|---|
| tener | tenga | no tenga | tengan | no tengan | ten | no tengas |

# The Verb *Venir*

The verb *venir* is a lot like *tener*. It is very irregular in the Preterite but also is a stem changer. An irregular *yo* form in the present tense affects the command forms.

venir = to come

gerund form = *viniendo*

past participle = *venido*

## Present tense

yo vengo

tú vienes

él viene

ella viene

usted viene

nosotros/nosotras venimos

vosotros/vosotras venís

ellos vienen

ellas vienen

ustedes vienen

## Preterite tense

yo vine

tú viniste

nosotros/nosotras vinimos

vosotros/vosotras vinisteis

| él vino | ellos vinieron |
|---------|----------------|
| ella vino | ellas vinieron |
| usted vino | ustedes vinieron |

## Imperfect tense

| yo venía | nosotros/nosotras veníamos |
|----------|----------------------------|
| tú venías | vosotros/vosotras veníais |
| él venía | ellos venían |
| ella venía | ellas venían |
| usted venía | ustedes venían |

## Command forms

| Infinitive | Usted Affirmative | Usted Negative | Ustedes Affirmative | Ustedes Negative | Tú Affirmative | Tú Negative |
|------------|-------------------|----------------|---------------------|------------------|----------------|-------------|
| venir | venga | no venga | vengan | no vengan | ven | no vengas |

# The Verb *Jugar*

*Jugar* is the only *u>ue* stem changer. It also has a *g>gu* spelling change in the command forms and the *yo* form of the Preterite.

> *jugar* = to play (a sport or game)
> gerund form = *jugando*
> past participle = *jugado*

## Present tense

| yo juego | nosotros/nosotras jugamos |
|----------|---------------------------|
| tú juegas | vosotros/vosotras jugáis |
| él juega | ellos juegan |
| ella juega | ellas juegan |
| usted (Ud.) juega | ustedes (Uds.) juegan |

## Preterite tense

yo jugué

tú jugaste

él jugó

ella jugó

usted jugó

nosotros/nosotras jugamos

vosotros/vosotras jugasteis

ellos jugaron

ellas jugaron

ustedes jugaron

## Imperfect tense

yo jugaba

tú jugabas

él jugaba

ella jugaba

usted jugaba

nosotros/nosotras jugábamos

vosotros/vosotras jugabais

ellos jugaban

ellas jugaban

ustedes jugaban

## Command forms

| Infinitive | Usted Affirmative | Usted Negative | Ustedes Affirmative | Ustedes Negative | Tú Affirmative | Tú Negative |
|---|---|---|---|---|---|---|
| jugar | juegue | no juegue | jueguen | no jueguen | juega | no juegues |

# The Verb *Dormir*

The verb *dormir* is a typical *–ir* verb with an *o>ue* stem change. All forms have regular endings, and they follow normal stem-changing patterns. Note that it follows a different stem-changing pattern in the preterite.

> *dormir* = to sleep
> gerund form = *durmiendo*
> past participle = *dormido*

## Present tense

yo duermo

tú duermes

nosotros/nosotras dormimos

vosotros/vosotras dormís

| | |
|---|---|
| él duerme | ellos duermen |
| ella duerme | ellas duermen |
| usted duerme | ustedes duermen |

## Preterite tense

| | |
|---|---|
| yo dormí | nosotros/nosotras dormimos |
| tú dormiste | vosotros/vosotras dormisteis |
| él durmió | ellos durmieron |
| ella durmió | ellas durmieron |
| usted durmió | ustedes durmieron |

## Imperfect tense

| | |
|---|---|
| yo dormía | nosotros/nosotras dormíamos |
| tú dormías | vosotros/vosotras dormíais |
| él dormía | ellos dormían |
| ella dormía | ellas dormían |
| usted dormía | ustedes dormían |

## Command forms

| Infinitive | Usted Affirmative | Usted Negative | Ustedes Affirmative | Ustedes Negative | Tú Affirmative | Tú Negative |
|---|---|---|---|---|---|---|
| dormir | duerma | no duerma | duerman | no duerman | duerme | no duermas |

## The Verb *Pedir*

*Pedir* is an *–ir* verb with an *e>i* stem change. Note that it follows a different stem-changing pattern in the preterite.

> *pedir* = to request
> gerund form = *pidiendo*
> past participle = *pedido*

## Present tense

yo pido

tú pides

él pide

ella pide

usted pide

nosotros/nosotras pedimos

vosotros/vosotras pedís

ellos piden

ellas piden

ustedes piden

## Preterite tense

yo pedí

tú pediste

él pidió

ella pidió

usted pidió

nosotros/nosotras pedimos

vosotros/vosotras pedisteis

ellos pidieron

ellas pidieron

ustedes pidieron

## Imperfect tense

yo pedía

tú pedías

él pedía

ella pedía

usted pedía

nosotros/nosotras pedíamos

vosotros/vosotras pedíais

ellos pedían

ellas pedían

ustedes pedían

## Command forms

| Infinitive | Usted Affirmative | Usted Negative | Ustedes Affirmative | Ustedes Negative | Tú Affirmative | Tú Negative |
|---|---|---|---|---|---|---|
| pedir | pida | no pida | pidan | no pidan | pide | no pidas |

# The Verb *Decir*

The verb *decir* has some irregularity in nearly every form and in every tense.

> *decir* = to say, tell
> gerund form = *diciendo*
> past participle = *dicho*

## Present tense

| | |
|---|---|
| *yo digo* | *nosotros/nosotras decimos* |
| *tú dices* | *vosotros/vosotras decís* |
| *él dice* | *ellos dicen* |
| *ella dice* | *ellas dicen* |
| *usted dice* | *ustedes dicen* |

## Preterite tense

| | |
|---|---|
| *yo dije* | *nosotros/nosotras dijimos* |
| *tú dijiste* | *vosotros/vosotras dijisteis* |
| *él dijo* | *ellos dijeron* |
| *ella dijo* | *ellas dijeron* |
| *usted dijo* | *ustedes dijeron* |

## Imperfect tense

| | |
|---|---|
| *yo decía* | *nosotros/nosotras decíamos* |
| *tú decías* | *vosotros/vosotras decíais* |
| *él decía* | *ellos decían* |
| *ella decía* | *ellas decían* |
| *usted decía* | *ustedes decían* |

## Command forms

| Infinitive | Usted Affirmative | Usted Negative | Ustedes Affirmative | Ustedes Negative | Tú Affirmative | Tú Negative |
|---|---|---|---|---|---|---|
| decir | diga | no diga | digan | no digan | di | no digas |

# The Verb *Seguir*

The verb *seguir* has some irregularity in nearly every form and in every tense.

> *seguir* = to continue, to follow
> gerund form = *siguiendo*
> past participle = *seguido*

## Present tense

| | |
|---|---|
| yo sigo | nosotros/nosotras seguimos |
| tú sigues | vosotros/vosotras seguís |
| él sigue | ellos siguen |
| ella sigue | ellas siguen |
| usted sigue | ustedes siguen |

## Preterite tense

| | |
|---|---|
| yo seguí | nosotros/nosotras seguimos |
| tú seguiste | vosotros/vosotras seguisteis |
| él siguió | ellos siguieron |
| ella siguió | ellas siguieron |
| usted siguió | ustedes siguieron |

## Imperfect tense

| | |
|---|---|
| *yo seguía* | *nosotros/nosotras seguíamos* |
| *tú seguías* | *vosotros/vosotras seguíais* |
| *él seguía* | *ellos seguían* |
| *ella seguía* | *ellas seguían* |
| *usted seguía* | *ustedes seguían* |

## Command forms

| *Infinitive* | Usted *Affirmative* | Usted *Negative* | Ustedes *Affirmative* | Ustedes *Negative* | Tú *Affirmative* | Tú *Negative* |
|---|---|---|---|---|---|---|
| *seguir* | *siga* | *no siga* | *sigan* | *no sigan* | *sigue* | *no sigas* |

# APPENDIX C
# IDIOMATIC EXPRESSIONS

Learning the idiomatic expressions listed in this appendix will help you enhance your Spanish-speaking skills. For the expressions that contain a verb, the verb can be used in different tenses if it is always conjugated in the same form (usually the *él* form) that is shown. It is also common to see a verb in its infinitive form as part of an idiomatic expression. Usually these verbs stay in the infinitive form, but there are exceptions to the rule. If the verb must be conjugated to match the subject of the sentence, the infinitive will be shown in the expression with an asterisk (*) placed next to it.

## Introduce a Topic

| | |
|---|---|
| *a propósito de* | by the way, concerning |
| *acerca de* | about, concerning (preposition) |
| *en cuanto a* | as for, in regards to |
| *tiene que ver con* | it has to do with |
| *tocante a* | in reference to, with regards to |

## Transitions

| | |
|---|---|
| *a lo largo* | in the long run |
| *a lo menos / al menos* | at least |
| *a ver* | let's see |
| *además de* | besides, in addition to |
| *al parecer* | apparently |
| *claro* | clearly, of course |
| *conforme a* | according to |

| | |
|---|---|
| *del mismo modo* | likewise |
| *desde luego* | of course |
| *en efecto* | in effect |
| *en efecto* | as a matter of fact, in reality, in fact |
| *en serio* | seriously |
| *es decir* | that is to say |
| *mejor dicho* | better said, in other words, rather |
| *ni siquiera* | not even |
| *por ejemplo* | for example |
| *por supuesto* | of course, naturally |
| *por lo demás* | furthermore |
| *por lo menos* | at least |
| *por lo mismo* | for that very reason |
| *por lo visto* | apparently, evidently |
| *por otro lado* | on the other hand |
| *por un lado* | on one hand |
| *también* | additionally, also |

## State an Opinion

| | |
|---|---|
| *a mi (tu, su, nuestro) juicio* | in my (your, his, our) opinion |
| *a mi (tu, su, nuestro) parecer* | in my (your, his, our) opinion |
| *a favor de* | in favor of, in behalf of |
| *al contrario* | on the contrary |
| *anda de boca en boca* | is generally known |
| *de acuerdo* | in agreement |
| *de ningún modo* | by no means |
| *de ninguna manera* | by no means, no way |
| *en mi (tu, su, nuestra) opinión* | in my (your, his, our) opinion |

| | |
|---|---|
| *en virtud de* | by virtue of |
| *estar\* harto de* | to be fed up with |
| *la desvantaja de* | the disadvantage of |
| *la ventaja de* | the advantage of |
| *llevar\* la contraria* | to contradict, take an opposite point of view |
| *no hay más remedio que* | it can't be helped that |
| *no importa que* | it's not important that |
| *no tener\* razón* | to be wrong |
| *no tiene arreglo* | it can't be fixed |
| *no tiene pies ni cabeza* | it makes no sense |
| *poner\* en ridículo* | to make look ridiculous |
| *por desgracia* | unfortunately |
| *por lo que a mi me toca* | as far as I'm concerned |
| *por mi parte* | as far as I'm concerned |
| *tanto mejor* | so much better |
| *tener\* la culpa de* | to be to blamed or blameworthy for |
| *tener(le) por* | to take (someone) for |
| *tener\* razón* | to be right |

## Conclusions

| | |
|---|---|
| *a fin de cuentas* | after all |
| *al fin y al cabo* | in short |
| *de todos modos* | anyway, at any rate |
| *en breve* | in short |
| *en fin* | in short |
| *en resumidas cuentas* | in short |
| *en suma* | in short, in a word |
| *por último* | finally |

## Contrasts

| | |
|---|---|
| *a diferencia de* | unlike |
| *a excepción de* | with the exception of |
| *a la vez* | at the same time |
| *a pesar de* | in spite of |
| *al contrario,* | on the contrary |
| *aún cuando* | even though |
| *de otro modo* | otherwise |
| *en cambio* | on the other hand |
| *en contra de* | contrary to |
| *en lugar de* | instead of |
| *en vez de* | instead of, rather than |
| *no obstante* | nevertheless, however |
| *por contraste* | in contrast to |
| *por lo contrario* | on the contrary |
| *por otra parte* | on the other hand |
| *sin embargo* | nevertheless |

## Cause and Effect

| | |
|---|---|
| *a causa de* | due to/because of |
| *a fin de que* | so that, in order that |
| *a fuerza de* | by the efforts of |
| *de esta manera* | thus |
| *para que* | so that |
| *por culpa de* | the fault of |
| *por eso* | therefore |
| *por motivo de* | on account of |
| *por consecuencia* | consequently |

| | |
|---|---|
| *por consiguiente* | accordingly |
| *por lo tanto* | consequently, therefore |

## Location

| | |
|---|---|
| *a bordo* | on board |
| *a campo raso* | in the open |
| *en casa* | at home |
| *a la vuelta de la esquina* | around the corner |
| *a lo largo de* | alongside of |
| *a lo lejos* | in the distance |
| *a los cuatro vientos* | in all directions |
| *a pocos pasos* | at a short distance |
| *al aire libre* | outside |
| *al final de la calle* | at the end of the street |
| *arriba* | upstairs |
| *de arriba abajo* | from top to bottom |
| *en casa* | at home |
| *en ninguna parte* | nowhere |
| *en todas partes* | everywhere |
| *por allá* | around there, that way |
| *por aquí* | around here, this way |
| *por dentro y por fuera* | inside and outside |
| *por todos lados* | all over, everywhere |
| *por todas partes* | on all sides, all over, everywhere |

## Time

| | |
|---|---|
| *a cada instante* | at every moment |
| *a eso de* | about (a certain time, date, etc.) |

| | |
|---|---|
| *a fines de* | at the end of (day, week, month etc.) |
| *a la madrugada* | at daybreak |
| *a la semana* | per week |
| *a la vez* | at the same time |
| *a más tardar* | at the very latest |
| *a medianoche* | at midnight |
| *a primera luz* | at dawn |
| *a principios de* | at the beginning of |
| *a tiempo* | on time |
| *al amanecer* | at dawn |
| *al anochecer* | at nightfall |
| *al cabo* | in the end, at last, finally |
| *al cabo de* | at the end of |
| *al día* | up to date |
| *al día siguiente* | on the next day |
| *al fin* | finally |
| *a(l) mediodía* | at midday (noon) |
| *al mes* | a month, per month |
| *al mismo tiempo* | at the same time |
| *al principio* | at first |
| *de aquí en adelante* | from now on |
| *de atemano* | ahead of time |
| *de ayer en ocho (días)* | a week from yesterday |
| *de cabo a rabo* | from beginning to end |
| *de día* | by day |
| *de día a día* | from day to day |
| *de madrugada* | at dawn |
| *de noche* | at (during the) night |

| | |
|---|---|
| *de sol a sol* | from sunrise to sunset |
| *de vez en cuando* | from time to time |
| *en adelante* | from now on |
| *en cuanto* | as soon as |
| *en el momento preciso* | in the nick of time |
| *en este momento* | at this moment |
| *en esto* | at this point |
| *en eso* | at that point |
| *en la actualidad* | at this time |
| *. . . en punto* | sharp (telling time) |
| *en seguida* | at once, immediately |
| *por ahora* | for now |
| *por aquel entonces* | at that time |
| *por esa época* | at that time |
| *por lo pronto* | for the time being |

## Manner and Adverbial Expressions

| | |
|---|---|
| *a ciegas* | blindly |
| *a fondo* | thoroughly |
| *a escondidas* | stealthily, on the sly |
| *a espaldas* | treacherously |
| *a gatas* | on all fours |
| *a la española* | Spanish-style |
| *a la francesa* | French-style |
| *a mano* | by hand |
| *a pierna suelta* | without a care |
| *a regañadientes* | reluctantly |
| *a sabiendas* | knowingly |

| | |
|---|---|
| *a solas* | alone |
| *a todo correr* | at full speed |
| *al azar* | by chance |
| *al oído* | confidentially |
| *de algún modo* | in some way |
| *de broma* | jokingly |
| *de buena fe* | in good faith |
| *de buena gana* | willingly |
| *de esa manera* | in that way |
| *de ese modo* | in that way |
| *de esta manera* | in this way |
| *de este modo* | in this way |
| *de golpe* | suddenly |
| *de mala gana* | unwillingly |
| *de memoria* | by heart (memory) |
| *de otra manera* | in another way |
| *de otro modo* | in another way |
| *de pie* | standing |
| *de prisa* | in a hurry |
| *de puntillas* | on tiptoe |
| *de repente* | suddenly |
| *de rodillas* | kneeling |
| *de súbito* | suddenly |
| *en broma* | jokingly |
| *en voz alta* | in a loud voice |
| *en voz baja* | in a soft voice |
| *paso a paso* | step by step |
| *poca a poco* | little by little |

| | |
|---|---|
| *por separado* | separately |
| *sin aliento* | breathless |
| *sin cuidado* | carelessly |
| *sin novedad* | the same as usual |
| *uno a uno* | one by one |

## Means of Transportation

| | |
|---|---|
| *a pie* | on foot |
| *a caballo* | on horseback |
| *de viva voz* | by word of mouth, in a loud voice |
| *en autobús* | by bus |
| *en bicicleta* | by bike |
| *en coche* | by car |
| *por avión* | by plane |
| *por barco* | by boat |
| *por computadora* | by computer |
| *por correo* | by mail |
| *por correo electrónico* | by e-mail |
| *por escrito* | in writing |
| *por fax* | by fax |
| *por ferrocaril* | by train |
| *por medio de* | by means of |
| *por teléfono* | by phone |

## Other Useful Expressions

| | |
|---|---|
| *a medio hacer* | half done |
| *a la larga* | in the long run |
| *a lo mejor* | maybe (used like *tal vez* or *quizás*) |
| *a lo menos* | at least |

| | |
|---|---|
| *a menudo* | often |
| *a oscuras* | in the dark |
| *a propósito* | on purpose |
| *a saltos* | by leaps and bounds |
| *a ver* | let's see |
| *al contado* | cash |
| *al contrario* | on the contrary |
| *al día* | current, up to date |
| *al menos* | at least |
| *al parecer* | apparently |
| *al pie de la letra* | to the letter |
| *aparte de* | aside from |
| *caer\* en cuenta* | to realize |
| *con tal de que* | provided that |
| *darse\* cuenta de (que)* | to realize, become aware (that) |
| *dar\*(le) vueltas a algo* | to think something over thoroughly |
| *de acuerdo* | in agreement |
| *de hecho* | in fact |
| *de mal en peor* | from bad to worse |
| *de mal humor / buen humor* | in a bad mood / good mood |
| *de manera que* | so that |
| *de moda* | in style (fashion) |
| *de modo que* | so that |
| *de nuevo* | again |
| *de oídos* | hearsay |
| *de todos modos* | anyway, at any rate |
| *de todas maneras* | anyway, at any rate |
| *de (un) golpe* | once and for all |

| | |
|---|---|
| *de una vez por todas* | once and for all |
| *de veras* | honestly, really, truly |
| *en breve* | in short |
| *en balde* | in vain |
| *en cambio* | on the other hand |
| *en caso de (que)* | in case of |
| *en cuanto a* | in regards to |
| *en efecto* | as a matter of fact |
| *en lugar de (que)* | instead of |
| *en marcha* | under way, on the way |
| *en otros términos* | in other words |
| *en pleno día* | in broad daylight |
| *en pro de* | on behalf of |
| *en pro y en contra* | for and against |
| *en resumen* | in brief |
| *en suma* | in short, in a word |
| *en vez de* | instead of |
| *ir\* al grano* | to get straight to the point |
| *llevar\* a cabo* | to accomplish, carry out, complete, finish |
| *por completo* | completely |
| *por poco* | nearly, barely |
| *sin disputa* | without question |
| *sin duda* | without a doubt |
| *sin falta* | without fail |

# Index

## A

*a* (letter), pronunciation, 6–8
*a* (personal *a*), 105, 154–157
*a* (preposition), 154–157
*a él / a ella,* 110–111
*abrazar,* 193
accent marks, 8–9, 21–22
adjectives
    adverbs from, 91–95, 97
    apocopated, 82–83
    that change meaning, 84–85
    comparisons with, 98–99
    demonstrative, 87–89
    and gender, 77–81
    nationality, 79–80
    in negative sentence, 202
    number and, 81–82
    placement of, 82–84
    possessive, 85–87
    superlatives, 100
    types of, 85–89
    use of, 76–85
    from verbs, 90
adverbial expressions, 263–265
adverbs. *See also* comparisons
    comparisons with, 100–102
    forming from adjectives, 91–95
    intensifiers, 97
    of manner, 96
    modifying adjectives or adverbs, 97
    placement in sentences, 95–97
    shortened, 97
    of time, 95–96
affirmative commands
    irregular verb forms, 194
    with reflexive pronouns, 192, 194
    regular verb forms, 189–191
    *tú,* 184–187
    *usted/ustedes,* 188
    *vosotros,* 187–188
affirmative words, 197

*agradar* (to please), 114
*algo,* 197
*alguien,* 197
*algún,* 83, 202
*alguno(s)/alguna(s),* 83, 197
*allá,* 89
AllExperts, 212
*allí,* 89
*almorzar,* 190
amusements vocabulary, 227–228
*–ando* (ending), 39
animal vocabulary, 218
apocopated adjectives, 82–83
*aquel/aquella,* 88–89
*aquél/aquélla,* 182
*aquello,* 182
*aquellos/aquellas,* 88–89
*aquéllos/aquéllas,* 88–89, 182
*aquí,* 89
*–ar* verbs, 32, 119, 137
    command forms, 186, 187, 188, 190, 232
    imperfect tense, 136–138, 232
    past participle, 90, 232
    present participle, 39, 40
    present tense, 34–35, 232
    preterite tense, 118–119, 121–125, 231
    stem-changing, 55, 58–59, 246–247
articles
    changing, 14–15
    definite/indefinite, 10, 11, 12, 19
    suffix changes, 14–16

## B

*b* (letter), pronunciation, 5
*bastante,* 83
*bastar* (to suffice, to be enough), 114
*bien,* 84, 94, 95
*The Big Red Book of Spanish Idioms,* 211
body vocabulary, 218–219

books, 211–212
*bueno,* 83, 94, 101
building vocabulary, 224–225
*buscar* (to search for), 193

# C

*c* (letter), pronunciation, 2, 3
C-NOTE acronym, 62–63
*caer* (to fall), 51, 125, 243–244
*caerse* (to fall down), 194
*–car,* verbs ending in, 122–124, 189
*cargar* (to load), 193
case (pronoun), 25–29
cause and effect, idiomatic expressions
     for, 260–261
*ch* (letter), alphabetization in
     dictionaries, 6
clothing vocabulary, 220
cognates, 2–3, 8
*comer* (to eat), 36, 120, 190, 232–233
comma, in numbers, 45
commands
     irregular verbs, 184, 185
     regular verbs, 184–186, 190
     stem-changing verbs, 190
     *tú* form, 184–187
     *usted/ustedes* form, 188–194
     verb charts, 230–256
     verbs ending in *–go,* 189, 191
     verbs ending in *–zco,* 189, 191
     verbs with spelling changes,
          189, 193
     *vosotros* form, 186–187
     with reflexive pronouns, 192, 194
     *yo* form, 189, 191, 193–194
*¿cómo?,* 69, 71
comparisons of equality, 99
comparisons, 98–102, 206. *See also*
     adverbs
compound nouns, 22
compound prepositions, 169–170
compound words, 22
*con* (preposition), 161–162, 181
*The Concise American Heritage
     Larousse Spanish Dictionary,* 211
conclusions, idiomatic expressions
     for, 259

conjugation, 31, 32, 33, 34–37,
     230–256. *See also* irregular verbs;
     regular verbs; *specific verbs*
conjunctions, 43–44, 202–203
*conmigo,* 181
*conocer* (to know), 52, 63, 145, 191
consonants, 1–6
*construir* (to build), 126
contrasts, idiomatic expression for, 260
*crema* (accent mark), 4
*cruzar* (to cross), 124
*¿cuál?/¿cuáles?,* 69, 70, 72
*cuando* (when), joining verbs with,
     149–150
*¿cuándo?,* 69, 71
*¿cuánto(s)?/¿cuánta(s?),* 69, 72, 73

# D

*d* (letter), pronunciation, 5
*dar* (to give), 48, 133, 194, 236–237
days of the week vocabulary, 161, 221
*de* (preposition), 157–159, 169–170
*¿de quién?,* 158
*decir* (to say, tell), 131–132, 185, 191,
     253–254
DEEMMMS acronym, 165–168
*defender* (to defend), 56
definite articles, 10, 11, 19
*del,* 159
*demasiado,* 93, 94
demonstrative adjectives, 87–89
demonstrative pronouns, 181–182
*desaparecer* (to disappear), 191
Deuber, Julianne
     *1001 Spanish Pitfalls,* 211
*diéresis* (accent mark), 4
dipthongs, 7–8
direct object, 103, 104–105
direct object pronouns, 103, 105–108,
     117, 155–156
distances, demonstrative adjectives
     and, 89
diversions vocabulary, 227–228
*doler* (to pain), 114
*¿dónde?,* 69
*dormir* (to sleep), 127, 251–252
*dormirse* (to fall asleep), 194

double consonants, pronunciation, 2
double negatives, 199
double object sentences, 114–116

# E

*e* (conjunction), 44
*e* (letter), pronunciation, 7–8
*e* to *i* stem change, 61, 127–128,
    252–253
*e* to *ie* stem change, 55–58, 127,
    247–248
*él/ella*, 27, 28, 29, 37, 38, 39, 86, 177
*el/la*, 11, 14, 19
*ellos/ellas*, 27, 28, 29, 37, 38, 39,
    72, 177
*en* (in, on), (preposition), 160–161
English subject case pronouns,
    25–26, 28–29
equality, comparisons of, 99
*–er* verbs, 32, 120, 138, 232–233
    command forms, 186, 187, 188,
        190, 233
    imperfect tense, 138–139, 233
    irregular *yo* form, 4, 49–51
    past participle, 90, 232
    present participle, 39–40
    present tense, 35–36, 232
    preterite tense, 120, 125, 232
    stem-changing, 49–50, 51, 56–57
*escribir* (to write), 37, 121, 190,
    233–234
*ése/ésa*, 182
*ese(s)/esa(s)*, 89
*eso*, 182
*esos/esas*, 89
*ésos/ésas*, 182
*estar* (to be), 39, 49, 62–63, 194,
    237–238
*este/esta*, 89
*éste/ésta*, 182
*esto*, 182
*estos/estas*, 89
*éstos/éstas*, 182
exclamation point (!), 45
*explicar* (to explain), 193

# F

*f* (letter), pronunciation, 4
*faltar* (to be lacking), 114
family vocabulary, 221
feminine nouns, 11–19
first person, 27, 28–29
*501 Spanish Verbs* (Kendris and
    Kendris), 211
food vocabulary, 221
formal "you," 27, 28–29

# G

*g* (letter), pronunciation, 3–4, 121
*–gar*, verbs ending in, 121–122, 189
gender
    and adjectives, 77–81
    article and suffix changes, 11–12
    basic rules of, 12–14
    compound nouns, 22
    definite articles, 10, 11, 19
    demonstrative adjectives, 87–89
    indefinite articles, 10, 12, 19
    irregularities, 16–18
    of nouns, 10–22
    number and plurality, 19–22
    possessive adjectives, 85–87
    subject pronouns, 25–29
*–go* verbs, 49–51, 189, 191
*grande*, 83–84, 101
*gustar* (to please), 111–113

# H

*h* (letter), pronunciation, 4–5
*hablar* (to speak), 35, 119, 190,
    231–232
*hacer* (to make/to do), 49, 130,
    150–152, 185, 191, 238–239
hard *g*, pronunciation, 4, 121
health vocabulary, 218–219
Holt, Marion Peter
    *1001 Spanish Pitfalls*, 211
home vocabulary, 222–223

# I

*i* (letter), pronunciation, 7, 8
*i* to *y* change, preterite tense, 125–126
i-stem verbs, 130–131
idiomatic expressions, 145–146,
    150–152, 168–169, 257–267
*–iendo* (ending), 39
imperfect tense
    indicators, 142–143
    irregular verbs, 140–141
    regular verbs in, 136–140
    usage, 141–142
    use with preterite tense, 148–150
    verb charts, 230–256
    verbs that change meaning in,
      145–147
indefinite articles, 10, 12, 19
indirect objects, 103, 104, 108–109
indirect object pronouns, 108–114,
    117, 155–156
inferiority comparison, 98–99
infinitives, 31–32, 41, 52, 116, 163,
    170–171
informal "you," 27, 28–29
intensifiers, adverbs, 97
Internet resources, 212
interrogative pronouns, 69–72
*ir* (to go), 47, 132, 140, 185, 194,
    234–235
*–ir* verbs, 32, 120, 138
    command forms, 186, 187, 188,
      190, 234
    imperfect tense, 138, 139–140, 234
    past participle, 90, 233
    present participle, 39–40, 233
    present tense, 36–37, 232–233
    preterite tense, 120–121,
      125–126, 232
    stem-changing, 57–58, 126–128,
      247–248, 251–254
irregular affirmative *tú* commands,
    185–186
irregular adverbs, 94–95
irregular comparisons, 101–102
irregular verbs
    command forms, 185–186, 194
    common, 47–48
    confusing verbs, 62–65
    imperfect tense, 140–141
    i-stem verbs, 130–131
    j-stem verbs, 131–132
    overview, 46, 94–95
    present tense, 46–66
    preterite tense, 128–133
    stem-changing verbs, 54–61
    u-stem verbs, 129–130
    verb charts, 234–256
    in *yo* form, 48–54, 121–126
i-stem verbs, 130–131

# J

*j* (letter), pronunciation, 4
j-stem verbs, 131–132
*jamás*, 197
*joven*, 101
*jugar* (to play [a sport or game]),
    60, 190, 193, 250–251

# K

*k* (letter), pronunciation, 1, 3
Kendris, Christopher and Theodore
    *501 Spanish Verbs,* 211

# L

*la/el*, 11, 14, 19
*lavar* (to wash), 175
*lavarse* (to wash oneself), 177, 194
*le/les*, 110, 115–116
Learn-Spanish-Language, 212
Lingolex, 212
*ll* (letter)
    alphabetization in dictionaries, 6
    pronunciation, 2
*llegar* (to arrive), 158, 193
*llevar* (to take), 64–65
location, idiomatic expressions for,
    261
*lo(s)/la(s),* 19, 106, 115–116

# M

*mal*, 94
*malo*, 83, 94, 101
manner, 96, 263–265

*más,* 84, 93, 94, 98
masculine nouns, 11–19
*mayor,* 101
*me,* 106, 110, 176
means of transportation, idiomatic
    expressions for, 265
*mejor,* 95, 101
*menor,* 101
*menos,* 93, 94, 98–99
*–mente* (ending), 91–93, 95, 96, 97
*mentir* (to lie [to tell an untruth]),
    57, 127, 190, 247–248
*mí,* 180, 181
*mi/mis,* 85
*mientras,* joining verbs with, 148–149
*mío(s)/mía(s),* 86
months of the year vocabulary, 224
*mucho,* 93, 94
*mucho(s)/mucha(s),* 82
*muy,* 84

# N

*ñ* (letter), alphabetization in
    dictionaries, 6
*nada,* 197
*nadie,* 197
nationality, adjectives indicating,
    79–80
natural stress, 8
nature vocabulary, 224
*–ndo* ending, 39–40, 116
negative commands
    irregular verbs, 185–186, 194
    with reflexive pronouns, 192, 194
    regular verbs, 185–186, 190,
        222–225
    *tú,* 186–187
    *usted/ustedes,* 188
    *vosotros,* 187–188
negative superlatives, 100
negatives
    adjectives, 202
    conjunctions, 202–203
    overview, 196
    pronouns, 200–202
    sentences, 198–200
    words and expressions, 196–198
neighborhood vocabulary, 224–225

neutral demonstrative pronouns, 182
*ningún,* 83, 202
*ninguno(s)/ninguna(s),* 83, 197,
    200–202
*ni . . . ni,* 197
*no,* 198–200
*nos,* 106, 110, 177
*nosotros/nosotras,* 27, 28
nouns
    compound, 22
    definite articles, 11, 19
    gender, 12–18
    indefinite articles, 11, 19
    masculine/feminine endings, 14–18
    number of, 19
    overview, 11
    plural forms of, 20–22
    possessive adjectives, 85–87
    replacing with subject case
        pronouns, 29
*nuestro(s)/nuestra(s),* 85–86
number and plurality, 19, 20–22,
    81–82
numbers, punctuation and, 45
*nunca,* 197

# O

*o* (or), (conjunction), 43, 44
*o* (letter), pronunciation, 7, 8
*o* to *u* stem change, 126
*o* to *ue* stem change, 58–60, 126–127,
    251–252
*obedecer* (to obey), 191
object pronouns
    adding two to verbs, 116
    direct objects and direct object
        pronouns, 104–108, 117,
        155–156
    double object sentences, 114–116
    indirect objects and indirect object
        pronouns, 108–114, 117,
        155–156
    objective case, 103–104
objective case, 103–104
*ofrecer* (to offer), 191
*1001 Spanish Pitfalls* (Holt and
    Deuber), 211
*o . . . o,* 197

opinion, idiomatic expressions for, 258–259
*os,* 106, 110, 177
*–oy,* verbs ending in, 48–49

# P

*p* (letter), pronunciation, 3
*pagar* (to pay), preterite forms of, 122
*para* (preposition), 154, 163–165
¿*para qué?,* 69
*parecer* (to seem [look like]), 114
past participle, 90, 230–256
past tense
    expressions of time, 150–152
    overview, 144
    preterite-imperfect formulas, 147–150
    verbs that change meaning in preterite, 145–147
*pedir* (to request), 128, 190, 252–253
*pensar* (to think), 55, 137, 246–247
*peor,* 95, 101
*pequeño,* 101
*perder* (to lose), 56, 139
period, in numbers, 45
*pero* (but), (conjunction), 43, 44, 202–203
person. *See* first person; second person; third person
personal *a,* 105, 154–157
*placer* (to please), 114
plural forms, 19–22, 26–28
*poco/poca,* 82, 93
*poder* (to be able), 59, 146–147
*poner* (to put), 50, 185, 191, 239–240
*por* preposition, 165–169
¿*por qué?,* 69
possessive adjectives, 85–87
*preferir* (to prefer), 57
prepositional pronouns, 180–181
prepositions. *See also specific prepositions*
    compound, 169–170
    defined, 153
    idiomatic expressions, 168–169
    *para* and *por,* 154, 163–169
    simple, 153–162

    using with verbs, 170–173
    verbs after, 173
present participle, 39–40, 116, 230–256
present progressive, 39–41
present tense
    common, 47–48
    irregular verbs 46–54, 225–248
    overview, 46, 94–95
    regular verbs, 34–39, 222–225
    stem-changing verbs, 54–61
    *tú* commands, 184–186, 189–194, 230–256
    verb charts, 231–255
    *yo* form in, 48–54
preterite indicators, 134–135
preterite tense
    defined, 118
    indicators, 134–135
    irregulars in, 128–133
    *mientras* and *cuando,* 147–150
    regular verbs in, 118–121
    situations, 133–134
    stem-changing verbs in, 126–128
    usage, 133–135
    use with imperfect, 147–150
    verb charts, 230–256
    verbs that change meaning in, 145–147
    *yo* forms in, 121–126
preterite-imperfect formulas, 147–150
*primero,* 83
PRODDS acronym, 163–165
*producir* (to produce), 53
*promover* (to promote), 60
pronouns. *See also* object pronouns
    adding to end of infinitive, 116
    answering questions with, 74–75
    case, 25
    defined, 24
    demonstrative, 181–182
    direct object, 104, 105–108, 117, 155–156
    formal/informal, 27, 28–29
    English subject case, 25–26, 28–29
    indirect object, 108–114, 117, 155–156
    interrogative, 69–72

pronouns *(continued)*
   negative, 200–202
   prepositional, 180–181
   pronunciation, 1–9
   reflexive, 176–178, 192–194
   subject, 186
   subject case, 24, 25–29
   use of, 24–25
pronunciation, 1–8, 204
punctuation, 9, 44–45

# Q

*qu* combination, pronunciation, 3
quantity, adjectives of, 82
*que*, expressions of time, 150–152
¿*qué?*, 69, 70, 71
*quedar* (to remain), 114
*querer* (wanted), 147
question marks (?), 44
questions, asking and answering
   interrogative pronouns (question
      words), 69–72
   question words as subjects, 72–74
   using pronouns to answer
      questions, 74–75
   yes or no questions, 67–69
¿*quién?/¿quiénes?*, 69, 70, 71

# R

*realizar* (to realize), 193
reciprocity, 177–178
recreation vocabulary, 218
reflexive pronouns, 176–178, 177,
   192–194
reflexive verbs, 175, 178–180
reflexivity, 175
regular affirmative *tú* commands,
   184–185
regular verbs
   command forms, 184–185, 190
   in imperfect tense, 136–139
   in present progressive tense, 39–41
   in present tense, 34–37
   in preterite tense, 118–121
   verb charts, 231–234
resources, 211–212
*rr* (letter), pronunciation and spelling, 2

# S

*saber* (to know a fact), 54, 145–146,
   194, 242–243
*sacar* (to take), 64–65, 193
SAFE acronym, 133–134
*salir* (to leave), 50, 158, 172, 185,
   191, 240–241
school vocabulary, 225–227
*se*, 115–116, 177
*–se* verbs, 175, 178–180
seasons vocabulary, 228–229
second person, 27, 28–29
*seguir* (to continue, to follow),
   255–256
*sentarse* (to sit down), 194
sentences/sentence structure
   adjective placement, 82–84
   adverb placement, 95–97
   conjunctions, 43–44
   direct object of, 104–105
   double object, 114–116
   indirect object of, 109
   negative, 198–200
   overview, 42–43
   preterite and imperfect together,
      147–150
   punctuation, 44–45
*sentir* (to feel), imperfect tense forms
   of, 139, 140
*ser* (to be), 48, 62–63, 86, 87, 132,
   186, 194, 235–236
*servir* (to serve), 61
shortened adverbs, 97
*si*, 197
*siempre*, 197
simple prepositions, 153–162
*sino*, 202–203
*sobrar* (to be left over, to be an
   excess), 114
*Spanish For Dummies* (Wald), 211
Spanish subject case pronouns, 26–29
Spanish Unlimited, 212
spelling, 1–9, 204
sports vocabulary, 227–228
SRID acronym, 176–177
stem-changing verbs, 125–128
   command forms, 189–190
   defined, 51

*e* to *i,* 61, 127–128, 252–253
*e* to *ie,* 55–58, 61, 127, 247–248
*i* to *y,* 125–126
imperfect tense, 132
*o* to *u,* 126
*o* to *ue,* 58–60, 126, 251–252
in present tense, 54–61
in preterite tense, 128–223
*u* to *ue,* 60, 250–251
stress, 8–9
strong vowels, 8, 9
*su/sus,* 85
subject, in sentence structure, 42–43
subject case pronouns, 25–29
subject pronouns, 177
subjects, question words as, 72–74
suffix changes, 14–16
*suficiente,* 82
superiority comparison, 98
superlatives, 100
*suyo/suya,* 86
*suyos/suyas,* 86

# T

*t* (letter), pronunciation, 5
*también,* 197
*tampoco,* 197
*tan . . . como,* 99
*tanto,* 93, 94
*tanto . . . como,* 99
*te,* 106, 110, 177
*tener* (to have), 58, 129–130, 186,
    191, 248–249
tenses. *See specific tenses*
*tercero,* 83
thematic vocabulary, 218–230
third person, 26, 27–28
*ti,* 180
tilde (´), 6
time
    adverbs of, 95–96
    expressions of, 150–152
    idiomatic expressions for, 261–263
TLF acronym, 63
*tocar* (to play / to be someone's turn),
    114, 123, 190, 193
*tomar* (to take), 64–65
*trabajar* (to work), 40, 138

*traer* (to bring), 51, 244–245,
    248–249
transitions, idiomatic expressions for,
    257–258
transitive verbs, 108
travel vocabulary, 228
*tú,* 27, 28
*tú* commands, 184–187, 189–194,
    230–256
*tu/tus,* 85
*tuyo/tuya,* 86
*tuyos/tuyas,* 86

# U

*u* (or), (conjunction), 44
*u* (letter), pronunciation, 3, 7, 8
*u* to *ue* stem change, 60, 250–251
*–uir,* verbs ending in, 126
umlaut (¨), 4
*un/una,* 12, 19
*uno,* 83
*unos/unas,* 19
upside-down punctuation marks,
    44, 45
useful expressions, 265–267
*usted/Ud.,* 27, 38, 180
*usted/ustedes* commands, 188–194,
    222–246
u-stem verbs, 129–130
*ustedes/Uds.,* 27, 38, 180

# V

*v* (letter), pronunciation, 5
*valer* (to be worth), 50
*Velázques World Wide Spanish English
    Dictionary,* 212
*venir* (to come), 58, 130–131, 158,
    186, 191, 249–250
*ver* (to see), 53, 133, 141, 241–242
verb(s), 33–34. *See also –ar* verbs;
    *–er* verbs; *–ir* verbs; irregular
    verbs; regular verbs; stem-
    changing verbs; *specific verb
    tenses; specific verbs*
    adding two object pronouns to, 116
    adjectives from, 90
    *–ar,* 32, 34, 119, 137

verb(s) *(continued)*
   that change meaning in preterite,
      145–147
   charts, 230–256
   choosing correct form, 37–39
   command forms of, 189–192
   confusing verbs, 62–65
   conjugation, 31
   direct object placement, 106–108
   double object placement, 114–116
   ending in *–car,* 122–124, 189
   ending in *–gar,* 121–122, 189
   ending in *–go,* 49–51, 57–58,
      189, 191
   ending in *–oy,* 48–49
   ending in *–uir,* 121–122
   ending in *–zar,* 124–125, 189
   ending in *–zco,* 52–53, 189
   endings for irregular preterite, 129
   *–er,* 32, 35, 120, 138
   followed by an infinitive, 31–32,
      63–64
   following prepositions, 164, 173
   with indirect object pronouns,
      111–114
   *–ir,* 32, 36–37, 39–40, 57–58, 120,
      126–128, 138, 186, 187, 188
   i-stem, 130–131
   joining with *cuando,* 149–150
   joining with *mientras,* 148–149
   j-stem, 131–132
   past participle, 90
   preposition use with, 170–173
   reflexive, 175, 178–180
   in sentence structure, 42–43

   with spelling changes, 193, 194
   transitive, 108
   u-stem, 129–130
*viejo,* 101
*vivir* (to live), imperfect tense forms
   of, 139
vocabulary, thematic, 218–230
*vosotros* commands, 187–188
*vosotros/vosotras,* 27, 28, 29
vowels, 6–8
*vuestro(s)/vuestra(s),* 85, 86

# W

*w* (letter), pronunciation, 1
Wald, Susan
   *Spanish For Dummies,* 211
WATERS acronym, 141–142
weak vowels, 8, 9
weather vocabulary, 228–229
work vocabulary, 229–230

# Y

*y* (and), (conjunction), 43, 44
*y* (letter), pronunciation, 7
yes or no questions, 67–69
*yo,* 27, 28, 38
*yo* commands, 189. 191, 193–194
*yo* forms, in preterite tense, 121–126

# Z

*–zar,* verbs ending in, 124–125, 189
*–zco,* verbs ending in, 52–53, 189, 191